IN DEFENSE OF WOMEN

NANCY GERTNER

IN DEFENSE OF WOMEN

MEMOIRS OF AN UNREPENTANT ADVOCATE

Beacon Press · Boston

Beacon Press
25 Beacon Street
Boston, Massachusetts 02108-2892
www.beacon.org

Beacon Press books
are published under the auspices of
the Unitarian Universalist Association of Congregations.

15 14 13 12 11   8 7 6 5 4 3 2 1

This book is printed on acid-free paper that meets the uncoated paper
ANSI/NISO specifications for permanence as revised in 1992.

Text design and composition by Wilsted & Taylor Publishing Services

Library of Congress Cataloging-in-Publication Data
Gertner, Nancy.
In defense of women : memoirs of an unrepentant advocate / Nancy Gertner.
p. cm.
ISBN 978-0-8070-1143-0 (hardcover : alk. paper) 1. Gertner, Nancy, 1946–
2. Lawyers—Massachusetts—Biography. 3. Judges—Massachusetts—Biography.
I. Title.
KF373.G467A3 2011
340.092—dc22   [B] 2010047337

*To Sarah, Stephen, and Peter
for their endless love and patience*

CONTENTS

The women students at Yale Law School sponsored a panel in the late 1990s. What they wanted to know was how one became a judge. They didn't want a general perspective. These young women wanted answers to very concrete, very specific questions—what courses, what jobs, what contacts?

There were two panelists; Judge Sonia Sotomayor and me. I had been a judge of the U.S. District Court in Massachusetts for only a few years. Sonia was then on the Second Circuit Court of Appeals in New York City. We were both Yale Law graduates—I in the class of 1971, she in the class of 1979.

Sonia went first, speaking deliberately: How does one become a judge? You graduate this fine institution with a stellar record. You work as a prosecutor in the celebrated Manhattan District Attorney's Office and then as a corporate lawyer in New York. You have clear principles, but you take care not to be publicly associated with controversial causes. Rather, you speak your mind carefully, cautiously, within existing institutions. You demonstrate in every way, in word and deed, that you can be a neutral, temperate jurist. And then you are nominated to become a judge.

———

Her story was compelling. In fact, in little more than a decade, she would be confirmed to the highest position that the American legal profession has to offer: the U.S. Supreme Court, an extraordinary tribute. And everything about her background—her hard-won and hard-fought career, certainly, but also her modest beginnings in the projects of the Bronx—would predict that she would be a superb judge.

It was my turn. I paused. How does one become a judge? I paused again. Yes, you graduate this fine institution with a stellar record. But then—and I paused for effect, ever the trial lawyer, my voice getting louder, the cadence quicker—you represent the first lesbian, feminist, radical, anti–Vietnam War activist accused of killing a police officer you can find; that would be your first major case in prime time. You take every abortion case in the Commonwealth of Massachusetts; you speak out on the major hot-button legal issues of the day in successive rallies on the Boston Common, or on television, or in the editorial pages of the newspapers. You represent defendants of all stripes, from those in political corruption cases to high-profile murder cases, and for the final coup de grace, you marry the legal director of the American Civil Liberties Union in Massachusetts. In short, after doing everything that, in this political culture, in this epoch of strident judicial politics, should disqualify you for the position, you become a judge.

Sonia turned to me, laughing. The students, at first a bit stunned, then joined in.

———

There is no right way, no clear path. Numbers of lawyers were oh-so-cautious throughout their legal careers and were never rewarded with a judgeship because of the vagaries of politics. Nor does your path predict the kind of judge that you will be. To be a judge, every lawyer needs to move to neutral. The issue is less where you start than where you end up and what you have spent your life doing. The fact is, I could not have lived my life any other way.

———

After almost twenty-five years as a civil rights and criminal defense lawyer, I was nominated for a federal judgeship in the spring of 1993. I was told to go through all the records of my career to see if there was something wrong, something that would embarrass President Bill Clinton. And so I did. I started with the "Sexist Tidbits" file. From the beginning of my career, I had compiled a growing file called "Sexist Tidbits," in which I kept personal notes as well as diaries, and through which I chronicled the pain of breaking into this male profession, of proving, first to myself and then to others, that I was capable. I wrote down what I was feeling because I did not allow myself the luxury of saying these things out loud— that I feared that I would never be up to snuff, that the skeptical comments by the male lawyers I met about women trial lawyers mirrored my own self-doubts.

I went through every transcript, all the videotaped sound bites hastily blurted into microphones outside courthouses; I had saved them all. I went through all the clippings, the speeches, the articles, the causes, the clients. It seemed like everything I'd done in the last twenty years could embarrass the president. What was clear to me, however, was that none of it should.

And when it was apparent that I would be confirmed, I wanted to memorialize these stories, if only for my kids, my friends, myself. I had been there, done that. It had been quite a ride; important lessons had been learned personally and professionally; and maybe—just maybe—some good had been done.

Being a judge, it was said, was the pinnacle of one's career. But I worried that that identity, important though it was, threatened to obliterate all traces of the earlier one. It was as if conceiving of me in my new judicial role required wiping out the memory of the advocate, the activist, the trial lawyer—roles that had meant so very much to me, representing people whom I had cared so much about, causes that I had taken so much to heart.

Shortly after I was confirmed, a woman toll taker on the Mass. Pike recognized me as I was blazing through on my way to work. She was about my age. She told me that she had followed my career from the beginning and congratulated me on becoming a judge. Then there was another, and another, in a grocery store, behind the counter at Lechmere's, in a bookstore, at a party, in letters that flooded in after my nomination was announced. They too knew of my work, from the first celebrated murder case to this moment. Why?

———

Charles Black, a professor of mine at Yale Law School, wrote of the importance of telling the stories of the excluded, what others have called the "outsider stories." He reminded us that it was only one generation ago that there were people whose living grandparents had been slaves.

Perhaps I should tell my story, I thought. The gains of women in the past two decades were so recent, and so fragile. People—especially women—need to be reminded that it had been only twenty years since women had entered this profession in force, that in the memory of those of us in our fifties and sixties were the painful slights and insults of the 1960s and 1970s, a sense of exclusion not subtle, not vague, but palpable and overt. The public had to guard against being fooled by the fact that some of our number—like me, like Justice Sotomayor—had made it to high-status positions. It seemed especially important now, when the media touted the end of the women's movement, when younger women were said to be rejecting feminism and the choices of my generation.

It was also important to tell the stories of civil rights and civil liberties lawyers and the principles they embodied as legal services to the poor were at risk, as more and more law students, buried under loans, eschewed public service, as lawyers appeared less and less like members of a revered profession and more like ordinary businessmen and businesswomen. New lawyers need to see that you can do what you set out to do, make principled decisions, align your heart and your work, and reject money as the only measure of value.

———

When I was interviewed by Senator Edward Kennedy, who was to propose a candidate for the president to nominate for a federal judgeship, I thought it unlikely that I would ever make the cut. I ended the interview by saying: "Senator, I have a bone to pick with you" (a pretty impertinent comment for one seeking a federal judgeship). I said that "if you value the things you say you do, at some point—perhaps not even with me—you need to propose a civil rights lawyer as a judge, to validate this career path." He did.

And I began to write this book.

It is, in some ways, a coming-of-age account from the Lower East Side of Manhattan, a beginning not unlike Justice Sotomayor's—far from a wealthy or high-status background—ending in a success story. But it is also a woman's story: a story of breaking into and succeeding in the quintessential man's world in the late twentieth century and its personal costs. And that story is set within the movements of the 1960s and 1970s, legal and political, told by one of many women who desperately tried to put her fancy legal skills at the service of society's most maligned members. Finally, it is the story of our justice system, and what it takes to wrest rudimentary fairness from it, a lesson that I take with me to this day.

CHAPTER ONE

The Revolutionary
and the Radical Lawyer

When I was twenty-nine and she was twenty-five, I defended Susan Saxe, an anti–Vietnam War activist accused of robbery and murder. The judge persisted in calling me "Susan Gertner." Even Susan's own mother, Rose Saxe, confused me with her daughter. The prosecutor assumed that since Susan was gay, I was gay. And that rumor persisted for twenty years; a husband and three children later, when I was nominated to be a federal judge, there it was. I identified with my clients deeply, and Susan even more than most, but I was the lawyer, not the client. Empathy was a given. Detachment was what I had to learn.

On September 23, 1970, five people robbed the State Street Bank in Brighton, Massachusetts. Stanley Bond, age twenty-six, William Gilday, known as "Lefty," age forty-two, and Robert Valeri, age twenty-five. Bond was a Vietnam veteran. All three were enrolled in a special program at Brandeis University for ex-cons. Two were young women and Brandeis seniors: Susan Saxe, twenty, and Katherine Power, twenty-one.

This was no ordinary robbery. Their goal was to raise money for the anti–Vietnam war effort. But the robbery turned tragic when Officer Walter Schroeder, age forty-two, responded to a silent alarm. Lefty Gilday, the lookout, unaware that the robbery was over and the participants long gone, shot Officer Schroeder in the back. The men were caught immediately. The two women became fugitives.

———

On March 17, 1975, I was at home, alone, in a one-bedroom apartment on Harvard Street in Cambridge, Massachusetts, half-heartedly watching the news, when I heard of Susan Saxe's capture in Philadelphia. I too had been an antiwar activist of sorts—demonstrations, teach-ins, and, as undergraduate president of Barnard College, a signatory of the 1967 "student leaders" letter to President Lyndon Johnson protesting the Vietnam War. I had been at meetings when frustration at the pace of change in America bubbled over into talk of violence. But that's where I stopped—marches and talk.

It never dawned on me that I might be asked to represent Susan. I had been a member of the bar for only a little over two years, since December 1972. Although a partner in a small civil rights/criminal law firm, I was a novice. What's more, I believed I was not long for trial practice. I wanted to be a law professor.

Sonia Dettman, a client and a friend, called to talk about Susan's capture. She was Stanley Bond's widow; they had married while he was in prison on another charge, after the State Street Bank robbery. Although she had never met Susan, she wanted to help in whatever way she could. Susan would need representation; would I do it? "Of course," I said, without hesitation. Writing this now, I try to understand how I had the nerve to say yes.

———

Susan Edith Saxe, along with the other four, was indicted for the 1970 robbery and the murder of a police officer.

Almost immediately after it occurred, the bank robbery had become a cause célèbre when Valeri told the police that it had been committed to fund the anti–Vietnam War effort. The five, he said, planned everything at two apartments that they had rented in Boston's Back Bay. As he described it, on the day of the robbery, Susan, Bond, and he drove to the State Street Bank and Trust Company, at the intersection of Everett Street and Western Avenue in Brighton. Susan went in first, to "case" the scene. She returned with Bond and Valeri. Bond had a 9-mm handgun; Valeri, a shotgun and a handgun; and Susan, a .30-caliber carbine. Bond demanded money from the teller, who complied without resistance. They took $26,000.

Gilday was in another car, parked opposite the bank on Everett Street. His job was to guard the escape. He had an automatic rifle and a clip of thirty .45-caliber bullets. Some blocks away, on Colerain Street, Kathy Power was waiting, with the "switch car."

The robbery over, Susan, Bond, and Valeri fled in a car that they had parked nearby; they heard no shots and saw no police. According to Valeri, they assumed that Gilday had left when they had. They met up with Power and got into her car. Later, on the "switch car" radio, they heard, to their utter horror, that a police officer, Walter Schroeder, had been shot in the back and was fighting for his life.

The men were caught immediately, tried separately, and within a year were behind bars. Valeri cooperated with the government in exchange for a lesser sentence of imprisonment. Gilday was sentenced to life. Bond was convicted of an earlier armed robbery in Evanston, Illinois, and died in prison trying to build a bomb while awaiting trial on the Brighton robbery and murder. The two women, however, eluded capture. Within a month, two letters from Susan were turned over to the Federal Bureau of Investigation. Written days after the robbery, one was to Susan's rabbi, another to her father, Eliot Saxe. They were heartrending, filled with a sense of impending doom and death. One began, "I'm writing this letter because I'll never see you again and probably won't write anymore. In a few days, you will have a rather garbled, but basically accurate version of what 'your little girl' has done with her life." In so many words, Susan admitted her involvement in the crime.

The FBI could not find the women anywhere. The press reported that they had become lovers and escaped into a "women's underground" that the FBI could hardly understand, much less infiltrate. Five years later, Susan was captured. Kathy surrendered almost twenty years after that.

———

Ironically, my path had crossed with Susan's once before, although I didn't know it. On Saturday, May 2, 1970, a demonstration was held on the New Haven Common and both of us were there, the future lawyer and the client-to-be.

The Saturday demonstration in New Haven had been planned to protest the trial of Bobby Seale, Erica Huggins, and other members of the Black Panther party, charged in the murder of one of the group. Representing Huggins was Katherine ("Katie") Roraback, an extraordinary lawyer, one of two women to graduate from the Yale Law School over twenty years earlier. Part of a raft of eager law students, I volunteered to work for her.

The day before, May 1, 1970, the headlines announced a new U.S. "incursion" of Cambodia, a major escalation of the Vietnam War. In response, students at Kent State burned down an ROTC building. A nationwide student strike was announced. In the Yale Chapel, a meeting was held to form the National Strike Information Center (NSIC). It would be based at Brandeis University, in Waltham, Massachusetts.

On May 2, New Haven Common was filled with demonstrators from all over; tear gas wafted throughout the city, into the law school halls and classrooms, clinging to our clothes. Someone tried to burn down the Yale Law School Library. New Haven felt as if it were about to explode, and from my sheltered vantage point, so did the country. By Monday, our worst fears were confirmed; while New Haven had escaped major violence, the Ohio National Guard had fired on a group of Kent State students, killing four, wounding nine.

Finishing my second year at Yale Law School, I was a legal observer—my way of participating, but without risk. I wore an identifying armband. If there were arrests, I was to provide an "independent" perspective of what had happened. In fact, I had actually studied the "law of mass arrests." I knew considerably more about that bit of esoterica than the standard law school fare.

Yale Law School had always been progressive, but those years won the prize. I had taken Spanish for law school credit, thinking I might represent migrant workers in California. But by the spring of 1970, all I knew how to say was "Les policia attaco les etudiantes" (the police attacked the students). I couldn't ask to find a bathroom in Spanish if my life depended on it. And whatever traditional curriculum there was, I missed. When I took the Massachusetts bar exam, I thought dying "intestate"—a common legal term for dying without a will—was a disease, related to the prostate or some such thing. But however little law I knew, I was determined to do my small part somehow.

Susan was very much a participant, not an observer. An honor student, she was poised to graduate from Brandeis in another month. She happened into the NSIC meeting, got hooked, and then stayed on at Brandeis after graduation to work on the student strike effort. Kathy stayed on, too, and in short order, they met Bond, Gilday, and Valeri. The men were part of the Student Tutor Education Program (STEP), under which they had studied at Brandeis while they were on parole.

Fast-forward a year. In May 1971, I graduated. I was poised to start a prestigious clerkship with Luther M. Swygert, Chief Judge of the Seventh Circuit Court of Appeals, a prelude to an academic career. After my clerkship year, I wanted to get a taste of practicing law before returning to the ivory tower. Turning down offers from Wall Street law firms—money was irrelevant to a great many of us in 1971—I joined a small civil rights/criminal defense firm in Boston, Zalkind & Silverglate. Within a year, the firm broke up and Harvey Silverglate, one of my bosses, offered me an equal partnership share in a firm he was forming with Tom Shapiro, another young lawyer from a like-minded law practice. I accepted. Having neither experience nor money, my only contribution was my brains and my commitment. (My capital contribution to Silverglate, Shapiro, and Gertner—a $600 check—bounced.)

In May 1971, Susan Edith Saxe, honors graduate from a prestigious university, eldest daughter of a respected upper-middle-class family, was a fugitive, indicted for robbery and first-degree murder. She had become one of the first women to make the FBI's Ten Most Wanted list. While I was settling into my new firm, practicing law and teaching law school part time, she was on the run somewhere in the United States, with a different name, a different life, and unimaginable fear.

———

On March 27, 1975, Susan was apprehended walking down a Philadelphia street with her lover, Byrna Aronson. It was just good police work, so the newspapers reported, a beat cop who claimed to recognize Susan from a wanted poster. The identification was cinched when he somehow managed to notice a distinctive beauty mark in Susan's eye.

Susan was to be tried in Philadelphia first on several federal bank robbery charges. Two weeks before the Boston robbery that lead to the death of Officer Schroeder, the Bell Federal Savings and Loan Association in West Philadelphia had been robbed. And shortly before that, so had the National Guard Armory in Newburyport, Massachusetts. Susan and all the others were implicated in all three crimes. The government's plan was to try the Philadelphia federal charges first, then the Newburyport federal charges, and then the Massachusetts state murder/robbery charges.

Her lawyer, Katie Roraback, who also had been on the New Haven Common that day five years before, already had a team of talented, progressive lawyers, David Rudovsky and Hollie Maguigan, but she needed someone to advise her on Massachusetts law for Susan's eventual return to Boston. It was a small, supporting role, perfect for a beginner. When she scoped out what she wanted me to do, I was almost relieved.

En route from Boston to Philadelphia, for my first meeting with the legal team and Susan, I studied the law of bail and rendition, the procedures governing the return of a prisoner from one state to another. Although it's second nature to any experienced lawyer, this material was all new to me. I memorized everything, trying to sound not just knowledgeable but confident.

Soon it was clear to me that no matter what happened in Philadelphia, Susan's future would be determined by the Boston charges, which were life imprisonment felonies. (Massachusetts had no death penalty.) The Philadelphia and Newburyport charges were considerably less serious. Because of the vagaries of the law, if Susan were sentenced on the federal charges first and then convicted on the state charges, consecutive sentences were likely.

Katie negotiated a guilty plea for both of the federal cases which Susan could not refuse. The sentencing of the two federal cases would be put off until after the Boston state case had been resolved. With the judge's approval, the prosecutor would recommend ten years to be served concurrently with whatever sentence the Boston judge meted out. (Although no one said so, everyone expected Susan to be convicted for the Boston crime, which was bound to result in a lengthy prison term, perhaps even life imprisonment.) Most important of all, Susan did not have to give the government any information about Kathy Power, who was still at large, or the people who had sheltered both of them for nearly five years. In fact, the grand juries investigating the charges of harboring a fugitive would be dissolved. This was paramount in Susan's thinking.

With the federal charges resolved, Katie surprised everyone by deciding not to represent Susan in Boston. She did not want another long trial away from her New Haven home. And, as she told me, she already had experienced her "Susan Saxe" when she represented Black Panther Erica Huggins, a woman about whom she cared deeply. Katie recommended me, and even more important, urged me to take the case. "It is not often that your work and your heart come together," she told me. "Don't let this chance pass you by."

However much I disagreed with what Susan was charged with doing, whatever different choices I had obviously made, she had acted out of conscience and now faced spending the rest of her life in prison. I simply could not turn down a chance to make a difference to her—someone my age, my generation, even my background, and someone whom, over time, I grew to love. Teaching, my intended direction, could never measure up. Furthermore,

I could not admit how frightened and overwhelmed I felt at the prospect of representing her. Because the inevitable "they" (my father, my professors, my legal "colleagues," society) thought that women were not tough enough for criminal defense work, I also had to prove that "they" were wrong. Susan had taken far greater risks than I ever had, greater than I had ever imagined. The Vietnam War was over. Whatever passions had moved her and others in 1970 were, even to many of those who once had been in the antiwar movement, a distant memory. Her acts were bound to be viewed through a different, far more critical, lens.

Despite the odds, Susan turned out to be every bit as committed as a defendant as she had been as an activist. With her entire future at stake, she wanted to use her case to advance yet another progressive cause. She insisted on a woman lawyer, no matter how green. She was determined to have her defense team represent her feminist values as well as her case. How could I turn her down?

Did I think about how little experience I had? I tried not to. This profession had been far harder than I had imagined at Yale— far more hostile, far more bigoted. In my first jury trial, representing an African American woman accused of not stopping for a white policeman after he signaled her to stop, the judge instructed the jury, "Black people have rights, but no more rights than anyone else." And then: "To acquit this woman, you have to find an officer of the Commonwealth was a miserable liar!" The jury convicted in a nanosecond. And when I asked another judge if a woman law student could sit with me at counsel table, he quipped, "One woman in a courtroom is bad enough." And those were the judges who were honest.

Did I worry that little or no money was involved? No, but my partners did. The case, likely a loser, could take down the new practice. But after a small contribution from Susan's parents, and much agonizing, my partners agreed. Harvey would keep the firm afloat. Tom, with perhaps three years' more experience than I, would keep up his practice, but he also work with me on the case.

Did I think about the family of the slain officer, and the enormous toll that his death took on them? I think about it now—a great deal now—but I did not then. I thought I wasn't supposed to.

I thought advocacy meant putting on blinders and focusing only on my client. Candidly, that approach was functional. It was too hard for a young lawyer to separate the personal from the professional, a human being's empathy from an advocate's single-minded focus.

Did I think about the political implications? Not much. I had a well-worked-out, if abstract, theory about political trials which had been part of the "law of mass arrests" curriculum. But I also knew that the violence of the early 1970s had threatened to undo whatever popular support there had been for the antiwar movement. Still, to do what I had to do—what I now wanted to do—I had to be monomaniacal. I wanted to save this young woman's life and somehow believed I could.

When Susan asked me how many jury trials I had done, I rounded off three to the nearest ten. When she asked me how many years I had practiced, I once again rounded up the three to the nearest ten. She knew better. It was the last time I wasn't totally honest with her.

———

"Life" was everything that was supposed to be ahead of Susan and me—love, adventure, career, children. But a conviction for felony murder—a theory of first-degree murder—carried a mandatory punishment of life in prison, without parole.

This was my first serious felony trial, so my learning curve would be on prime time. The publicity was anti-student, anti-Semitic, anti-lesbian. And it was unrelenting; it started in 1970, when the robbery took place, flourished during the prosecution of the male co-defendants, and continued unabated while the women were underground. Susan was a caricature of everything that the public had grown to fear during the years of Nixon/Agnew—a feminist, radical revolutionary, and a lesbian to boot. The newspapers linked her with Cathy Wilkerson and Kathy Boudin, who had survived the March 1970 explosion of a Greenwich Village townhouse where bombs were supposedly being assembled for the antiwar effort, and who then disappeared into what came to be known as the Weather Underground. Also underground was Bernardine Dohrn, charged in the 1972 "Days of Rage," when the Weathermen, an antiwar group, battled police in Chicago. Dohrn soon joined Susan on the FBI's Ten Most Wanted list.

Officer Schroeder, in contrast, was justifiably lionized. He was the very best of the force—decorated for bravery, a religious Catholic, with nine young children, each of whom would follow his footsteps into public service. Schoolchildren, one paper reported, were being given civics lessons in which the name "Schroeder" was synonymous with "heroism, dedication, and service." He had been caught, as another described, "in the crossfire of a surly end-of-the-world campus mood."

The judge, Walter McLaughlin, had been on the bench for decades. He had a reputation for being a bright, no-nonsense judge who carefully controlled the courtroom. But as Bill Homans, a noted civil rights lawyer, said, he would not get "high marks for compassion." He had presided over the prosecutions of Valeri and Gilday and had every reason to believe that the Saxe case would simply follow the same script. He was slated to retire at age seventy, and this was to be his last major case.

The prosecutor, John Gaffney, was reputedly one of the best in Suffolk County, having lost only one of the 200 murder cases that he had prosecuted since joining the DA's staff twenty years earlier. He had beaten the legendary F. Lee Bailey five times. He was fifty-six, born and raised in Boston, and lived with his wife of thirty-one years and two of their four children. A graduate of Boston College and Northeastern University Law School, he too was a religious Catholic, as well as a wounded World War II veteran with a Purple Heart and a Bronze Star. He was "one of the boys," with the enthusiastic support of the courthouse gang, from the police, to the DA's staff, down to the court officers and elevator operators.

And as for me, I was invisible. The day the trial began, after two years of high-profile pretrial hearings in which I made almost all the court arguments, the headline read:

> Susan Saxe Trial Opens Today;
> Prosecutor Called Able, Tough

Me? If they mentioned me at all, I was the "lady lawyer" or "Ms. Gertner; she prefers that designation."

Butting heads with Gaffney was like dealing with the catcher "trash-talking" the batter at the plate. When I wore a loose-fitting dress to court, he cracked that I had "no business" looking pregnant while I was representing "that lesbian." At a hearing to determine the admissibility of a survey of the attitudes of potential jurors, he asked only one question of the woman PhD who headed the survey team: "Were any of the surveyors gay?"

To the press, he bragged that he'd spent only a fraction of the time that I was pouring into the case. He'd "been through it all once before" with Gilday, and could "probably try it in his sleep." Asked if he had ever tried a case against Nancy Gertner and Thomas Shapiro, Susan Saxe's defense team, he replied: "Have they ever tried a case before?"

Yes, but only a few; you have to start somewhere.

CHAPTER TWO

The All-Women Team

I was born on the lower East Side of Manhattan, the second daughter of Moishe and Sadie Gertner. The four of us lived in a tenement until I was seven, sleeping in the same room, with me in a crib because there was no space for another bed. Flushing, Queens, was a move up—to a lower-middle-class community in the flight path of LaGuardia Airport.

My grandparents had been immigrants, Orthodox Jews from Poland and Hungary at the turn of the century. And although my parents were American citizens, they—my father in particular—had Old World attitudes toward women. He was left back in the first grade because he could only speak Yiddish. He had one semester of college and then quit to support his family in the linoleum business (the Gartner Floor Covering Company—"Gartner" rather than "Gertner" because the midwife who had delivered him misspelled his name on the birth certificate). My mother graduated from high school and took secretarial jobs. When they married, he insisted that she quit. He would not even let her learn to drive.

My sister, Roz, and I were similarly tethered, or so my father thought. He urged Roz to take commercial rather than academic courses at Flushing High School; an academic course would be "wasted" on a woman, he said. We could not go "out of town" to

13

college, he insisted: "Girls are supposed to live in their father's house or their husband's."

We didn't listen. My sister took that academic path and went to Barnard College, then on to graduate school. As the second child, I had even more ambitious plans. But working on civil rights struggles in the South in the early 1960s, just for the summer? Out of the question. Going to Radcliffe College in Cambridge, Massachusetts? Never. Barnard, because it was in New York City, because my sister had gone there, was my only choice.

Barnard, it would seem, betrayed his trust. I entered the school as Flushing High School's valedictorian, on the one hand, and yes, cheerleader, and homecoming queen (actually, second runner-up), on the other. I left a feminist, antiwar activist, determined to have a career. Betty Friedan's *The Feminine Mystique* was required reading when I arrived; marches a regular activity when I left. And after graduation, I fled for New Haven, then Chicago, then Boston, unmarried and seemingly unrepentant.

Still, my father and I were very, very close. No matter what he said—and said often—he acted differently. It was as if there were a text and a subtext. The subtext I sensed every night after television's *Eleventh Hour News with John Cameron Swayze* went off and we debated—actually, fought—about every political issue of the day—"Red China's" admission to the United Nations, then the war, then women's rights. What his engagement with me said was that I was important, that my thoughts were to be reckoned with, that I could do anything. And because I loved him so very much, I learned how to fight and love, confront and respect, disagree but cherish. When I faced a jury in later years, Moishe's rules resonated, his candor, his common sense, his principles. I would have to struggle with them, just as I had struggled with him all my life.

So I called my father about Susan's case. How would this play in Queens with his Sunday-morning paddleball group (four middle-aged men, playing ball half the time, arguing ferociously the other half) and my mother's Friday-night poker game (twelve mostly overweight women, one hour of cards, chain smoking, two hours of highly caloric "snacks")? Not to mention their respective pinochle and mahjong buddies on Tuesday nights? How would the rest of the family, still on the Lower East Side, react? Would he be embarrassed? He said: "Embarrassed? Not at all. I want you to take the case, to work as hard as you can, to win, and be praised by all. Then I want Susan to get out of jail, cross the street—and be hit by a car." Moishe, in a nutshell.

———

Susan came from an upper-middle-class family in Albany, New York. Also Jewish, she was the oldest sibling, her brother five and a half years younger. She was the first in her immediate family to finish college. Her mother, Rose, a high school graduate, had chosen to be a homemaker. Her father, Eliot, went to the University of Mississippi, but he left school to support his family. He went into a manufacturing business with his two brothers and was quite successful.

Susan was the golden girl, excelling in school from the outset. She entered kindergarten at four because she had already learned to read. And unlike my family, in hers the old expectations for women were sprinkled more liberally with the new. They wanted her married, to be sure, but with the best education they could afford—even if that meant she went "out of town" to Brandeis.

Although there had been no contact during her five years underground, her family never wavered after her arrest: "We'll stick by her through this mess," her mother would say, "and then I'll kick her teeth out for being such a damned fool when it's all over." Not unlike Moishe.

Had we run into each other that New Haven weekend in 1970, Susan and I would have been fast friends. Five years later, one in jail, one outside, we were.

———

Young lawyers have no filters. The "I've heard it all before," "do I believe him or her," or, later, the "how would it look for me to do that" kind of feelings had not yet emerged. I had even fewer filters than most my age. I was opposed to what I thought "professionalism" meant. It wrongly separated the lawyer from the client, encouraged elitism. I refused to carry a briefcase, the emblem of the professional. No, I would carry my papers in a paper bag. There would be no desk between me and my clients; we would sit on the same side of the table. And I would trudge into court in a miniskirt, hair down my back, one step from a flower child.

I would communicate with my client constantly, sharing the decision making. The lawyer-client relationship, I believed, should not replicate the powerlessness that may have pervaded the rest of the client's life. The *process* of representation was every bit as important as the *outcome*.

Happily, I made some accommodations before the Saxe case. I gave up on the paper bag when something personal, shall we say, popped out while I was reaching for my papers in court. And I learned to be more skeptical of my clients when a defendant I was interviewing on the same side of the desk helped himself to my wallet. I traded the flower child wardrobe for suits because courtrooms were heated with men's clothing in mind, and I also needed pockets to keep my hands from flailing about.

But nothing else. If I had to wear suits, they would be bright red. I would dote on my clients, and, in the parlance of the day, "empower" them.

With Susan, empowering was not a problem. She was bright and articulate, with definite ideas about her representation, more definite than mine. She believed that because she was likely to spend the rest of her life in jail and then be forgotten, she wanted her brief moment on the public stage—her trial—to be without compromise. Every part of the legal team was to reflect her feminism. While there could be men on the team, I was to lead.

And so, there was "Nancy Drew Associates," the investigative team that we organized and named after the crackerjack fictional teenage detective, composed of Sherry Edwards, an artist and teacher, and Cookie Rudolfi, who first came to us as a member of the National Jury Project. The NJP was a consulting firm charged with gathering information and giving advice about the Saxe jury. What these two young women lacked in experience, they made up for in determination and panache.

Women had to run the jury consultant team even though its founder, Dr. Jay Shulman, was a pioneer, with a string of victories in cases involving other antiwar and prison activists. Dr. Shulman could help, but the women on his staff, Elissa Kraus and Diane Wiley, had to take responsibility. That's just the way that our client insisted we run her defense.

So it wasn't simply Gertner, the novice. Susan was prepared to risk everything on an entire team of women novices, whose careers—mine included—would never be the same. There was Cathy Bennet, who would scrutinize the potential jurors, their affect and their interactions, and advise us as to their selection; she went on to consult for William Kennedy Smith, the nephew of Senator Edward Kennedy who was tried and acquitted in a high-profile rape case in 1991. Elissa and Diane would do survey research of attitudes in Suffolk County, on which we would base our selection decisions; they later became successful jury consultants in a wide range of cases. Sherry, soon joined by Cookie, would investigate everything, literally everything, and ultimately list "Nancy Drew" associates on their resumes.

Because Susan saw herself as part of a political movement— the antiwar movement, the women's movement, the gay rights movement—the trial also had to reflect the input of those groups. A defense committee was organized that was mostly women, activists, many gay. While Officer Schroeder's death, the guns, and the threatened violence deeply troubled them, they were committed to Susan and concerned that there could not be a fair trial for someone like her. I was supposed to consult with them regularly, without somehow risking FBI infiltration or the disclosure of client confidences. It was a thin line. (My father understood the defense committee even less then he understood Susan. Years later, when I represented more traditional clients, shareholders suing corporations, defendants accused of white-collar crime, he would quip, "And what does the defense committee think of all of this?")

Organizing everyone was Byrna Aronson, Susan's partner. While Byrna was as surprised by Susan's arrest as anyone—she had not known Susan's real identity—she was a stalwart. She was

Susan's voice—communicating her wishes, her feelings, just as a spouse would do. She had set aside her life for this trial, working as a paralegal for us. I was so impressed with her that when the trial was over, I hired her as the firm's investigator. She didn't look the part—openly gay, short, cropped hair, given to wearing leather, with keys on a chain at her side—but none of us looked our parts. It was just a question of degree.

Beyond the "Nancy Drew Associates," the defense committee, and Byrna, there was Susan's family. Late at night, probably after her father had gone to bed, her mother would call. She wouldn't talk to Tom or Harvey, only to me. Sometimes the calls reminded me of my debates with Moishe after the *Eleventh Hour News:* What's wrong with the treatment of women, or gays, or prisoners in this country? What is this junk about being called "Ms."? Didn't she realize that this country was better than any other? She should be happy she lives here and not in Russia or Cuba!

And then she would grill me: Did Susan act like a lady in court? Why did she have to dress like a lesbian? And who was Byrna Aronson? Why couldn't Susan have been a lawyer like me? Could she go to law school after the trial was over? What about Yale? And so it would go—on and on—Susan and me, our loves, our choices, even our looks. But no matter how much she would merge the two of us in her mind, I was not Susan.

To the press, I was invisible. To Gaffney and the police, I was a rabid feminist/radical, representing everything that they reviled. To the lesbian feminists around me, I was "terminally heterosexual," a feminist with eye makeup, shaved legs, and a bright red suit, a carnivore while they were vegetarians, far too moderate, too much the compromiser. To Susan's family, I was her proxy. And while representing Susan aligned with my politics and my heart, I felt I was neither fish nor fowl, neither a member of the lawyers' club nor of the defense committee, neither Susan's friend nor "just" her lawyer. It was a lonely perch.

All that was clear was that Susan could not afford a merely symbolic defense—a woman lawyer, the right gestures, a political show trial. While I had to reflect her goals, her principles, I somehow had to win.

You walk into a courtroom. You are the only woman, years younger than anyone else. The court officer checks your credentials—yours alone, among all those waiting for a case to be called.

"You a lawyer?" he asks, sometimes incredulous, sometimes sarcastic. What he is really saying is, "Hey lady, you don't fit in." Professor Randall Kennedy of Harvard Law School talks about the crime of being "out of place," the black man accosted by the police because he is walking in the white neighborhood at night, the black woman who is not buzzed in to the fancy upscale clothing store. These are the ceremonies of exclusion, made all the worse because they are self-fulfilling prophecies. You *feel* "out of place." You come to believe that you don't really belong there.

Add this: you are representing someone everyone seems to hate. The court elevator man is silent when you enter. The court officer can't make small talk without adding a sexist joke or two, perhaps an antigay comment, just to test you. "Who the hell are you?" is unspoken. How dare you make all this fuss when we all know she's guilty? A beloved police officer, a hero, died. You should be ashamed of yourself.

Susan's voice within me: Ignore them. Be aggressive, even when Moishe and Sadie raised you not to be. Be a leader when you think you haven't the foggiest notion what you are doing. Critique yourself: Why did you let so-and-so monopolize the conversation? Why did you sound so tentative? Wake up early. Practice your arguments in the shower until your skin is wrinkled and the hot water runs out. Lower the register of your voice. (You sound like Minnie Mouse when you are nervous.) Put your hands in your pockets. Wear red. Breathe.

Work was my armor. I read everything about the previous trials, every transcript, every piece of evidence, even every newspaper article. I critiqued the performance of the previous lawyers. If I liked what they did, I memorized it. If I liked Judge McLaughlin's rulings in the earlier cases, I said: "But Judge, this is what you did in the Gilday case, on x date, y page!" If I did not like the earlier decision, I filed a brief against it, carefully researched and argued. With my female paralegals and investigators, I would unearth facts that no one had come up with before. I would raise legal issues not raised in the men's cases, and in some cases, never raised before in Massachusetts courts.

The problem was, we had no idea how to defend the case.

———•———

I was late for the first hearing—not a propitious start. Outside the courthouse, a dozen women demonstrated on Susan's behalf. A bare-chested young man unfurled a banner reading, "Free Saxe—Jail U.S. Military for Vietnam War Crimes."

My job was to fight for bail on behalf of a woman who had been a fugitive for five years, who had been on the FBI's Ten Most Wanted list, and who was charged with the first-degree murder of a police officer. Not likely.

My second salvo in the case was even less promising: filing a motion to have McLaughlin removed from the case on the basis of bias, essentially attacking a respected judge. Gaffney admitted that he had met alone with McLaughlin while the case was in Philadelphia to see if the judge would accept a plea for Susan to a reduced charge, manslaughter. (McLaughlin reportedly would not at that time.) Ex parte—one-sided—communications are totally improper; they compromise a judge's ability to be fair. Not wanting to burn bridges, though, we moved to seal the motion, and our flat-out challenge to his impartiality was couched in legal language deferential to the judge.

Indignantly, McLaughlin denied the motion. How dare we question his ethics? But for all his indignation, I learned twenty-five years later that he continued to meet with Gaffney regularly, in the judge's private chambers, even during the trial itself. The judge would criticize Gaffney's performance the previous day and make suggestions about how to improve it. Gaffney would try to predict what I would do, and the two would strategize. As paranoid as we were, we hadn't imagined anything like this was taking place.

Nothing was what it seemed. The first time I visited Susan at the Worcester County House of Correction, she whispered, "They're listening," and gestured in the direction of the guards. Paranoid, I thought, the tiresome paranoia of the left. That couldn't happen in 1975; attorney-client communications were privileged.

But I agreed to investigate. So I coyly talked to Sheriff Joseph A. Smith—yes, coyly. "Sheriff, you have such a modern place here—all of these neat devices. Tell me about them." And he did. Puffing up his chest, he showed "the little lady" around. "Here," he told me, "is where we can listen to what goes on in the jail." "Does that include conversations that take place in that little room over there?" I said, pointing to the attorney-client conference room. "Yes," he answered, proudly.

Bingo. Susan was right. In fact, as Smith later explained to the judge at a pretrial hearing, he could not understand why we interviewed Susan in the attorney-client room when he offered us the chaplain's office. The chaplain's office had no "monitor or other devices, quite obviously because of the confidentiality of confession and the communications between clergymen and those seeking their help." So that's it. The only privilege that this man respected was the priest-penitent privilege; the attorney-client privilege took a decided back seat. The judge ordered that we be permitted to conduct our interviews in the chaplain's office.

Rumors swirled. In October 1975, the *Worcester Telegram*, quoting Sheriff Smith, insinuated that "more" was going on in that room than legal work: *Pax Centurion*, a Boston police union newspaper, railed in a March 1976 article about "the incongruity of that setting—the priest's vestments, religious books, holy articles—seemingly ignored." The sheriff sent a copy of Susan's visitor log to the police newspaper; the names of all paralegal visitors were announced, including one occasion when Byrna, not on a legal visit, signed in as "lover." The judge, to his credit, interceded; hearing about these travails with considerable patience, he approved the list of paralegals, including Byrna.

———

I saw Susan all the time, whether there was a professional reason or not. I didn't want her to feel alone or abandoned, as I would have in her shoes. I told her that I wanted her to have tea with me in my Cambridge apartment, not just sometime in the future but now, while we were both young. I felt guilty when we were not in touch, pained every time the prison gates closed behind me, leaving her in and me out. Sometimes I would get a wake-up call from her. I would say, "Susan, can I see you today?" She would answer, as if she had a crowded calendar, "Just a minute, let me check. Yes, I'll be here."

And after we discovered the bugging, whenever she would write to us, she would write on the outside of the envelope: "Attorney-Client Correspondence (if you turkeys must open this, could you at least keep the tuna stains off the letter)."

———

Process was as important as outcome, I insisted. I filed a motion to have Susan be co-counsel; denied. Then I filed a motion to have her sit with Tom and me at counsel table, at the very minimum. Again, motion denied. (In those days, prisoners were supposed to sit in a dock, which was nothing more than a cage, a medieval throwback. Two years after Susan's trial, the dock was eliminated.) After that came a motion, Harvey's brainstorm, that suggested— seriously—that if she could not be moved out of the dock, the legal team would move into it. Also denied. We even moved to withdraw on the eve of trial so that Susan could take on her own defense, with us as standby counsel. Denied. We appealed to Massachusetts's highest court—unsuccessful.

———

Enough already, enough about process, and participation, Tom said. What's the defense? Still working on it, I insisted. How about challenging the government's case, in advance of trial, molecule by molecule? That's a start.

There are many reasons why a lawyer raises issues pretrial. Some challenges must be raised before the jury is selected. Sometimes a lawyer wants to raise complex issues in a more deliberative setting. It is difficult to give careful consideration to legal challenges in the midst of the pressures of a jury trial, where the jury is patiently waiting to hear the evidence (and all the more difficult if it is sequestered, to boot) and especially when the case is a high-profile one. Sometimes the motions are for the judge and the public: you may think this case is open and shut; it is not.

I had additional reasons. The prosecutor, and to a degree the judge, believed that this would be the Gilday trial redux, that my novel legal challenges were just minor diversions on the road to Susan's inevitable conviction. I had to prove them wrong. But beyond the legal strategy, I needed both the time and the setting. I had to slow down the proceedings so that I could prepare everything—and hopefully, learn the craft. And just as I had to script everything in advance, I had to raise legal issues in a setting in which there could be extended legal argument and briefing. The truth was that I was more comfortable there than before a jury. That would change.

We challenged the government's first-degree murder theory, the felony murder rule, the first such challenge in Massachusetts. Susan, while not accused of actually shooting Officer Schroeder, could still be held responsible for his murder. Anyone who intentionally took part in certain felonies, like armed robbery, was guilty of murder if a killing took place in the course of its commission or attempted commission. The theory was a throwback to a time when all felonies were punished by death. Directly participating in the murder made no difference to the outcome. Nor did it matter if the defendant had no intention of committing a murder, or if she had tried to prevent it. She would be held responsible even if the shooter had killed accidentally.

In fact, the shooter was treated more fairly than other participants. He would be charged with standard first-degree murder, not this vicarious liability version. Evidence of *his* intent—what the law calls mens rea—could be offered in mitigation, and, if the jury agreed, could lead to conviction of second-degree murder or manslaughter, which carried lesser penalties. The non-shooter, however, was either a knowing participant in a felony from which a killing resulted, or she was not—first-degree murder, or acquittal.

In a sense, severe punishment turned on a fortuity. Someone

who, while robbing a bank, wants to kill every guard he sees but can't get his weapon to fire will get off "only" with armed robbery. Someone who wanted to avoid bloodshed but winds up in the middle of a police shootout is convicted of murder. The rule, we insisted, violated due process, equal protection, and the Eighth Amendment's protection against cruel or unusual punishment.

The hearing was classic: I would lay out the argument, chapter and verse. Gaffney would spoof, sarcasm dripping: "This is an excellent treatment of some law school issue, but not in the case of Saxe and the gang she was hanging around with. They prepared to go into the bank armed with the clear intent, if anyone got in their way, to kill them. That's what the government will show." I wasn't a real lawyer, he was saying, I was bookish, not gritty or tough. What did I know? Sometimes the judge would join in, with a sarcastic remark or even an argument that Gaffney left out. I pressed on, pretending that I had their respect.

McLaughlin upheld the murder charge, but he opened a window, wider than had been opened before, allowing the defendant to "rebut the evidence of intent to commit the felony and the evidence of causation." Perhaps the defense could show—if our client would let us, and that was a big if—that she was horrified at the murder, that she did not intend to kill anyone, that the shooter had acted in a fashion inconsistent with his instructions. In addition, we might be able to show that the felony was long over when the murder took place. There was some chance—however slight—that an issue as simple as timing would enable us to defend the murder charge.

And there was an additional benefit to making these arguments. The public now knew that Susan was not the shooter—a fact that the media, incredibly, had largely ignored. Maybe now it would be harder to demonize her.

Then we whittled away at the government's evidence. One of the two Beacon Street apartments in the Back Bay had been unlawfully searched. When the police officers' illegal entry yielded evidence that looked interesting (guns and ammunition), they invented an informant to justify their actions in the warrant application to the judge. And they gave their invention a Jewish name,

"Ralph Applebaum," of course, a Jew hanging out with the other students from Brandeis, a Jewish university.

The lie was transparent. No Mr. Applebaum could be produced; by the time of the hearing, he had conveniently died. (Susan had never heard of him.) Nor did the police have any idea how Mr. Applebaum came upon his information. Had he ever been in the Beacon Street apartment? When? And while the warrants to search the two Beacon Street apartments linked to the robbery were applied for at the same time and executed on the same day, there was something fishy. The date stamp on the "Applebaum warrant" was six days later than the date stamp on the other, supposedly contemporaneous, search warrant. Rather than being numbered sequentially, as they would have been had the officers obtained their warrants at the same time, the two were four numbers apart.

Judge McLaughlin suppressed the fruits of the "Applebaum" search, but it was only a symbolic victory. None of the weapons found there had been tied to the Brighton robbery. Still, it was not a futile gesture. Maybe the public was beginning to understand that the investigation had not been entirely fair.

So far, so good. By keeping out some of the government's evidence, and challenging the bona fides of what was left, maybe we could argue that the evidence against Susan was not as overwhelming as the media reported, not beyond a reasonable doubt. But argue to whom? Reasonable doubt was a hard-enough concept for ordinary citizens to grasp. For the likely jurors in the Saxe case, it seemed well nigh impossible.

Someone who is well known to the public, and indeed, respected before being charged with a crime, can begin a trial clothed in the presumption of innocence. The public's views of him or her are shaped beforehand, untainted by information about the criminal charge. But in a high-profile case, with an unknown defendant, the public learns about him or her only in terms of the crime charged. She's a murder defendant, not a person. And that information is rarely balanced. Pre-arrest, the only information likely to be released is prosecution-friendly information: police facts (so-and-so wanted for this charge), the status of the investigation (all points bulletin issued for so-and-so's arrest), the results of searches (biggest drug bust in the galaxy in so-and-so's house), the wanted posters (so-and-so on the Ten Most Wanted list). Few defendants have a lawyer to counter the charges before they are arrested. Once charges are brought, the rules change, and there are formal limits on what the attorneys for either side can say. By then, however, the damage to the defense case has already been done. The defendant is stigmatized; the presumption of innocence is at risk of evaporating.

I was prepared to do whatever the NJP suggested to ensure the fairest possible panel of jurors. Jury "science" was in its infancy, but that hardly mattered. The NJP had more of a track record than I had.

I moved to dismiss the case because of the virulent publicity. My staff and I collected reams of publicity, in chronological order, from 1970 through 1975. We subpoenaed television records and radio tapes. We did a fancy content analysis of the coverage—the numbers of times that certain derogatory words were used (*radical, revolutionary, terrorist, violent, underground, fugitives, sick, sexual preference*), government sources were quoted (FBI's Ten Most Wanted list, interviews with police officers and FBI agents), uncharged crimes in other states, inflammatory headlines, and so on. There had been 424 articles as of the end of 1975—49,689 lines of newsprint.

We arranged for an opinion survey of potential jurors in Suffolk County. More than 90 percent were familiar with Susan Saxe. Her name recognition was higher in Boston at the time she went to trial than that of Attorney General John Mitchell when he went to trial for the Watergate break-in in Washington, D.C. More than three quarters of them (76 percent) believed that she was guilty of one or more of the crimes with which she was charged; and 62 percent, or two thirds, believed that she needed to prove her innocence.

Voir dire, the questioning of jurors before they were selected, would not make any difference in this regard. When polled, 59 percent of the sample agreed that they could be fair and impartial jurors. Yet, of the very people who stated that they could be impartial jurors, 74 percent admitted that they believed that Susan had participated in the offense, 57 percent stated that she should prove her innocence, and 42 percent said she should be severely punished! If a hypothetical jury had been selected from those who announced they could be "fair and impartial," nine would believe that the defendant probably took part in the crime, seven that she had to prove her innocence, and five that she deserved severe punishment.

At last, Judge McLaughlin was impressed. While he would not dismiss the charges, he would take special measures to assure a fair jury. The jury would be sequestered during the entire proceeding; they would not be allowed to go home after court each day. There would be lawyer voir dire "in appropriate instances" after the court's questioning, something unprecedented in Massachusetts, where only judges questioned jurors. And the defendant would have thirty-two peremptory challenges to the government's sixteen (the usual number in a murder case). (Peremptory challenges are challenges for which the defense does not have to give a reason.) Given the prejudice in the jury pool, we argued that questioning— whether by judge or lawyer—would not suffice to ferret out bias. Not only did we need a greater number of challenges than usual, but we needed proportionally more challenges than the government, to match the bias in the potential juror pool.

By the spring, most of the pretrial matters had been resolved. The trial likely would begin in June.

CHAPTER THREE

Saving Her Life, Inventing Mine

At the end of April, Sheriff Smith started acting up again, limiting paralegal visits just when we needed them most. There would be a meeting to discuss this problem in Judge McLaughlin's chambers in the new Suffolk County courthouse. (Only in Boston does a "new" courthouse date from the 1930s.)

I parked my car and entered the old courthouse, which was adjacent to the new courthouse, where Judge McLaughlin had chambers. It was April 22, 1976, and I was late, again. As I ran through the basement connecting the two buildings, an explosion rocked the corridor. Then there was silence, the smell of fire, and the sound of people running and screaming. A bomb had been placed in the second-floor probation office. Someone waiting for the elevator—where I would have been had I been on time—was badly injured. I was shaken and frightened; there was a lunacy in the air that seemed to put everyone at risk. When I returned to my office, the press called, asking me if Susan had been behind this. I answered, "If she were, she was trying to get rid of me!"

The trial was postponed until September. For me, it was a reprieve; five more months to learn.

——•——

I spent the summer like an athlete in training. I worked day and night, and when I wasn't working, I exercised—biking, running, or swimming—as if I were about to embark on a marathon. I took every fact, every case, every theory of relevance and reduced it to a litigation notebook, indexed and exhaustive. By the time I finished the trial notebook, I felt strangely confident, even calm: I had done everything possible to prepare.

It was like learning a language; you begin to know it so well that you can use idiomatic expressions, be creative, even be inspired. A trial is just the same. You see the whole and where the pieces fit in. You can be flexible and extemporaneous. And you can speak poetry.

But I still did not have much to say. There was still no defense, no different version of what had happened that day or where Susan had been. And Susan imposed profound limitations on almost every defense theory I suggested. There were words she would not allow me to use, defenses I could not mount, because they were inconsistent with her principles, because they cast aspersions on people who had supported her, or because they took advantage of sexist stereotypes. It did not matter if these words or this approach would help her defense, or even that they were true. It did not matter if they would have little or no impact on defendants yet untried, like Kathy Power, or defendants who had already been convicted, like Lefty Gilday.

I could not emphasize that it was Gilday, not Susan, who pulled the trigger. Nor could I suggest that she was somehow coerced by the "older" men, the ex-cons, the "poor vulnerable woman" approach. She would not be painted as anything other than the architect of her own fate; she would not point the finger at anyone else. Still, while she wanted to take responsibility for her acts, she was not about to plead guilty.

It was a hard line for many to understand. She participated in this crime, believing she was doing the right thing at the time, trying to end the war. She would not denounce anyone else or play the "woman" card, even if those were believable defenses. She would be accountable in her way, but that did not mean pleading guilty. It was, after all, five years after the crime, a very long and significant five years. In this interim period, Susan had lived an ordinary life, with friends and a new family, a quiet, law-abiding existence. Not only had the world changed, but she had changed as well. And a guilty plea, even to second-degree murder, would still mean life imprisonment, with eligibility for parole only after fifteen years.

Besides, she did not *have* to plead guilty. She fully expected to be convicted. So did everyone else—except, perhaps, me. I wanted nothing more than to save her life. So, the dilemma: I had to find a way to defend her without taking refuge in the symbols that she had rejected all her life. The pretrial challenge to the felony murder rule was acceptable because that rule disadvantaged many defendants: every "wheelman" whose cohorts kill inside the store unbeknownst to him, every young woman who went along with her boyfriend's shenanigans and found herself in the middle of a shootout. I could challenge illegal searches, like that of the Beacon Street apartment, or unfair procedures, like bugging the lawyer-client room at the Worcester jail. But what about emphasizing timing, that the robbery was over when the shooting of Officer Schroeder took place? Or her reaction when she learned of it? Would she let me defend her against the murder charge at the very least, even if I could not defend her against the robbery charge?

Of course, there was always the political defense—justifying Susan's acts as part of the antiwar movement, as other activists had done. While that was true to her politics in 1970, by the time of the trial I knew better. In any event, we (Tom and I, Susan and Byrna), understood that if it came to that, all was lost. There was no meaningful "political" defense to bank robbery or worse, murder.

We were supposed to provide the government with a witness list in advance of trial. If a name were not on that list, we ran the risk of the judge excluding him or her. On the other hand, we were not required to call everyone on the list as a witness. To keep our options open, however disagreeable they were, we turned in a witness list replete with all the icons of the antiwar movement: Daniel Berrigan, the antiwar Catholic priest; Howard Zinn, a radical professor from Boston University; Patricia Swinton, arrested, tried, and acquitted of crimes deriving from the Weather Underground. Newspaper columns went on and on about the relationship between Susan, her offenses, and the antiwar moment. Letters to the editor were written on her behalf by antiwar leaders. We did nothing to stop the speculation about our "defense."

I say "we," especially from this point on. Tom and I, Byrna, and the other paralegals met each and every day with Susan to go over the day's events and to strategize. And Harvey went from interjecting his irreverent ideas from time to time to being a regular contributor.

I lost weight and then bought a whole new collection of red suits. Sadie was pleased.

———

When the trial started on September 15, 1976, the courtroom was filled to capacity.

People had lined up for hours before the doors opened. A special, high-security corridor and metal detector—the first in the state—had been installed on the eighth floor of the new courthouse.

I invited my parents. In the middle of a heated argument at sidebar about a juror, I saw my father out of the corner of my eye, talking to a reporter. Oh, no! I thought. Filling him with stories about my bedwetting, no doubt. No such luck. A reporter had strode up to him, pad in hand. "You are Nancy Gertner's father?" he demanded. "No comment," my father replied, taking his cue from the politicians we watched on TV. Wonderful. Now he was denying paternity.

We received the list of potential jurors—some 800 names— in advance, but it had little information beyond the juror's occupation and address. The NJP prepared index cards for each, with whatever information the pretrial survey had disclosed: "This juror lives in such and such neighborhood"; "this juror works for a company that is heavily unionized," etc. Using a large network of volunteers, the NJP investigated the jury pool directly, although the volunteers were told not to talk to any juror, or any member of their family, or any of their close friends. We had more information about this jury pool than any Massachusetts lawyer had ever had.

Did we "hand-pick" this jury to make it tilt to the defense side? Hardly. Hand-picking was impossible. As I said before, the overwhelming majority of the potential jurors believed that Susan was guilty. And those who did not were hardly pro-Susan. We could not even count on a potential juror's assurance of impartiality. The survey showed that even those who believed they were impartial also insisted that Susan was guilty. We needed finer tools— scalpels rather than the usual meat axes—to carve out those who had not followed the case, or if they had, could somehow disentangle their current thoughts from their earlier impressions. And even with those tools, the most we could do was challenge jurors at the margins, the ones most obvious about their biases. For Gaffney, selection was a breeze. In this climate, almost any twelve people would do.

Each juror was questioned individually, in open court, by the judge. Judge McLaughlin was constantly impatient, rattling off the questions in legal language, as one newspaper noted, "like a priest leading a rosary hour." One potential juror reported that she had seen a "lovely" article in the *Boston Globe* the week before the trial began. When asked whether she could be fair and impartial, notwithstanding that article, she assured the judge that she could. I literally begged for lawyer voir dire. I knew that article. It had a drawing of a hand with a gun pointing at an officer's back—as if that were Susan's hand—and it went downhill from there. "All right," the judge said to me. "You can question." I hadn't the foggiest idea where to begin.

I took a breath and asked quietly, every inch the demure young woman: "When you read the newspaper, it is natural that you formed some impression. So when you read the paper on Sunday, did you get any impression about the defendant?"

She responded: "I don't even know Miss . . ." She searched for the name.

"Saxe," I offered.

"Yes, Saxe. I don't even know her case history. . . . I just know what she had done. . . ."

"When you say that you have only read about 'what she has done,' what do you mean by that?"

She answered: "Well, we all know what she has done. You know, we all know what she has done, so it is now up to the courts."

"Well," I said, "I am not sure what you mean when you say we all know what she has done."

"Well, we all know the girl went in and held up the bank and the policeman was shot here," the woman blurted out.

The judge excused her.

After the judge found that a juror was impartial based on his or her answers to the judge's questions, Tom, Susan, and I would caucus with the all-woman jury selection group, compare the information that came out in the questioning with the information from the survey and from the investigation. Sometimes we would also confer with the paralegals who had done the investigation.

Gaffney was exasperated by all this from the beginning. "I would like the court to set some limitation on these conferences. Are they going to go on indefinitely?" he protested. The judge, drumming his fingers against a microphone, replied, "I have it under consideration; you can be sure of that." A scant ten minutes after the selection process began, the judge and I clashed. At one point, he shouted: "I'm not going to ask what two hundred jurors have been discussing while waiting two days to be called. Miss Gertner, you've gone as far as you can push."

"I thought that was my job," I argued.

"Perhaps you're overdoing your job," he countered. To McLaughlin, our slowing down the pace of the selection, so that we could make informed judgments, was like the scratching of fingernails against a blackboard. *Perry Mason*, it was not.

After nearly a week, we finally had a jury. Twelve of the sixteen jurors were under the age of thirty-five. Two were not even twenty. It was the youngest jury ever to sit on a murder trial. Three jurors were black; seven were women. One juror was gay, we believed, based on the investigation. Another who seemed like a perfect prosecution choice, a young legal secretary living near her parents' home, may well have been involved in progressive causes. Maybe, just maybe, these jurors had not heard about the case, or if they had, it had not registered. And maybe, just maybe, some of them would identify with me, and more importantly, with Susan.

Identify with what, though? We still didn't have a defense.

—·—

By chance, the presentation of evidence at trial began on September 23, 1976—the sixth anniversary of the robbery and shooting. The bank witnesses came first: the tellers, branch manager, security guard, and two customers in the parking lot. Some had testified in the Gilday trial; they had identified only the male participants, if they had identified anyone. True to form, they had paid no attention to the woman in the bank. One of our investigators, Wendy Kaminer (now a famous social critic), had spoken with them, confirming that there would be no in-court identification. No dramatic "She's the one! I am sure." The only question now was how close Gaffney would skirt the line.

He tried. The woman in the bank wore a purple dress, one said. A purple dress had been found in a bag, together with bags from the State Street Bank and Trust Company, in a trash can at Logan Airport. To each witness, Gaffney would ask, "Is this the dress?"

"Can't tell."

"Well, is it this color?"

"Not sure."

"Does it resemble this color?"

"Maybe."

When things appear hopeless, it is easy to be creative. And for me, it was a clean slate. I had no "this is how I always do it" to get in the way. So I asked a number of women in the courtroom, including my secretary, then seated at counsel table, to wear various shades of purple to court the next day. One witness agreed that the color of my secretary's dress resembled the dress worn by the woman in the bank. In fact, as the jury could see, her dress was a different color from the dress found by the police. Another witness testified that the woman in the bank wore a purple dress, then called it a purple sweater, and finally said it was a purple skirt.

And those witnesses who paid any attention to the woman at

all described her only in the vaguest terms. I had an idea. Cross-examining Alton Otis, a teller, I pursued the following line of inquiry:

Q. And that description again, 5' 3" to 5' 5", that's about my height, would you say?

A. Well, she might have been shorter. I don't know.

Q. But you said 5' 3" to 5' 5". *(And then I kicked off my shoes and walked around in the courtroom in my stocking feet.)* I am about 5' 4". Would you say I am about the range of the woman?

A. Somewhere in that vicinity, yes.

Q. And this is very delicate, but you said this woman weighed between 125 and 135 pounds. *(In fact, most of the witnesses had described the woman as "stocky" or "hefty build.")*

A. Yes.

Q. It is usually hard to admit it, but would you say that's about my weight?

A. Well, maybe somewhere in that vicinity *(laughing)*.

Q. So what you are saying, Mr. Otis, is that the description fits me!

A. . . . Somewhat, yes . . .

I had learned by now that humor levels the playing field, defuses a tense trial, and humanizes the lawyer. In one of my first trials, representing a union suing the St. John of God Hospital for unfair labor practices, the judge asked me how it felt to be suing "St. John of God." I said, without missing a beat, that I took some consolation from the fact that it was "St. John of God, *Inc.*"

And humor was especially helpful for a feminist lawyer no one ever heard of, representing a radical lesbian "self-styled" revolutionary, as the papers described her. If the jurors liked me, maybe they would like her, too.

The description *did* fit me. The size, the build, even the color of the hair matched mine. All along, Susan's mother, the judge, even the prosecutor had confused the two of us. Now, even the bank witnesses joined in.

There were no eyewitness identifications of Susan, even after the barrage of publicity, the numerous times that her face had appeared in the paper or on television. Nor were there fingerprints identified as hers, or guns traced to her, or bank photographs of her during the robbery, even though there were photographs of the men. There was a single, blurry photograph of a woman, unaccompanied by anyone else and without weapons, which Gaffney claimed was Susan, casing the bank in advance. We dared to be hopeful. But the co-conspirators were yet to come—Valeri, an ex-con, who took part in the robbery, and a second man, Michael Fleischer, a Brandeis student who had helped plan it. Then there were the letters to her rabbi and her father. Surely, our mood would change.

When Valeri testified, he stuck to the script. It was his second retelling of the story; the first had been against Lefty Gilday in his trial. Valeri linked some of the physical evidence to Susan, as no other witness had—including the purple dress. He identified the blurry photograph of the woman in the bank before the robbery as Susan. But with no evidence independently corroborating his testimony, if the jury did not believe him and the links he was making, we still had a chance.

Cross-examination is a skill. It comes to some with experience, while others never get it right. There was what I have come to call, the "Aha! style," associated with some male lawyers. They bark at the witness, intimidating him with their physical presence or roaring their disapproval.

"Isn't it a fact that today is Wednesday, Mr. Witness?"

"No, sir. It is Tuesday."

"Aha!" exclaims the lawyer, pretending he had made some headway when in fact the detail was irrelevant.

I was not the barking, roaring, physically intimidating type.

Other lawyers are more subtle, learning to anticipate where a witness is likely to go, shifting tactics to meet new information, flexible yet focused, the tone at worst pointed and sarcastic. I was not certain I could do this because it meant going off the pre-arranged script, counting on my instincts. (And exactly what instincts were those?)

But I had several cards that Gaffney did not. Valeri was Susan's age, twenty-seven. He had come to court dressed in the costume of the 1960s—colorful headband, long hair. (These were his "court clothes," not the usual prison garb.) He seemed to have derived some meaning from his encounters with the Brandeis students and the antiwar movement. He seemed to want to please the defense as much as he could without endangering his government deal. In fact he had tried to call me before the trial (not the usual behavior of a government witness) and left a message protesting that he was being coerced into cooperating, that he "wanted out."

And so I began. Here were the ingredients for the classic "Aha!" examination: Valeri had a lengthy record, with previous incarcerations, and he had been in trouble with the law since his teens. He had been captured immediately after the robbery and charged with the murder of a police officer at a time when Massachusetts had a death penalty. He was facing additional federal robbery charges and a parole violation. "Aha!" I could say. He's just lying to please his captors. He'll say anything the government wants, whether or not it's true.

Effective enough on the surface, with all the right moves and gestures that an "Aha!" lawyer would love, that line of cross-examination still felt like running in place to me. The jury was bound to ask: Why name Susan Saxe, out of all the women Valeri knew? So I probed, seeking innocent details, the kind he might guilelessly provide. Valeri had a girlfriend, Linda LaMontagne, to whom he had given gifts purchased from his share of the proceeds of the robbery. That put her at risk of being a suspect, right? And to protect Linda, he pointed the finger at Susan as the woman in the bank. And why Susan Saxe? She had been part of the group from the NSIC, the antiwar group at Brandeis where they had all met. She had hung out at the two Beacon Street apartments where the robbery was planned. Given her background, if he accused Susan the police just might believe him, my questions suggested. No, no, he insisted, accepting some of the facts, but not my conclusions.

I needed more. Assuming that he felt guilt over Officer Schroeder's death but wanted to help Susan, I questioned him about the crime. I ventured into this area gently, fearing Susan would stop me short. He described the getaway—that he had not heard any shots, that he knew nothing at all of the murder. In fact, he testified, he, Bond, Kathy Powers, and Susan did not learn of the killing until they had left the bank, switched cars, and were well on their way. "[S]omewhere around Newton or Waltham," miles from the bank, they heard a news flash over the radio that revealed that a police officer had been shot during the robbery. Susan was "very upset." Later, when they rendezvoused, Bond tried to calm Susan and Valeri, who were agonizing over it—Why did a police officer have to be shot? Was there a need? What was the purpose of it?

On the stand, Valeri communicated their utter horror at the deed, and happily, Susan let me elicit this testimony. At least— the very least—Valeri's testimony was helping us disentangle the murder from the robbery, set the stage for a compromise verdict of some kind. The more headway I made, the more Gaffney interrupted. Every time I left the script—the cross-examination of Valeri in the Gilday case—he objected. It's a familiar tactic. Break your opponent's rhythm. Interrupt the narrative so that the jury can't follow the story. And if your opponent is a young, green woman, sound really indignant; she can't possibly be sure of what she is doing.

Objection! Gaffney would roar—he definitely was the roaring, barking type. Judge McLaughlin would sustain it. I would argue and argue, cite reams of case law to back up everything; with this judge, I couldn't count on just my powers of persuasion. I would ask the question a different way; another objection sustained. "You know when you ask that question that I am going to exclude it, and you go ahead and ask it anyway. . . ." Judge McLaughlin chided me, in front of the jury.

If we were making progress, as we thought we were, it was lost on the media. While F. Lee Bailey was described as "aggressive" in his representation of Patty Hearst, I was described as being "reprimanded" and "scolded" by the judge, like a child.

Testifying after Valeri was Michael Fleisher. He had been present in the two Beacon Street apartments before and after the crime, and he was charged with accessory after the fact of murder. He was not an ex-con, like Valeri. In fact, this was his first offense. He had married Helen Zelitch, another member of the NSIC, attended graduate school, and become a social worker. Unlike Valeri, he eschewed the '60s costume, cut his hair, and looked like a young, law-abiding professional. Most striking of all, in the Gilday trial, it appeared that he had gotten no benefit for his testimony, only that he thought cooperation would be "helpful." There were no deals, nothing that the government disclosed or experienced counsel in the previous trial had uncovered.

I talked to Fleisher's lawyer, Ben Lerner, before the trial. Again, I found a connection: Lerner and I had mutual friends in Philadelphia's progressive legal community—Susan's original lawyers in the Philadelphia case, David Rudovsky and Holly Maguigan. Lerner, now a public defender, would take my calls, and like Valeri, express his discomfort at the role he was playing. Still, he was fiercely protective of his client.

It was inconceivable that Lerner would have allowed his client to testify "cold," without some agreement. Between the charges in 1970 and this trial, nothing had happened—no motions, no hearings. Fleisher had simply gone on with his life, obviously "assuming" that he was protected from criminal prosecution. When I pressed Gaffney, he reiterated that there were no deals. When I questioned Fleisher about what he might have told his lawyer to get for him, Gaffney objected. "Attorney-client privilege," he argued. I, like all the previous defense lawyers before me, hit a wall.

I dug. I found a case that sounded similar: a lawyer was given assurances by the government that his client would get leniency, but he was told not to share this with the client. The lawyer told his client: "I can't disclose the details, but, don't worry, everything is taken care of." When the "Aha!" defense lawyer pounced—So, you have a deal!—he could say "No" without committing perjury. For the DA, it was perfect. The government got the benefit of the witness's cooperation without having to compromise the witness in front of the jury.

One court—not in Massachusetts—called the arrangement unconstitutional, a bargain made expressly to avoid the disclosure requirements. The jury had to know that a witness had made a deal, and the terms of that deal, to evaluate his or her testimony. In any case, Gaffney's argument was actually wrong as a point of law. What the client told his lawyer to bargain for with the DA was not confidential. It was not intended to remain private—in fact, it was specifically intended to be communicated to a third party, the prosecutor. And the assurances that the lawyer got back from the DA that he transmitted generally to his client were also outside the privilege. One way or another, I argued, the deal between Fleischer and the Massachusetts DA had to be disclosed.

McLaughlin agreed. For the first time, Fleischer was obliged to testify that he told Lerner to get not only an assurance of leniency, but an assurance that he would not get a criminal record. And Lerner got it. Amazing: charged with nine counts of accessory after the fact of murder, Fleischer would implicate the co-defendants and then just walk away.

Why did he name Susan? There was another woman hanging out with Bond, Valeri, and Gilday—Helen Zelitch, who would later become Fleischer's wife. Fleischer conceded that she had stayed in the two apartments a few times, but that he had never mentioned that to the police. He even agreed that he had directed someone to destroy a letter that Helen had sent to Kathy Power or Susan Saxe, to keep her from being a suspect. Again, I could argue that he, like Valeri, put Susan in the thick of this to protect his girlfriend, now wife, Helen Zelitch.

And what about the murder? Like Valeri, Fleischer did everything he could to distance himself and the others from it. When Susan learned of the shooting, Fleischer testified, she screamed: "Why did you do that? You shouldn't have done that!" And later, when the group met after the robbery, Susan ripped into Gilday for being "trigger-happy, foolhardy, and stupid." Again—the Valeri theme and variation. The theme: Susan was not there; the variation: she was not associated with the murder.

Court officers, elevator operators, and police may have been part of the "old boy" network. The government's star witnesses were younger, part of a different world—like me—and I took advantage of it.

———

On Friday, October 1, Gaffney announced that his case was almost over. He could finish on Tuesday. Monday was a Jewish holiday, Yom Kippur; the court would not be in session.

I observed the holiday in Boston. I did not have time to join my parents in New York. In the late afternoon, the lawyers and defense team met to strategize. We had a list of fifteen to twenty witnesses. Several had signed a letter claiming that Susan was a "prisoner of war" in a war that the government declared was over. They had to be interviewed; the defense team had to make its final plans. Father Daniel Berrigan, Pat Swinton, and others were expected on Tuesday. Howard Zinn would be on call. Various prison witnesses who would contradict Valeri were summonsed. What would the defense look like? Finally, we had to decide.

There was unanimity about only one thing: if the letters Susan had written to her rabbi and to her father did not come in before the DA rested, we would rest. If Gaffney was holding these letters in reserve, to spring them on the jury in his rebuttal, we would head that off. Nothing we could do on defense—and we really had nothing—compared to the impact of those letters. Susan surely could not testify; Gaffney would introduce the letters into evidence in a nanosecond. There was no debate on the matter. Still, no one truly believed that Gaffney would rest without using the letters. And even if we rested, the judge would let him reopen the case, if he pressed the matter.

That Monday night, I prepared for the remaining witnesses, thought about the defense, and researched the reopening question. But mostly, I practiced my closing—my fourth or fifth ever.

The government testimony went quickly—a purple dress had indeed been found in a brown paper bag with bank bags in Logan Airport; Bond had been arrested with money from the bank and the guard's gun, and blank Brandeis identification cards; Gilday's fingerprints had been found in one of the abandoned cars; ballistics testimony linked the spent cartridges in the bank with guns found in one of the cars. But the only evidence specific to Susan was that she had been picked up in Philadelphia in 1975 using an alias. At the end of the day on Tuesday, Gaffney had only one more witness. He represented to the court that he would be done Wednesday morning, October 4.

Tuesday night, with my heart in my mouth, I met with one or two defense witnesses for a short time; but again, I worked on my closing. Susan would write some of it. I would read what she had written, making it clear that these were her words, a way of letting her connect with the jury even though she was not testifying. By the time I went to bed that evening, I feared that I had made a terrible mistake in not spending more time on a defense.

The next day, Gaffney presented one witness, Alan McGrory, a man who had met with Bond, Gilday, and Valeri—but not Susan— the night before the robbery. McGrory had decided not to participate; indeed, he tipped off the FBI to Valeri's participation, which led to Valeri's arrest the evening after the robbery.

Then, after twenty-four witnesses, Gaffney rested at 10:47 a.m. We asked for a sidebar conference. We moved to strike the blurry picture of the unarmed woman in the bank, which Valeri claimed was Susan. We claimed that there was no evidence where the photo was taken, or when. Denied.

Then I said: "If that's the Commonwealth's case, Your Honor, then the defense rests as well."

"Defense rests?" McLaughlin asked incredulously.

"That's right," I said.

"Are you ready for argument?" McLaughlin asked.

"I am."

Tom added, "We would like just a few minutes, ten minutes or so."

Of course I was ready for argument; I had prepared the night before. Gaffney was silent. He wouldn't admit that he needed to reopen his case or prepare a closing. After all, he had told the press that he could try this case in his sleep. This time it *was* like TV's *Perry Mason*. As the *Boston Phoenix* reported:

After Gaffney had closed his case, the prosecution and defense teams huddled with McLaughlin in the front of the courtroom for yet another of the bench conferences that had punctuated the trial. Reporters were expectant, waiting for a new, and they hoped, more interesting phase of the trial to begin. The next major event would be Gertner's opening statement, which would at last disclose the nature of the defense strategy. Instead, as the conference breaks up, the judge, looking stunned, announces to the court, "I have been advised that the defense rests." There is a moment of silence and then a murmur swells in the courtroom. "He means the *prosecution* rests, doesn't he?" inquires one puzzled reporter of another. But the half-smile on Nancy Gertner's lips as she returns to the defense table confirms that the judge has not misspoken. In a bold, dramatic gesture—perhaps an all-or-nothing gamble—Saxe and her attorneys have decided to send the case to the jury without calling a single witness in her defense.

———

I strode to the jury box and stared directly at them. I knew their profiles. I addressed them by name, not a usual tactic, but then again, I had no "usual" approaches. I was their age, their generation. I attacked; I cajoled; I paced, and came close to crying. I was completely at ease. I was speaking that foreign language, but it was no longer foreign. Without notes, the words flowed. I saw nothing but the jurors and Susan.

"[A]fter two and one-half weeks of listening to the Government's case, we decided that the Government had proved our case. We didn't have to do any more. . . . [T]he government has shown a parade of witnesses, neutral people, who were inside the State Street Bank and Trust Company. . . . None of it had anything to do with Susan Saxe. And if they didn't put on those people, we would have, but they did our job for us. . . . There was no need to have you people locked up any longer.

"There were witnesses inside and outside the bank who could not identify Saxe; fingerprint experts who could not produce the fingerprints of anyone; ballistics and guns that had no relationship to Susan, and "a purple dress that no one, except one man, Valeri, connects to Susan Saxe."

There was "a picture of a woman Valeri says is Saxe, [that] looks like me, or [*pointing to one of the jurors*] it looks like you.

"What have they proved? That there was a bank robbery on September 23, 1970, and unfortunately, really unfortunately, a police officer was killed."

Then I lit into the cooperators. Valeri was like a Pavlovian dog, rewarded when he cooperated, punished when he did not. And I suggested—improperly, to be sure—that he was facing the same punishment as Susan, "life imprisonment with no parole." Gaffney objected; you are not supposed to let the jury know the potential punishment of the defendant. The judge was furious. I apologized and went on. Fleisher, who was in this whole thing up to his ears, would walk away—as if he had done nothing wrong.

Each was trying to protect a girlfriend—Linda LaMontagne for Valeri, Helen Zelitch for Fleisher. Again the judge interjected, this time without an objection from Gaffney. "That is improper argument; there was no evidence against Helen Zelitch." I did not apologize; I objected.

"Why did they identify Susan Saxe?" Because she was linked to the National Strike Information Center. "That's why Valeri named her, and that's why the government believed him." But "you are not supposed to convict someone because of their associations, because of their political beliefs, because of who they know." Why then did Saxe run away, and live for years under an alias? For the same reason that Fleisher fled: he believed that because of his associations, he would be "nailed." So did Susan.

I went on, now reading from a paper that I took from Susan's hands in a dramatic gesture: "It's 1970 and there's a war going on, and there are people who are speaking out against that war. . . . There are people who are joining associations, who are marching, who are organizing. There's the National Strike Information Center—nameless, faceless people you may or may not remember, people who were none too popular at the time, people who were deeply committed to ending that war, the war which we have since recognized . . ."

THE COURT: Now, no. Go ahead.

MS. GERTNER: . . . was a mistake.

THE COURT: No, I strike that. You had no right to continue after I indicated to you that you shouldn't. I didn't want you to indicate what the Strike Information Center was, because there was no basis in the evidence.

Still, I went on—about the murder, which took place long after the robbery, a murder that shocked Susan and the others. Again, I could not suggest—directly, at least—a compromise verdict: yes to robbery, no to murder. But that was the message if all else failed.

Then, my voice rose, close to tears: "You have . . . Susan Saxe's fate in your hands. And I hope, I hope that when this case is over, some years hence, your conscience will be clear. Because ladies and gentlemen of the jury, two weeks from today, it is going to be too late to come back and say, I made a mistake, Ms. Gertner. I made a mistake. It'll be too late . . ."

I cannot claim that this closing was original. In fact, I read every closing I could get my hands on, cut and pasted the best parts of each, memorized them, said them over and over again until the words just poured out.

The newspapers reported only that I had been "reprimanded" by the judge during the closing.

Gaffney rebutted just as I had predicted in my closing. He brandished the carbine rifle that killed Officer Schroeder. Valeri got no deal. He will be doing ten years on the federal charge, and then on this charge. There are two systems of law, one followed by most citizens and the other practiced by Ms. Saxe and her gang: "That system of law was to plan and carry out a holdup, in the course of which Walter Schroeder, a father of nine, was killed. There was no deliberation, no ruling on the evidence. They carried out their execution swiftly." All the testimony, he claimed, backed up Valeri and Fleisher. "When you review all the facts and the evidence, can there be any doubt?"

The alternates were selected, and then excused; the jury was brought to twelve. Ten members were between nineteen and thirty-five, two in their late forties. Their questions during deliberations were manna to the defense: They asked for clarification about Fleisher's role in loading the cars. Then they asked for clarification of instructions dealing with "credibility of witnesses" and "reasonable doubt."

We waited. Over a week passed. Each day, I went to the basement of the Suffolk County courthouse where Susan was held. She was guarded by state officials and a woman federal marshal, Darlene Therrien, because Susan was in the custody of both state and federal authorities. Darlene, Susan, and I bonded.

I came to court in my "lawyer costume," but in Susan's cell, I would change into a Minnie Mouse t-shirt and jeans. Once, while we were waiting, I snuck in Chinese food in my briefcase. We had nothing to do except be with each other and watch *Bonanza* reruns. I could be nowhere else, not in the courtroom with the other lawyers, not in my office on call.

There was one rumor that the jury was nine to three for acquittal; another had it ten to two. Still another reported it was eleven to one. The foreperson, Dennis Lee Milford, was quoted later as saying that the "the jury tended toward acquittal." Many on the jury wanted to acquit "to forgive and forget the passions of the antiwar, antiestablishment movements of years past."

One prosecutor was quoted as saying, "If Nancy Gertner wins, it will be the win of the century. If she loses, she will lose nothing because everybody expects her to lose."

Walking across City Hall Plaza to our office, after those rumors surfaced, Tom and I were exultant. We might actually win! It was a feeling like nothing else in my life.

After several days, the jury announced that they were unable to reach a verdict. The judge sent them back to deliberate. They asked for Valeri's testimony about Gilday's role, and then the testimony concerning the time between the getaway and the shots that killed Officer Schroeder. They returned and announced that they were still "hung." The judge declared a mistrial, reassuring them that "there is nothing wrong with [their] disagreement." "Jurors," he said, "must vote on the issues based on their conscience." He later changed his tune.

The government insisted on a retrial. And this time, the rules would be different. There would be no additional peremptories for the defense; no lawyer questioning of jurors. The first trial had persuaded Judge McLaughlin that a fair jury could be seated, that there was no need for these special advantages. There was another conclusion that he could have come to, though: that these rulings had been necessary to make selecting a fair jury possible.

And those changes, we thought, would be McLaughlin's last acts having to do with this case. He was slated to retire at the end of January 1977. The new judge, James C. Roy, was described in the press as a "hanging judge." This was a squeeze play, one paper reported, designed to force a plea.

But neither the prospect of a new judge nor the new rules moved us. We knew that Gaffney would not make the same mistake twice; Susan's letters to the rabbi, to her father, would be center stage now as part of his case-in-chief. Still, while Gaffney had boasted that there would be another trial, that he would never negotiate, he could not risk another defeat and a costly retrial. The negotiations proceeded in strict confidence—no defense committee, no discussion with Susan's parents until the end. Susan had certain preconditions. No cooperation, no information, no testimony. Period. There would be no minimum and maximum terms of imprisonment, to eliminate the hold that parole officials might otherwise have had over her. (A prisoner is parole eligible based on the lower range of a term.) When she left prison, her time would be over; the concept was "maxing" out.

On January 17, 1977, Susan pled guilty to two counts of armed robbery and one count of manslaughter. The sentence was twelve to fourteen years. She would be returned to Philadelphia to be sentenced on the earlier armed robbery, for which she would receive ten years. Taking into account time off for good behavior and time already served awaiting trial (nearly two years), the Boston trial netted little additional prison time for Susan.

Four members of the Saxe jury were in the courtroom to witness the plea. Earlier, they had invited me and members of the defense committee to a party at the home of the foreperson, Dennis

Lee Milford. I went. Some told me that they wished Susan were there, how disappointed they were when the judge declared a hung jury, that they thought she should have been acquitted.

In his statement, before accepting Susan's plea, Judge McLaughlin directed his ire to them:

"You now know at least that Susan Saxe was in that bank, and you saw fit to disbelieve Valeri, you saw fit to disbelieve Fleisher. As long as justice is administered by jurors who refuse to believe accomplices because they turn state's evidence, then turn them out in the streets if you want to, and let that message go forth. . . . Let our banks continue to be robbed, our police officers continue to be murdered and our citizens plundered. It is high time our jurors exercised a little common sense and wisdom, and understand that we can't produce nuns and priests and ministers as witnesses, not when you are dealing with vicious crime."

This had been one of the most expensive of any trial held in Suffolk County, the judge said. He said it was understandable that a jury would be uncertain about the relationship between the murder and the robbery. It was conceivable that another jury would mistry the case as well on that issue. He then turned to Susan. He would accept her plea to manslaughter because of her exceptionally good record before this point, no evidence of lawbreaking afterwards, and her supportive family.

Finally, he turned to me and asked if I had anything to say. "No," I said. "Not this time."

He smiled. "It is the first time in seven weeks that you have said nothing."

One month later, McLaughlin retired. I would miss him. I'm told he had the same reaction about me.

———

The plea, and the relatively light sentence, was a victory for Susan and me. Was it a victory for truth, as the public demands? Or had I just learned crass manipulation, the trade of the hired gun? What about the principles that had prompted me to be a lawyer?

The felony murder charge was not "the truth." It was a legal contrivance. There was no "truth" treating Susan as if she had been the shooter, facing a first-degree murder conviction, and no sentencing alternative but life in prison. Nor was there "truth" in the phony search of the Beacon Street apartment or the secret deal with Fleischer. In fact, this trial had fleshed out more information about what had actually happened that September in 1970 then the extraordinary media coverage had come close to revealing.

But was "truth" even an attainable goal? After all, there had been many proceedings in this case, with different lawyers, different prejudices, and different outcomes, which may or may not have reflected the true culpability of the participants. Valeri's role was minimized because he advanced the government's case. Gilday, the first to be tried, was judged when the public's rage was at its height and without the benefit of the rulings that Susan got. Kathy Power pled guilty, after turning herself in twenty years later, in exchange for the same term of imprisonment as Susan, even when the evidence against her was far less substantial than the evidence against the others.

Perhaps, while we aim for "truth," the best that we can hope for most of the time is a result that everyone will accept, just because a jury pronounced it, or because certain procedures were followed. I was not fighting for Susan's right to do what she was accused of doing. I was fighting—with all my heart—for the obligation of the system to be fair, to follow the rules, no matter what the crime, no matter who the defendant. And given the overwhelming resources of the government, and the stakes for the woman I cared so much about, it was well worth the fight.

I was testing these limits, this new identity, weighing where it fit in the universe of my values. Who else would I represent with the passion with which I had represented Susan? And if I had only one speed—the "do everything there is to do" speed—who would I turn down?

As for the winning and the acclaim—candidly, it was seductive. The case changed my life. For a short time, it made up for all the slights, the snide comments, the skepticism about women lawyers in general and about me in particular. An older woman who worked down the hall in our office building, a secretary in an insurance firm, turned to me, took me by the shoulders, and said, "Congratulations. You have made us women proud." A female public defender told me that what I had done made a difference in her life. The judge's courtroom clerk, after the fact, said that we had tried one of the best cases he had ever seen.

Alan Dershowitz once told me that there were two fields closed to women when I started—brain surgery and criminal trial law. Because I wasn't particularly good at math, trial work was the logical choice. I had done it. I had crafted an identity in which I could live—at least for a time—funny, irreverent, dramatic, prepared—and wearing red.

Communicating with a jury was a special feeling, a feeling I had not anticipated, a kind of populism I relished, and a skill I had no idea I had. If I could communicate with Moishe, the crowd from the Lower East Side, McLaughlin, or this jury, I could reach anyone.

And as for Susan, we have been dear, dear friends from then on. "You saved my life," she said. In the final analysis, nothing else matters.

CHAPTER FOUR

You Want Me? I Want You!

Just one year after the Saxe case, six lawyers were on the cover of the *Boston Globe*'s weekend magazine. The title: "Boston's Criminal Law Superstars." Five were older male lawyers, realistically shown, hair thinning, obviously seasoned. And in the lower-right corner, there was a picture of a young woman—me—hair down her back, looking like a flower child.

To the Boston media, I had traveled in one year from invisibility to superstardom. It was feast or famine. The same media that could not see me at all before the trial had a hard time showing me realistically afterwards.

Away from the formality of the courtroom, I still felt like an outsider, cavorting around in someone else's skin. Lani Guinier describes it as having "insider privileges" and "outsider consciousness." Insider privileges accrue to lawyers as professionals, and now, in a fashion, to me. I "seemed" successful. "Outsider consciousness" involves that "peculiar sensation of always looking at one's self through the eyes of others."

I fell back on Professor Gary Bellow's advice. Gary was a truly inspired teacher and dear friend, teaching one of the first, and surely the best, trial advocacy courses at Harvard Law School. I had visited his class the year before the Saxe case. Being a trial lawyer, he told his class, was like being an actor or an actress. It is a role; the courtroom, a stage. You put on a costume on the morning—for me, it was the fire-engine-red suit—but importantly, you take it off in the evening. You decide the range of parts that you could conceivably play—within the limits of age, appearance, audience, and yes, gender. Try on this identity, reject that one. I could play the aggressive lawyer even if I wasn't an aggressive human being. And I could take the audience's prejudices about women into account without apology. Am I sounding too aggressive, too strident? Then let me tone it down. And I won't wear pants, lest there be one juror who thinks I'm acting too masculine. Which stereotypes will I adopt; which ones will I reject? "Outsider consciousness" came with the territory. But while I would struggle with certain stereotypes in my style, my dress, my manner, especially when someone's liberty depended on me, there were clear limits. I wrote a letter protesting a column in the *Massachusetts Lawyers Weekly,* the lawyers' newspaper. The columns recounted a mythical interview with an attorney and his secretary. In response to the secretary's complaints about short lunch hours, the attorney said, "Unfortunately, emergencies are a way of life in this profession, and occasionally jury charges or contracts must take precedence over Tillie's appetite or the girdle sale at Burdine's. Secretaries, like the girdles, must learn to give a little."

"As an attorney, and as a woman," I wrote, "I heartily resent both the characterization of the boss and of the secretary in these colloquies." The boss was an aggressive, highly competent professional, plainly a male; the secretary was a lazy worker, plainly a female. (The letters to the editor poured in; I was accused of being humorless. Guilty as charged, at least when it came to this kind of humor.) In a large commercial case that I was handling as lead counsel in my early years of practice with my partner, Harvey Silverglate, every time the opposing lawyer didn't like my answers to his demands, he called Harvey. We both wrote him indignant letters warning that we would not deal with him until he emerged from the dark ages and starting dealing with me as his equal. My letter, actually, was pretty strident:

While at the outset, I was willing to understand—although not condone—such behavior as the product of old habits and deeply ingrained stereotypes—after two years [of litigation] I can do that no longer. It both angers me and saddens me, that there can be people who can be so obtuse that they do not see change when it is upon them. Perhaps you and your colleagues will change when your myopia once again leads you to sadly misjudge a woman opponent, to lose substantially because you have undervalued your opposition. (Others in Boston have already learned this lesson.) I don't believe that you will change out of magnanimity.

One afternoon, a U.S. District Court judge (a member of the same court on which I now sit) invited my legal team into his lobby, the private area of the courtroom where he held conferences. Along with John Reinstein, legal director of the Massachusetts branch of the American Civil Liberties Union (ACLU), and Jim Hamilton, another lawyer volunteer, I represented two women who needed abortions and two doctors, on the staff of the Hale Hospital in Haverhill, who wished to perform them against the wishes of their employer. It was 1973, one year after *Roe v. Wade,* the landmark Supreme Court decision legalizing abortion. Lawyers for the Hale Hospital argued that a neighborhood hospital, even though a public one, had the option of declining to provide the procedure.

"Let's see," the judge said, going through the papers that we had filed. "One broad comes from New Hampshire and one from Massachusetts." "How dare he!" I shrieked to myself. "This is a women's rights case!" But I looked down, stared at my shoes, bit my lip, and just recorded the moment.

———

Building a practice was complex for a woman in the 1970s, even one who had had all the media exposure she could stand. Harvey Silverglate told me to pick only the very best cases and turn down the rest. You don't want to be wrapped up in the cases that you hate when the "good" one comes in the door. Over time, the cases that interest you will come. If you comment and write about the issues that you care about in the media and academic journals, you won't be forgotten.

It didn't work. All I got from waiting for the right case was silence. And when I wrote articles, I was seen as an academic, bookish, not a "real" lawyer.

Tom Dwyer, whose firm I joined many years later, advised me to network, join bar association groups and other organizations, attend receptions, mingle. Over time, you will get the calls from major firms, corporate counsel, people of influence.

That too failed. All I got from dinners and receptions was dates—no referrals, at least not from what was still a "boys' club."

For me, there was only one way. While young male lawyers could pass, play the role of a seasoned practitioner, even pretend to insider status, no one would assume that I was a trial lawyer unless they saw it—or so I believed. So I tried one case after another—jury trials or not, constitutional issues or mundane arguments, federal courts and state courts, municipal courts and appeals courts, Massachusetts and out-of-state cases, civil and criminal.

What was the principle behind my selections? Challenge, mainly.

Late one night, I was called by a relative of a woman sent to Bridgewater State Mental Hospital, the hospital for the "criminally insane." Bridgewater had never before taken women patients. I went out there immediately—I thought I *had* to—and promptly got hopelessly lost on the grounds. The place was dark; men were calling out from locked rooms with barred windows, sometimes shrieking, sometimes moaning. It took me more than an hour, but eventually I found my new client in the basement of the building, a locker room jerry-rigged to receive its only woman. She was highly medicated, barely able to communicate anything except "Get me out of here!" The next morning, leveraging the combined threat of litigation and media attention, I did get her out of there, having her transferred to Framingham, the women's facility.

I would rush to any police station, anytime, anywhere, when a potential client called. Armed with a map because I did not know Boston very well, and with my heart in my mouth, I drove to wherever. If it were late at night, in a high-crime area, I would park as close as I could to the police station—any spot, legal or illegal, sometimes in the middle of the street—canvass the entrance, and when no one was looking, lest anyone see the abject fear on the face of the "tough" defense lawyer, sprint in.

Requests from Walpole State Prison, the maximum-security all-male institution, were especially coveted. I'd go—past the razor wire, the parapets, the walls—and negotiate my way past the guards who refused to believe that I was a lawyer. After my experience with Susan's case, I insisted that I *had* to meet with my clients completely alone, away from prying guards. The first case was unforgettable. I asked this very large, powerful-looking man, affecting insouciance: "Tell me, Mr. X, what charges are you in here on?"

"Rape and unnatural acts," he said, with a hint of a smile.

"Control your face," I said to myself. "Just note where the door is."

Any—or rather, almost any—criminal case would fill the bill. They were challenges by definition. You want me? Really? Well then, I want you! The Jordan Marsh men's room case was emblematic. I represented a man accused of having sex with another man in the bathroom of Jordan Marsh, a large department store in downtown Boston. The police claimed that as soon as they entered the men's room, they saw four feet in a stall. They then banged on the door and arrested the men inside. Open and shut.

Here was one place I could not go. I begged a man I was then dating—luckily, an architect—to go to the men's room and draw it to scale. Although he was terrified that he would be arrested—or worse, accosted—he agreed, for my sake, which was surely an extraordinary dating ritual. So he went in with his architect's tools, entered a stall, sat on the toilet seat, and with a plumb line extended under the partitions, measured every part of it.

Given the height and the dimension of the room and the partitions, it was clear that the policemen had to stick their heads under the stalls before they could see any legs at all, let alone four. In short, they had to "search," invading the privacy of the men inside, before they had probable cause to believe that a crime had taken place. We could win.

On the day of trial, armed with charts and testimony, my reluctant beau on call, my client and I marched into the Boston Municipal Court. In the first row, I recognized a reporter from the *Boston Globe*. When I told my client that the press was there, he was appalled. Nothing was worse than letting the accusations against him become public. Vindication no longer mattered; he decided to plead guilty to a lesser offense.

These were not the big cases, the front-page headlines, but the everyday struggles, buried on page 20, or in the police blotter. These were the ordinary compromises, representing human beings, vindicating rights, struggling still with whatever "the truth" was. It was "true" that my client had violated a law, although it was troubling that conduct between consenting adults was criminalized. But it was also "true" that his rights had been flagrantly violated, and he felt powerless to resist it.

Murder cases were the biggest challenges. I was the only woman on the list of lawyers to be appointed by the state, but when I never got a single appointment after being on the list for a year, I complained, this time to the Superior Court of Massachusetts. Your selection process can't be alphabetical, I suggested, a tad snidely. Men with last names beginning with letters before and after "G" had received appointments. It can't be workload; some men received multiple appointments at a time. Could it be sex discrimination?

The response? I was assigned every hopeless, disgusting case that came along. A murder in Norfolk County, with the head in Plymouth County and the body in Suffolk County? Give it to Gertner! Great jurisdictional issues!

And if I was refused an appointment as the state-appointed defender on a complex case, I took it for free. A gay woman, probably drunk at the time of the crime, was convicted of aiding and abetting another woman and a group of men in committing a rape. I read about the case in the *Boston Globe*. The victim had been brutalized. While most of the men got off relatively lightly, the two women were sentenced to life imprisonment. Throughout the trial, the judge showed his disgust for their sexual preference—calling it "sexual perversion," suggesting that as lesbians they were more likely to be violent. Although the men had initiated the offense, forced the victim to have sex with them, and coerced the women not to interfere, the *Globe* reported that most of the judge's indignation was reserved for the female defendants. Concerned about his antigay comments, I got in touch with one of the women and offered to represent her on appeal. When the judge refused to appoint me, I entered my appearance (the formal procedure for representing a party in court) anyway. And when the judge refused even that—the right to donate my services—I sued him. (This would be the second time I sued a judge; there would be more.) In Massachusetts's highest court, I won the right to represent her, but I lost the case.

Still, criminal law was not totally satisfying, not then, not ever. Civil cases were more complex, the opponents—large law firms with myriad resources—more challenging. The underlying issues in many civil actions reflected my values more directly—discrimination law, First Amendment issues, civil rights. I represented a woman clerk who claimed that the U.S. District Court discriminated against her. She had been employed by the district court for years and years, passed over for promotion over and over again, generally ignored. This time, to bring her claim, I had to sue each and every one of the judges of the federal court, judges I had only just met in my still-young career. Over time, the court settled the case.

In a curious way, I began to exult in my "outsider consciousness"—the fact that I did not care about money or public criticism. I was in a position to make choices that others would not. No one else will take your case? I will. You can't afford a lawyer? No problem. No one has ever thought of bringing such a case? Terrific. Even better.

I had no political ambitions, no desire to work my way up the professional ladder. My friend and Yale classmate, Hillary Rodham (now Clinton), called me in 1973 to join her on the staff of the House Impeachment Committee investigating the charges against President Nixon. We had been close friends at Yale, and especially during her brief time in Boston, when she worked for the Children's Defense Fund. We shared a passion for politics, only of different sorts. She was focused on the electoral kind; I had been swept by the populism of the 1960s. Although I was profoundly anti-Nixon, the House Impeachment Committee seemed like just another resume-building step, another preparation for that great job. I wanted to finally do "that job," not assemble credentials. I declined her offer.

Like a kid in a candy shop, I was trying all the challenges that the profession could offer. While I had toyed with leaving practice before the Saxe case, I didn't. I couldn't admit that I had failed at this profession, at least in my eyes. And after the Saxe case, I was hooked. I couldn't admit that the Saxe case had not been an aberration. I was smitten with what I was able to do, whom I was able to help.

———

The rough outline of one year, 1977, five years into the practice, foreshadows the people and the issues that I would struggle with over the next sixteen.

January: Three days after Susan was sentenced, I represented Barbara White, an art history professor at Tufts University, in an emergency hearing, seeking a preliminary injunction. She wanted to enjoin Tufts from denying her tenure, thereby forcing her to leave an institution in which she had taught her entire career. It was the very first case applying the gender discrimination laws to an academic institution. While the Equal Employment Opportunity Commission was representing a class of women denied tenure, Barbara and another colleague, Christiane Joost, needed individual representation. In a reversal of the Saxe case, in this one there was no time to prepare. We won the preliminary injunction, and many years later, settled the case, permitting her to remain at Tufts. Instantly, I had a new specialty: academic discrimination cases.

These were easy choices. The women were me.

April: I began Marcia Y's case against a psychiatrist for having sex with her during therapy. And while that was being litigated, I represented a woman suing the city of Boston after she had been raped in a municipal parking lot. She had parked her car in the morning and returned at night, with no way of knowing that the lights above her parking space were defective.

These cases led to similar ones. I represented another woman who had been raped in a downtown hotel, when the rapist secured entry because a desk clerk mistakenly gave a man the key to her room. She was a virgin on her very first business trip. I represented another who was raped in the middle of the night in her apartment because the landlord used faulty locks.

Again, these were easy choices. I had parked in that lot, stayed at similar hotels, been vulnerable to cheap landlords and errant professionals.

May: I was in Concord, New Hampshire, with John Reinstein, legal director of the American Civil Liberties Union of Massachusetts, representing 1,400 demonstrators, members of the Clamshell Alliance who were arrested protesting nuclear power at the Seabrook Nuclear Power Plant. The demonstrators had been kept in makeshift "jails" set up by the New Hampshire National Guard armories. Bail, we claimed, had been ordered on the instructions of the state's then-governor, Meldrin Thompson, not for the purpose of ensuring their appearance at trial, which is what bail is for, but just to punish them for their civil disobedience; most of them weren't able to come up with it and were forced to stay in custody. So we sued the governor. Judge Hugh Bownes, a man of enormous compassion and integrity, took a "view" of the armories in which they were detained on Saturday and held emergency hearings the following week.

(We circulated a petition asking our clients to record what we expected would be horrible conditions. Along with some genuine horror stories, there were the following comments: "Insufficient gluten flour in the bread!" "No deep well water." "No green leafy vegetables." The New Hampshire officials, with the best of intentions, bought food from McDonalds for the "kids." A Big Mac, to this group, was poison.)

By the end of the week, the authorities released everyone. The publicity and the cost had been prohibitive.

Other "political cases" followed. I handled *Civil Liberties Legal Defense Fund v. Kliendienst,* a case about purported surveillance of the Cambridge antiwar organization. I advised the Coalition to Stop Institutional Violence, which tried to stop the placement of women at the all-male Bridgewater State Mental Hospital, as in the case of the woman I had visited. These issues were the legacy of the 1960s, and new specialties for a new lawyer—the law of mass arrests, of political surveillance, of legal reform.

July: I tried Sonia Dettman's lawsuit against a parole officer for wrongfully searching her home without her permission. (It was Sonia who had married Stanley Bond and, through that connection, had referred Susan Saxe to me.) She had been imprisoned for a short time and was on parole at the time of the incident. She won.

August: I conducted depositions in *Kolodney v. University of New Hampshire,* which involved sex discrimination in a tenure decision. I carried out discovery in a class-action suit involving African American women suing Riverside Press, a publishing company, for race and gender discrimination in blue-collar jobs.

I wrote a demand letter for Jane King, a woman challenging sex discrimination in a white-shoe Massachusetts investment house. (The rumor at the company was that Jane had hired some "Hebrew" woman lawyer to represent her. Talk about "outsider" status!) I wrote another demand letter for Dr. Joy Hochstadt, a woman scientist suing the Worcester Foundation for Experimental Biology for sex discrimination. (Ironically, this was the foundation that had developed the birth-control pill.)

And in some quarters, my reputation as an advocate was now preceding me. I counted on that. I sent a great many "oh shit" letters like this one:

Dear X:

I represent Ms. Y. My investigation suggests that Mr. Smith, a vice president in your office, discriminated against my client in the following ways. . . . Rather than proceeding directly to court (a draft complaint is attached), we would like to meet to avoid litigation if at all possible.

Sincerely,
Nancy Gertner

The lawyer was supposed to look at the signatory, remember the Saxe case, mutter "oh shit," and settle. Sometimes it worked.

October: There was the retrial of two defendants charged with distributing marijuana. At an earlier state trial, I had persuaded the judge to suppress the eight tons of marijuana found on their farm because the load had been seized without probable cause. In the federal case, however, the government did not rely on the seized marijuana, just the testimony of a co-conspirator that linked them to drug trafficking. We lost.

December: I represented Vicki Gabriner in the appeal of her case. Vicki, linked to antiwar activities, had been charged with and convicted of passport fraud. She won her appeal.

In between, there were domestic cases, representing lesbian mothers seeking to get, or keep, custody of their children; a stockholder's suit against the Gulf Oil Corporation for paying off officials abroad; even immigration cases. Plus, I taught a "Sex Discrimination and the Law" course at Boston University Law School, participated in various panels and programs, and, yes, somehow fit in some free time for playing guitar, biking, hiking, canoeing, the usual, stuffed into the interstices of this manic life. There was even time for a reading group with other academics on political theory. (Picture this: I am in the "First Session" of the Boston Municipal Court. That's where defendants are brought after spending the night in jail. The presiding judge sets bail on an assembly line— the "men's session," largely for accused pimps; the "women's session," for accused prostitutes—and me reading Hegel while listening for my case to be called.)

And money? I lived on whatever came in. Our offices were modest; overhead, low. The Harvard Street apartment in Cambridge was rent-controlled. I drove a ten-year-old Chevy named "Iphiginie," nicknamed, appropriately, "Iffy." (The blinker beeped just before she died.) There were middle-class defendants, charged with marijuana offenses, who could afford to pay for counsel. There were a few appointments here and there, a few civil cases settled after an "oh shit" letter or minimal litigation. Then the case against Gulf Oil settled. For a short time, their bad judgment endowed the office.

Family and social life? I adopted the families of others, my nephews, the children of my friends. Dates with men are penciled in the "Lawyer's Diary" after this brief, or that deposition. Some, like the guy I sent into the Jordan Marsh men's room, were enlisted to help the cause. I was hooked.

CHAPTER FIVE

Psychiatry, Malpractice, and Feminism

In 1977, the firm couldn't afford walls that went all the way up to the ceiling. Partitions covered three quarters of the space, with an open area at the top. There was one all-purpose, windowless middle-of-the-office room that served as a library, conference room, and lunch room, all rolled into one. We were a generally fairly rowdy bunch of about fifteen—sharing the work, the strategy, the wins and losses.

When I scheduled Dr. X's deposition in that less-than-private setting, I took special precautions. I asked my colleagues to take coffee breaks only at their own desks. No shouting across the room (our primitive version of an intercom system). No loud strategy sessions or running commentary about this or that case, I begged. I assured them all that I would give them a signal when I was about to ask "The Question." And when I did, staff, secretaries, paralegals, and lawyers alike silently lined up outside the door to hear "The Answer."

"Dr. X," I asked slowly, enunciating my words, the way you do when you are truly self-conscious, "do you have a small nodule on the left side of your penis, and a red mark, like a birthmark, on your left buttock?"

He paused. He looked at me, eyes first wide, then narrowed in contempt. And then he ran for the door.

"Let the record reflect," I said pretending to be calm, even nonchalant, "that the good doctor has just bolted."

My client, Marcia Y, was suing her psychiatrist, Dr. X, for malpractice. She claimed that he had had sex with her during their psychiatric sessions nearly every week. Her current psychiatrists referred her to me in the middle of the Saxe trial. Not because of my extraordinary experience with malpractice cases—I had none. It was gender that made me seem appropriate, the assumption that as a woman, I would believe her. That, and my reputation for fighting against the odds.

I *did* believe her. (True, at this stage, I believed almost everyone. There was the man who came to consult with me about a counterfeiting charge. I was so flattered. After an hour of advice, he thanked me and asked how much he owed. I said, "Fifty dollars." He left me a fifty-dollar bill, hardly common currency in the 1970s. Undoubtedly counterfeit. I was too embarrassed to put it to the test.)

I believed Marcia because her story was conceivable to me. I could imagine it happening. I had been treated by a dentist who insisted on using laughing gas, and just as I went under, started to touch my breasts. I had heard similar stories from other women about trusted male professionals. Given who I was, what I had lived through and heard, I was not about to say—as others had said to her: "No, a prominent physician, at a respected Catholic hospital, with a family no less, would ever do such a thing."

The fact that no one before had sued a psychiatrist on these grounds was no impediment. Nor did it matter that Dr. X had a major insurance company and a fancy corporate law firm behind him when I had my two partners, who knew even less about malpractice law than I did, and an office without floor-to-ceiling walls.

—•—

From 1971 to early 1973, Marcia saw Dr. X for depression. Thirty-two years old at the start, she had never enjoyed a successful, intimate relationship with a man. She felt deeply isolated and profoundly lonely. She sought out her priest, but when she needed medication, her priest referred her to Dr. X.

Nineteen months passed. She saw Dr. X every two weeks. He prescribed and monitored her antidepressants. His fee was thirty dollars an hour.

On January 19, 1973 (Marcia remembered the date precisely), Dr. X came around the desk, sat next to her, and suddenly kissed her—"to get her to talk," he said. Then he changed the frequency of the appointments. Now she would see him once a week, typically at the end of the day: 4:30, then 5:15, 5:30, and finally 5:45, after the secretary had left.

Kissing turned to undressing and fondling. Undressing progressed to oral sex and, by February 1973, intercourse. When she seemed hesitant, he told her that she should be "flattered" that someone like him was interested in her, that the relationship would improve her self-esteem. It was therapy, he assured her, a kind of therapy that would do her "a world of good." Sexual intercourse could "help her unwind." And he added that he loved her "a little" or else he "wouldn't be doing this to [her]."

Given that she had been a virgin, sex with the doctor seemed safe somehow. Besides, she loved him, or so she thought.

By March 1973, sexual activities of varying sorts were part of each and every weekly visit, always initiated by him. In short order, Dr. X reduced his fee from thirty dollars to fifteen. He told her that he really didn't want to charge her at all, but that if he did not, his secretary, who watched him "like a hawk," would be suspicious. Once, Dr. X suggested that they go out to dinner. If they met anyone, he warned, he would introduce her as his "educational consultant." Dinner was never arranged. In the fall, Marcia contracted trichomonas vaginalis vaginitis, an inflammation of the vagina caused by sexual contact. Dr. X diagnosed the infection and gave her a prescription for a drug known as "Flagyl," stating that he too needed to take it. Marcia was infected over and over again.

During 1973 and 1974, Marcia confided in Dr. X that she was growing more and more dependent on him. "Actually, you don't depend on me enough," he told her. "How does it feel to have an affair with a doctor?" he added.

But it was not an "affair." It was a "session."

In December 1973, her father died. Marcia was deteriorating. A schoolteacher, she began to feel incapable of working, soon incapable of functioning at all.

She turned to the same priest who had referred her to Dr. X originally. She confided in him about what was going on in her sessions with Dr. X. The doctor was his good friend, the priest told her, and he warned her not to confront him. (Later, the priest told me that he did not take her account "literally." Exactly, what other way was there to take it? Even worse, at the height of the priest sex abuse scandal, I read in the *Globe* that the church's response to the accusations was to send the offending priest to a psychiatrist. And who was that psychiatrist? Dr. X.)

In June 1974, Marcia signed herself into the hospital where Dr. X occupied a senior position and was the heir apparent to becoming the psychiatrist in chief. While there, she found out about another woman who claimed to be having "an affair" with Dr. X. When she confronted Dr. X, he told her that "his sexual escapades were none of [her] business." Days later, he prescribed shock treatments, although he was previously reluctant to use them. Marcia believed that shock treatments would hurt her memory. She refused and signed herself out.

At their next appointment, Dr. X told Marcia that he was not her problem, that she was "a global disaster" long before they met. True, he admitted, "marital fidelity" was not one of his outstanding virtues, and then boasted of having been involved with "a whole string" of patients, nurses, and secretaries.

By this time, Marcia had lost her moorings completely. Deeply depressed, preoccupied with suicide, she was desperate to continue seeing Dr. X.

In August, Dr. X gave her six sample boxes of Serax (a total of ninety-six pills) for her anxiety. As he gave her the pills, he added, "Now I don't have to worry about you, do I?" The medical literature urges "careful supervision of dose and amounts" of Serax, citing the possibility of overdose in susceptible persons. Giving samples guaranteed that there would be no paper trail. After the Serax "gift," Dr. X went on vacation.

Within weeks, Marcia was hospitalized again, this time at McLean Hospital in Belmont, Massachusetts, a well-known psychiatric hospital affiliated with Harvard University. After her first month of treatment at McLean, Dr. X called and told her that if she got out, she could see him every day. They would resume "playing games," which he said he "had always enjoyed." But, he said, she had to leave McLean first. By the way, he added, does the McLean psychiatric staff know about our relationship? When Marcia told him that they did, Dr. X became furious.

His panic was justified. The psychiatrists at McLean, to a man —and they were all men—believed her and condemned Dr. X. In a profession notoriously protective of their own and skeptical of patients claiming malpractice, they had referred her to me. While I wondered whether they would be so adamant if the psychiatrist had been a McLean doctor, or from some other high-status institution rather than a local Catholic hospital, I did not doubt their sincerity.

In December 1974, Marcia was discharged from McLean but was scheduled for frequent outpatient treatment, which would very likely continue for the rest of her life. Dr. X had exacerbated the very problems for which she consulted him. Her experience with him confirmed her worst and most neurotic fears about men, about the dangers of getting close to them, trusting them. When yet another important figure in her life abused her trust, the reaction was dramatic.

———

In a funny way, knowing little about malpractice was a strength. These were not traditional cases—the doctor who operates on the wrong kidney or leaves an instrument in the patient's belly. These cases had more in common with the race and sex discrimination claims with which I was familiar—an exploitative relationship between two people of different status and power, a victim not just hurt but dehumanized.

The exploitation, the dehumanization, were especially acute here: Dr. X's status gave him access to the patient's most intimate secrets, and as a result, enormous power. The patient—Marcia—was far more vulnerable than the worker claiming discrimination. She was needy, seeking psychiatric help, accepting whatever "treatment" he had to offer. Gender lines were reinforced by status lines. Dominance was couched as therapy. Marcia had been literally seduced by the most powerful figure in her world.

Denise Le Boeuf, writing in the *Harvard Women's Law Journal*, described it as a kind of "reverse prostitution," "the special humiliation of paying for this sexual 'therapy.'" She was not only "victimized sexually by [her] 'doctor,' but financially by [her] 'lover.'"

His power extended to the lawsuit as well. Dr. X and his lawyers had ammunition far beyond that of the ordinary defendant. He labeled her schizophrenic, claimed that she was hallucinating, even when the prelitigation records suggested otherwise. Although he was a litigant and the comments were self-serving, his "diagnosis" had the aroma of legitimacy, particularly to those who did not want to believe her to begin with.

In the late 1970s, there was hardly any place to go with these complaints. Few women came forward. The medical profession, for the most part, turned a blind eye. When Marcia went to the Massachusetts Psychiatric Society Ethics Committee, her complaint was dismissed minutes after the committee received Dr. X's version. Government regulatory boards, such as the Massachusetts Board of Registration in Medicine, were notoriously lax at that time.

The courts weren't any better. A clerk in the Middlesex Superior Court's office refused to send the file to the Medical Malpractice Tribunal. The tribunal had been established to help doctors by screening out the frivolous cases. Its review was a prerequisite to bringing a malpractice action. When I finally persuaded the clerk just to send it to the tribunal—it wasn't his business to make legal decisions—I had to convince the tribunal that Marcia's complaint even amounted to malpractice. Traditional malpractice involved negligence, an inadvertent or mistaken act. Dr. X's acts seemed intentional, willful even; insurance companies balked at covering such claims. As one company argued, the doctors in these cases "were doing things any butcher, baker, beggarman, or thief" was capable of doing. Without insurance coverage to provide the plaintiff with a settlement, the pain of the litigation would not be worth it.

But it *was* malpractice, I argued. Psychiatrist and patient are supposed to be in a relationship of profound trust, what the law calls a "fiduciary relationship." Central to it is the phenomenon of transference. The psychiatrist tries to have the patient transfer to the psychiatrist the emotional attachments that once linked her to important figures in her past in the hopes of resolving these attachments in a healthier way. Psychiatrists are trained to deal with transference and to control countertransference, the name given to the psychiatrist's own reaction to the patient. He is not supposed to use the patient to meet his own emotional needs; surely he's not supposed to seek sexual gratification at her expense.

This was malpractice because Dr. X mishandled the transference phenomenon and his own countertransference. He had called his behavior "therapy." His conduct took place during therapy sessions, and in the confines of his office. He told her that it would make her better, ease her pain.

Marcia was not capable of consenting to the sexual relationship. She submitted because of the very emotional problems for which she was being treated. She agreed to therapy, not sex. But for that therapy, there would have been no sex.

Finally, I argued, Dr. X was negligent on an even more basic level. He failed to treat Marcia's problems—her loneliness, her depression, her unresolved feelings toward men. She was doubly harmed—by what he did to her and by what he failed to do.

———

In 1990's *The Journalist and the Murderer*, Janet Malcolm compared litigation to therapy:

> From the lawyer who takes [the plaintiff] into his care he immediately receives the relief that a sympathetic hearing of one's grievances affords. Conventional psychotherapy would soon veer off into an unpleasurable examination of the holes in one's story, but the law cure never ceases to be gratifying; in fact,

what the lawyer says and writes on his client's behalf is gratifying beyond the latter's wildest expectations. The rhetoric of advocacy law is the rhetoric of the late-night vengeful brooding which in life barely survives the skeptical light of morning but in a lawsuit becomes inscribed, as if in stone, in the bellicose documents that accrue while the lawsuit takes its course, and proclaims with every sentence, "I am right! I am right! I am right!"

By now, I was a believer in the "law cure," the unequivocal language of advocacy, the feigned certainty of courtroom presentations. And my approach to clients—empowering them to participate in their own case as Susan Saxe had done—fit right in. In fact, in Marcia's case, the "law cure" was part of her recovery. She needed to announce unequivocally that what Dr. X had done to her was wrong. Without this validation, her doctors believed that she would be suicidal.

Each milestone in the litigation was critical to her; every hearing, every ruling. The "happiest moment of 1976" will be when the complaint is filed, she told me, "that somehow from under all the ashes in this holocaust, the wheels of justice are beginning to turn." "Please tell me the minute it is filed," she begged, "as I am literally living for that moment."

But there were costs. I shared Dr. X's records of his treatment with Marcia. They revealed next to nothing about the real life-and-death emotional struggles that she had gone through, her pain and dislocation. They were sentence fragments, bloodlessly recorded trivia, a completely cursory diary—"went to Los Angeles," "looked tan," "waiting for new house to be completed." In another case that I would try years later, my client cried when she realized the psychiatrist had taken her poignant love letters and filed them in her medical record. The "law cure" made Marcia's pain worse, but it also allowed her to focus her anger, which was, perhaps, an improvement. From his notes, she told me, he sounded like "a third-rate newspaper hack rather than a doctor."

But the law cure was bound to be inadequate. No matter how hard I worked, no matter what the breakthroughs, nothing I did seemed to be enough. I needed to buoy her up, to support her, but also to be critical, to analyze what we could prove and could not prove, how she might appear to a less supportive audience than I was. And I needed to learn about malpractice, psychiatry, even civil litigation. And if I should fail—what then? What would happen to her?

I assigned Byrna Aronson, Susan Saxe's partner, to Marcia's case as a paralegal. Her natural skepticism about authority and her profound passion for civil-rights causes made her the perfect choice for the job. I could count on her not being cowed by a professional man, the mumbo jumbo of psychiatry, much less the considerable odds of the case. They were an unusual duo, to say the least: Marcia was a very protected, inexperienced, and somewhat naive woman; Byrna, worldly wise, a lesbian, a ferocious critic and political activist. Marcia would dress up for her visit with me, conservative skirts and blouses, low heels. Byrna came to work in jeans, hair cut short, still with a huge keyring looped through her belt and often a leather vest with metal studs. They got along famously.

——

Once past the malpractice tribunal, the problem was the usual one—proof. Juries in the mid 1970s were still cynical about women alleging rape. Juries still assumed that a woman must have consented if she were dressed provocatively or didn't resist hard enough. I worried that the same kind of cynicism would spill over to a woman claiming sexual abuse at the hands of her doctor. After all, here was Dr. X, tall, distinguished, graying at the temples, wearing a nice suit. It was the "a man like that would never do such a thing" problem.

Marcia had corroborating witnesses, friends to whom she had confided. Indeed, one friend would report picking her up at Dr. X's office late in the afternoon and seeing a large wet spot on her skirt. Marcia had told her friend that she had simply spilled some "iced tea" on her skirt. (This was many years before President Bill Clinton's encounter with Monica Lewinsky; Marcia did not think to save the skirt.)

Dr. X's records were helpful but no slam dunk. They confirmed the change in the time of the visits as they moved later and later into the afternoon, and the inexplicable reduction in the fee. There were records of the Flagyl prescriptions for her gynecological ailments, an unlikely prescription for a psychiatrist.

But if Dr. X had weapons that other defendants did not have—his reputation, his standing in society, his financial resources—Marcia had a few in her arsenal, too. She had a diary—in actuality, her datebook. While it was a reflection of her pathology, her extraordinary compulsiveness, it was also extraordinary evidence. After every visit, Marcia wrote an amount and a symbol: the amount was what Dr. X charged; the symbol described the kind of sex act he performed, even the position. At one point, Dr. X claimed through his lawyer that his office was far too small to perform the physical acts that she described. She did a drawing of his office freehand, virtually to scale. It was big enough.

I was not satisfied. We sought out other women patients whom Dr. X may have seduced. While Byrna heard rumors of other affairs, no one would come forward. I still didn't like the odds.

———

I don't recall whether I asked the question or whether she just volunteered the information, but one day, Marcia described Dr. X's body in detail. She reported that Dr. X had a small knobby red growth to the left of his penis, and that he had a dark patch of skin on his left buttock, one that looked like a birthmark. She drew a picture, front and back, noting precisely where the marks were.

After the deposition in which Dr. X refused to answer "The Question" about his private parts and fled my office, I filed a motion to compel his response. After more delay, Dr. X agreed to resume his deposition, although he balked at continuing in my office, ostensibly because of the "hearing and noise problems." I insisted. It was symbolic, his having to come to our modest environs, face me, answer my inquiries. He arrived at the deposition, denied having any such marks, and left again.

His denials were not enough. I needed to look, or rather, have a professional examine him. I filed a motion for a physical exam in the civil motion session of Suffolk County, the same court where I had tried Saxe. (In the firm, we labeled this a "Motion to Take a View." We speculated how the trial might proceed. At the critical moment, would I direct the defendant to "moon" the jury?) The judge read the papers, looked at me, still the only woman in the courtroom, turned crimson, and took a break. Days later, we learned that he had allowed it. (Apparently, he was too embarrassed to say it out loud.)

Dr. X procrastinated. His own insurance company clamored for an independent exam. Marcia grew more and more impatient. Then, his counsel produced medical records, never seen before. Dr. X, it seems, had arranged for an examination on his own in February 1979, after he had answered my questions at the second session of his deposition. His handpicked physician concluded that there were no marks on Dr. X at all in the places Marcia indicated. Wasn't that sufficient? No, obviously not.

After all the delays, it seemed clear that a specialist would have to examine Dr. X. I assumed that, by now, he would have tried to cover up the marks. I retained Dr. John Constable, a well-respected plastic surgeon from Massachusetts General Hospital. Dr. Constable warned me that the marks on Dr. X's penis could be removed without a scar, but the mark on his buttocks could not be.

On December 13, 1979, Dr. Constable examined Dr. X at 6:30 p.m. I waited—inconspicuously, I thought—in the lobby of Massachusetts General Hospital. (I was the one in the red suit, pacing back and forth.) The entire case had come down to Dr. X's private parts. The insurance company threatened to disclaim liability if the marks were confirmed. If he had done the deed, they reasoned, it was not malpractice, just his "private pleasure." I didn't know if this was just posturing or for real. But for Marcia, the stakes were even higher. Insurance coverage or not, what mattered to her was my belief in her case. She feared that if there was no evidence of marks on Dr. X's body, I would just dump her. She confused my professional judgment and my personal support. She conflated the statement "This will weaken the case" with "I don't believe you anymore."

At 7:00 p.m., Dr. Constable met me in the lobby. We shook hands, but I was incapable of small talk. With his very English accent and regal demeanor, he reported to me that he had the proverbial "good news" and "bad news." "Where should I begin?" he asked. Bad, I said, give me the worst first. Indeed, he could find no red nodule on Dr. X's penis, and no scar. And the good? There was in fact a scar on Dr. X's left buttocks, precisely where Marcia had reported the birthmark had been. Dr. X had told Dr. Constable that he had gotten the scar by falling off a fence somewhere in Maine just that year. I didn't believe him, but his explanation was plausible enough for the insurance company to stay in the case.

Trial was scheduled for July 14, 1980. On July 10, the Friday before, we received more records from Dr. X's counsel—again, records that we had never seen before. They came from an emergency room in that small town in Maine. They showed that Dr. X had come into the emergency room in March 1979, claiming that he had fallen off a stone wall and landed on a broken bottle, the very story he had told Dr. Constable months before. The records showed that he had cut his left buttocks, precisely where Marcia said the mark was and where Dr. Constable reported a scar. The emergency-room doctor had sutured the cut.

Convenient. In February 1979, Dr. X's own doctor reported no marks on his private parts. By March, he "happened" to cut his left buttocks.

I could have raised holy hell about the timing of these records—on the eve of trial, six months after the "accident"—technical arguments to exclude them. But that wasn't good enough. Partly out of advocacy, partly because I needed to look for the ephemeral "truth" again, I put Byrna on the trail. I told her to interview the emergency-room doctor; perhaps he was a buddy of Dr. X and had completely contrived the records. Go to the site of the supposed "fall," take measurements and pictures of the wall, look for witnesses, find out about the weather, learn anything she could about the "accident."

Late on Saturday evening, July 12, 1980, Byrna called me at home. She knew I would be awake, obsessing about the case. I could only do things sequentially—work maniacally for days and days in a row, sleeping little, eating less, and then, when it was over, playing maniacally. She reported that the temperature was well below freezing in Maine on the day of Dr. X's "fall." There were fourteen or more inches of snow on the ground. Unless the doctor was walking around nude, or in shorts, rather than layers and layers of winter clothes, it was physically impossible for him to have fallen off a stone wall and cut himself in the fashion he described. I could have kissed her.

On July 14, I told Dr. X's lawyers what Byrna had found. Dr. X, they said, was prepared to settle. The settlement would include substantial money for Marcia, much of which was to come from the doctor's own pocket; the insurance company balked at paying it all. And, in an unusual move, the settlement would require that Dr. X meet with Marcia's therapist at McLean to address how he might deal with Dr. X's exploitation of her. Dr. X, of course, would admit to no wrongdoing in the formal papers, and the settlement amount and terms would remain confidential; standard terms, his counsel assured me. (Oh really? I called another lawyer to check whether that was the case. It was.) Marcia was to move to withdraw her complaint before the Board of Registration in Medicine. Dr. X wanted to continue to practice.

Ironically, settlement discussions were far harder for me than public courtroom fights. In the courtroom, I had the status of an advocate, and the protection of the formal rules. I wasn't "Nancy" with the high-pitched voice, congenial manner, and what I still thought was a fatal need to please; I was "Ms. Gertner," the one with *that* reputation, armed with the law books and legendary preparation, dogged in her determination to win. And for me to calculate what was fair in this case, which had no precedent, was excruciating. How could I predict what a jury would do? Or an appellate court? What monetary figure could possibly compensate Marcia for her pain? Was I just chicken to go to court? Did I fear losing this, my first malpractice trial? Like the classic nightmare of high-achieving people—this time your incompetence will be found out!—a loss, I feared, would show that Saxe was an aberration. I wasn't very good after all. What about the money? I had a contingency-fee agreement with Marcia, which meant that I would get a sizeable percentage of any settlement, but nothing if we lost in court. It would be easier to take the money then to run the risk of loss.

"Get your narcissism out of the picture," I shouted to myself. If I feared a trial, I had no business taking the case. In fact, because I tried both criminal and civil cases, I had more trial experience at this stage of my career than most other lawyers. By the time Marcia's case was scheduled, I had multiple jury trials and multiple victories under my belt. And the money? While money was getting more and more tempting the longer I eked out a marginal, single woman's existence, it did not compel me. My new guitar lessons were not expensive. (Guitar was just an excuse to warble totally unfeminist, "he-keeps-on-dumping-me-but-I-love-him!" songs in the privacy of my home.) The rent-controlled apartment on Harvard Street in Cambridge suited me, decorated in early graduate student, with shelves made of milk cartons, bricks, and boards. "Iffy," the car, was holding up just fine.

What about Marcia? She would be ground up in a trial. If she was rattled by each page of the doctor's record, or each small court defeat, what would each adverse witness, each negative evidentiary ruling do? And the publicity? The doctor's derriere, the "tea stain" on her skirt. He might be ruined, but what of her future? What if we lost? How would she feel?

And yes, settling felt all wrong. Your client screws her courage on to make her private indignities public, not just for herself, but, on one level, for all women. She loves it when you depict her case as a grand battle between good and evil. Then, after working our hearts out, we take our money, fold our tents, and retire quietly. No announcement that the doctor had wronged her, no protection for other women that he might abuse in the future. Hush money, plain and simple.

It was an old dilemma. Was the goal of litigation to resolve disputes, with almost any settlement seen a victory just because it ends the case? Or was litigation a public process, a way to announce a violation of social norms, so that others will be moved to conform their behavior?

I would not push her. True to my creed, I would lay out the

options; it was her decision and her decision only. I urged her to talk to her doctors. I made myself available to her day and night. To my surprise, Marcia wanted to settle. She was vindicated, knowing that he had to pay a substantial amount from his personal resources, and, at the very least, confess to her McLean therapist and acknowledge the pain that he had caused her. After the settlement papers were signed, even Dr. X's lawyer, in an extraordinary gesture, stepped out of his role and let Marcia know that he had believed her, too. She wanted her life back and her privacy. Suing Dr. X had not become a holy war. This was an act of health and sanity. She wrote me afterwards, about her case and more important, our friendship:

> I've always felt very proud that you were my attorney, and that was especially true during the finale. You swept into court with just the perfect balance of preparedness, confidence, and charm. You were 1000 percent ready to go forward with the trial and take on the world in order to make things right . . . When it came to the settlement, you orchestrated things beautifully, giving me courage when I had the stamina of oatmeal and being so gracious, right down to the wire, about whatever I wanted and my head needed . . . Quite apart from the legal victory, I learned a lot about becoming a person. I'm walking away feeling very uplifted and inspired by all that you are and all that you stand for.

Somehow everything between us—the usual ups and downs of representation—was all forgiven. She could look past my efforts to prepare her for the worst, as lawyers are supposed to do. I could forget the lengthy letters, written in a tiny, compulsive handwriting, letting me know what I had missed, what I had to do. We mainly remembered the jokes, all at Dr. X's expense, with occasional spoofs of Marcia's awful anatomical drawings.

The "law cure" worked for her in ways I could never have imagined. We have stayed in touch.

And while I was gratified and happy because she was gratified and happy, I had concerns about Dr. X. Marcia withdrew her complaint before the medical disciplinary board. So far as we knew, no disciplinary action was ever taken against Dr. X. And even when another woman sued Dr. X, Marcia declined to participate. (The confidential settlement could not prevent her from being subpoenaed to testify in a later legal proceeding. But when Marcia made it clear that she did not want to testify, no subpoena was issued.) She had, as they say, truly "moved on." Still, I wondered whether some part of her did not want to admit that there had in fact been others, that she meant so little to him, the enduring legacy of his humiliation of her. I would not push her to do anything that could hurt her so. Representing her—like all the people of my "causes"— always meant *thinking* on multiple levels—the importance of the case, the precedent it would set—but *acting* on only one: what's best for your client. While I was prepared to take risks with my career, to take on unpopular causes, to be as zealous an advocate as I could possibly be, I could not expect her to follow. I was troubled by what happened to Marcia's claim; the problem of abusive professionals seemed epidemic. And given their stature, they had the means to buy off their victims. Still, I knew I had to follow her wishes. My only solace was that this process had been so painful for Dr. X that he would be deterred from ever abusing his patients again.

———

On May 23, 1979, the *Boston Globe* reported that more than 10 percent of doctors in the United States not only engaged in "erotic contact" with female patients, but they also saw nothing wrong with it. Gynecologists were the worst, general practitioners second, and psychiatrists third. According to the report, 19 percent believed that the contact was even "useful to patients."

In time, I saw more and more of these victims. One woman believed that she was dying of cancer; her therapist told her that he had to do "vaginal rolfing," a technique involving massaging her genitals, to get the "healthy juices" flowing. By the end of the therapy, she felt confused and humiliated. The case was settled when it was clear that the "rolfing" therapist had many other victims.

A second, a student at a woman's college, was deeply depressed and needed counseling. Her psychiatrist became her guru, encouraging her dependence on him, above and beyond the therapeutic relationship. The case was settled when we sat down with the insurance lawyer and played the tapes that he had sent her, in which he gave her totally inappropriate advice, like a crazed, narcissistic swami. A third consulted a psychiatrist to deal with a troubled marriage; when the psychiatrist became interested in her, he abruptly terminated the therapy and seduced her; later she returned to therapy, with him now playing both doctor and lover. The doctor admitted the sex. Did you ever have sexual contact with my client? Yes, fellatio, and she loved it, he replied, almost proudly. The case settled when it was clear that he was about to retire.

Like Marcia's, these cases did not garner substantial publicity. Indeed, the rule, at least through the 1970s and early 1980s, seemed clear: the more press, the more difficult to settle. Disciplinary boards would be obliged to take harsher action in response to public pressure. When backed into a corner, the doctor would fight harder to preserve his livelihood. The central dilemma became even more intractable: how to contribute to the public debate, to expose this abuse, while still providing redress for the victimized women?

———

By the late 1980s, the debate shifted again. Finally, the problem of abuse by doctors was receiving widespread coverage; cases were brought from one end of the country to the other. Bar journals reported settlements and trials with substantial damage awards. Disciplinary boards were finally becoming stricter.

In response, insurance companies were carving out sexual assault from their malpractice policies, in unequivocal terms. There was a real risk that women would not be compensated for the damage inflicted by these physicians.

Women's advocates pressed for legislation that would make a doctor's conduct criminal. While it was important to announce in the strongest possible terms society's condemnation of this behavior, I was skeptical. Prosecutors, as in date rape cases, would be hard-pressed to bring accusations against respected psychiatrists. Juries would be unlikely to convict. The problems of proof would be exacerbated. On the civil side, a woman had to prove her case only by a fair preponderance of the evidence. On the criminal side, it would be the much more stringent "beyond a reasonable doubt" standard. If there was finally a prosecution, the risks would be extraordinary. A woman would take the stand, be obliged to recount the pain that she endured in excruciating detail, and likely face cross-examination even more aggressive than in the usual date rape case. The doctor, likely a well-heeled defendant, would pour resources into the case; his liberty would be on the line. In effect, the only way for him to "win" would be for her to "lose," to be discredited, or worse, demonized. And even a victory, with the doctor convicted, would be hollow. No insurance company would pay for damages arising from a criminal act. The one victory I garnered for Marcia, a financial settlement, would be gone. For the most part, thankfully no such criminal laws were passed.

In the early 1990s, a psychiatrist that I used as an expert witness in a murder trial asked if I would write an affidavit supporting his "good character" in the face of an accusation of sexual misconduct from a patient. I knew why he wanted me, of all the lawyers with whom he dealt, to do this. I did not know him the best, but I had legitimacy because of my women's rights practice. I knew him well enough to believe in his "good character." I provided him with the affidavit. I dealt with one human being at a time.

———

In the summer of 1997, I was having my hair done. The hairdresser, making conversation, reported that he had just been a juror in state court. The case was against a doctor for malpractice. The claim was that he had sex with a woman patient. The hairdresser said that while the jury felt for the woman, they simply could not believe her rather than him, especially because no other women complained. The doctor was exonerated. "What was the doctor's name?" I asked. It was Dr. X.

CHAPTER SIX

The Right to Choose
All of Life's Roles

Every single June between 1977 and 1980, it seemed, there was a woman's rights emergency. The Massachusetts legislature, like state legislatures around the country, was passing or seeking to pass legislation testing the limits of the 1973 *Roe v. Wade* decision, which had made abortions legal. John Reinstein of the ACLU and I would spring into action. We litigated almost every abortion case in the state. Working day and night, we would rush to court to seek a preliminary injunction. The idea was to keep the law in question from being implemented, even for a moment. If access to abortions were limited, we argued, women would face increased medical risks as their pregnancy continued, or worse, they would suffer at the hands of the back-alley abortion butcher.

In spite of its reputation as a progressive state, Massachusetts was among the most conservative on social issues at that time. Some of the new laws being proposed had no chance of passage, but they reflected a wider, decidedly antifeminist agenda. A resolution decrying the declining birth rate, for example. Or, more ridiculously, a resolution, filed at the request of a constituent but allegedly disclaimed by the sponsors, proclaiming that "males are the naturally dominant force in the family and should have the deciding say in family controversies."

Others struck close to the heart of the matter (and presaged the restrictive legislation of the 1990s). Among the most troubling then were the funding prohibitions that would effectively restrict the poor from getting abortions. Medicaid funds were prevented from being allocated for abortions; no public hospital would be required to perform abortions; no state funded insurance plans would cover the procedure.

There were also licensing proposals that would increase the cost of abortions even to the middle class. The procedure, no matter how routine, had to be performed in either a hospital or special facilities designed for the purpose. There were the regulations directly affecting the decision: informed-consent proposals required the doctor to provide details about the fetus's developmental stage, plainly to dissuade the woman from seeking termination of a pregnancy. There were even efforts to reinstate criminal penalties. One provided the death penalty for those who performed an abortion; another made it a crime to transport a minor across state lines to procure an abortion.

Part of the problem was with the *Roe v. Wade* decision itself. While the Court held that a woman's right to terminate a pregnancy by abortion falls within a constitutionally protected zone of privacy, it was not absolute. State regulations were permitted at certain stages of pregnancy where they were directed at protecting the health of the pregnant woman or fostering potential human life. In the first trimester, when the abortion procedure was relatively simple and the fetus was not viable, the decision of a woman to have an abortion and her doctor to perform it would be respected. In the second trimester, when the medical procedure was more complex, the state's interest in the woman's health permitted regulation but, because the fetus was still not viable, no prohibition. In the third trimester, when the fetus was viable and the procedure dangerous, the state could prohibit abortions except when the woman's life or health was threatened.

The most obvious flaw was that the right to choose pivoted on the viability of the fetus. It was at the mercy of medical technology, which was steadily moving the point of viability earlier and earlier. But there was a broader critique: limiting access to abortion, like limiting access to birth control, affected women's equality, a woman's right to participate as fully as men do in public and private life. It was not only about a medical procedure. It was about the right to be childless, though married; to be unmarried and sexually active; to pace the childbearing role to fit a career. In short, it was about the right to have all the choices that a man had.

I was fortunate never to have had an abortion. But I viscerally understood the significance of the right. It was about all the roles in life that I had chosen or was about to choose.

———

Sex discrimination does not always spring from malevolence or bad motives. It often lurks behind euphemisms like "chivalry" or humanistic-sounding phrases like "fetal rights." Even the Supreme Court recognized that sex discrimination was rationalized by a "romantic paternalism" which, in practical effect, put women "not on a pedestal, but in a cage." At its core, it derived from a woman's status as mother. Women were long excluded from politics and from the economic life of this nation because they were, could be, had been, or might become mothers. In 1869, for example, when Myra Colby Bradwell applied for admission to the Illinois bar, the Supreme Court ultimately rejected her claim in *Bradwell v. State,* with one of the justices citing the "Divine Order of Things":

> The constitution of the family organization which is founded in Divine ordinance, as well as in the nature of things, indicates the domestic sphere as that which properly belongs to the domain and function of womanhood. . . . The paramount destiny and mission of women is to fulfill the noble and benign offices of wife and mother. This is the law of the Creator.

That was neither the first nor the last time that the deity would be invoked to justify exalting the role of mother over all the other roles a human being might play. When women sought the vote, or to serve on juries, opponents argued that women should not be burdened with the obligations of public life given their significant obligations in private life. And when women entered the labor force in increasing numbers, their private obligations led to protective legislation limiting wages and hours, regulating working conditions—rules that initially applied only to women workers. That gender-based "protection," finally overthrown in the early 1970s, exacerbated sex segregation and gender inequality in the workplace. The exclusion of women from certain jobs was transformed into a set of cultural expectations and stereotypes that lasted well beyond the change in the laws.

Even after women got the vote, the Supreme Court continued to uphold statutes excluding women from participation in public life solely because of their potential for becoming mothers. In *Hoyt v. Florida,* the Court upheld a Florida statute that allowed women to be excluded from juries unless they voluntarily registered, while men were automatically included. "[D]espite the enlightened emancipation of women from the restrictions and protections of bygone years, and their entry into many parts of community life formerly considered to be reserved to men," the Court noted, "women are still regarded as the center of home and family life." This was in 1961. (By 1975, *Hoyt* was overruled.)

The issue was not anatomy. It was the social construction of motherhood. As then-Judge Ruth Bader Ginsburg noted in a 1985 lecture, quoting Kenneth L. Karst:

> Society, not anatomy, "places a greater stigma on unmarried women who become pregnant than on the men who father their children." Society expects, but nature does not command, that "women take the major responsibility . . . for child care" and they will stay with their children, bearing nurture and support burdens alone, when fathers deny paternity or otherwise refuse to provide care or financial support for unwanted offspring.

At stake, Judge Ginsburg wrote, was "a woman's autonomous charge of her full life's course," "her ability to stand in relation to man, society, and the state, as an independent, self-sustaining, equal citizen."

The separation of abortion from gender discrimination marginalized the right to choose. In short order, the Supreme Court held that this was a right that the state had no obligation to pay for and even public hospitals did not have to provide. While the state could not unreasonably burden the right to choose—most informed-consent and onerous licensing laws were rejected during the 1980s—it did not have to facilitate it.

Even more significant, the concept of an entity growing within a woman with interests adverse to hers, protected by the state, created new problems. Recasting the issue as a struggle of woman versus fetus undermined the moral authority of the woman, her right to make decisions about her body.

———

On June 13, 1979, Massachusetts governor Edward J. King, sporting a red rose (the symbol of the right-to-life movement), signed into law an abortion bill that prohibited the use of state or any other public funds for abortions, even for victims of rape or incest.

By the next day, John and I were in court moving to enjoin its implementation. The stories that we told were gripping: the woman with cancer who needed chemotherapy, a therapy that would endanger the fetus; the woman with chronic lung disease, where childbirth would accelerate the deterioration of her lung function; a woman with heart problems, or hypertension, whose body could not sustain the rigors of pregnancy and labor. Medicaid covered a range of medically necessary operations, including male-specific operations like male sterilization. It was discrimination, we argued, to carve out medically necessary procedures that affect women from medically necessary procedures affecting men.

But the U.S. Supreme Court rejected the federal constitutional challenge, the first indication of what would become a dramatic erosion of *Roe*. It validated restrictions on Medicaid funding of abortions as a matter of federal constitutional law, restrictions that soon went into effect around the country.

That is, except in Massachusetts. John and I turned to the state courts for relief.

The Massachusetts constitution predated the federal constitution. The Supreme Judicial Court of Massachusetts had begun to part company with the U.S. Supreme Court in a number of areas, interpreting its constitution in ways that differed from the U.S. constitution. It had held the death penalty unconstitutional when the Supreme Court refused to do so. It had ruled that discrimination against pregnant women was sex discrimination when the Supreme Court, in an astounding decision, had suggested it was not gender discrimination to distinguish between "pregnant persons" and "nonpregnant persons." It had been willing to ban the discriminatory use of jury challenges to eliminate African American jurors when the Supreme Court initially balked. Moreover, the Supreme Judicial Court had an even more expansive view of a citizen's right to privacy, particularly with respect to medical decisions, namely the right to refuse medical treatment. And at a time when efforts to pass the federal Equal Rights Amendment (ERA) were faltering, Massachusetts amended the state constitution to add an Equal Rights Amendment that expressly guaranteed the right to be free from gender discrimination.

We thought we had a good shot, but it meant another emergency, working around the clock. And another delicate balance—keeping the paying clients satisfied while pouring heart and soul into the Medicaid case (and fitting a social life into the interstices of the crises).

We garnered help from women's organizations all over the state. This would not be a case; it would be a mobilization. Women lawyers of my generation had just formed the Women's Bar Association (WBA), hoping that it would be more politically active than the traditional women's bar groups. It was not just about networking and cocktail parties. It was about abortion and equal rights. So the WBA's very first amicus curiae ("friend of the court") brief was in support of our position, claiming that it was required by the state equal rights amendment.

There were also briefs from medical organizations, physicians, professors who taught religion and constitutional law, abortion rights groups, the Boston Women's Health Book Collective, Inc., and other organizations promoting women's health.

At a cocktail party, before we filed our briefs, John and I heard that Eleanor Smeal, then the president of the National Organization for Women (NOW), was very anxious to talk with us. She was adamantly opposed to linking abortion to the Massachusetts equal rights amendment. The federal ERA had garnered the support of women who were anti-choice, who believed that reproductive rights were one thing, discrimination another. Linking the two, she insisted, would endanger the federal movement.

No, we said, two local lawyers talking to a national woman's rights figure. We had clients to represent here. Women were suffering. Having taken the case, we had to use all the tools at our disposal. Besides, if the ERA did not cover the right to choose, if it did not link gender discrimination and reproductive rights, it was not worth it. We had no intention of abandoning what we believed to be a significant theory of the case.

———

The lawsuit was successful beyond our wildest expectations. In February 1981, in a landmark 6–1 decision written by one of its most conservative justices, the Massachusetts Supreme Judicial Court held that there was a right to choose abortion under the Massachusetts constitution, and it described this right in sweeping terms. There was no trimester limitation, no tripartite system, no woman v. fetus dichotomy. The right at stake was the right to be free from "nonconsensual invasion of bodily integrity." And while the Supreme Judicial Court did not expressly call the state's regulation an example of gender discrimination, it came close. Citing Larry Tribe, Harvard's preeminent constitutional law professor, it stated:

> If a man is the involuntary source of a child [because] he is forbidden, for example, to practice contraception, the violation of his personality is profound; the decision that one wants to engage in sexual intercourse but does not want to parent another human being may reflect the deepest of personal convictions. But if a woman is forced to bear a child not simply to provide an ovum but to carry the child to term, the invasion

is incalculably greater. Quite apart from the physical experience of pregnancy itself, an experience which of course has no analogue for the male, there is the attachment the experience creates, partly physiological and partly psychological, between mother and child. Thus it is difficult to imagine a clearer case of bodily intrusion, even if the original conception was in some sense voluntary.

John and I were flooded with cards, letter, phone calls, even flowers, praising the victory. This was not just about one client's life; it was about all of us. And along with the WBA members who had helped, we celebrated for days.

———

Ten years later, in 1991, the attention to the abortion issue had died down, particularly in Massachusetts. Few people noticed when Elizabeth Levey was charged with manslaughter in Cambridge. Unmarried and troubled, she was in her last trimester of pregnancy. She got drunk and wrecked her car. Shortly thereafter, her fetus died and she was indicted for vehicular homicide. Nearby, in Brockton, Josephine Pellegrini was charged with distributing cocaine to her unborn fetus after traces of the drug were found in the baby's bloodstream at birth.

When I found out, I volunteered to represent Levey. Because Pellegrini was already represented by a lawyer, I submitted an amicus brief on her behalf for the ACLU's Women's Rights Project.

The television images were chilling—babies born addicted to cocaine, doomed to fetal alcohol syndrome, or worse, killed. The prosecutors suggested that these cases had nothing whatever to do with women's rights. These were "bad women," not "the rest of us," who followed the doctor's orders to the letter, who worked hard to maximize our children's chance for a healthy life. And, surely, they suggested, these prosecutions had nothing to do with the constitutional right to choose abortion. While the Pellegrini case was brought by a conservative district attorney in Plymouth County, the Levey case was brought by a liberal district attorney in Middlesex County. Indeed, the Middlesex district attorney, Scott Harsh-barger, was a strong supporter of the right to choose.

The reasoning of *Roe v. Wade*, ironically, seemed to justify the prosecutions. A woman and the fetus within her were described in *Roe* as different entities, their interests defined in relation to one another, a relationship that changed during the course of the pregnancy. In the first trimester of pregnancy, a woman's right to choose trumped the interests of the pre-viable fetus; and because the procedure was relatively simple, the state had a minimal interest in regulating it to protect a woman's health. In the second trimester, the fetus was still not viable, but a more complex abortion procedure justified state regulation in the interest of a woman's health. Post-viability, namely the third trimester, the balance shifted more dramatically; the fetus's interest outstripped the woman's—abortion was prohibited unless her life or health was endangered. In fact, at viability, some would say, the opinion seemed to suggest that the state could protect a fetus just as it did a child.

By now, the governor of Massachusetts was Michael Dukakis, also a strong supporter of the right to choose. Governor Dukakis had appointed me to his Anti-Crime Council as a representative of the civil liberties/civil rights community. The council was an extraordinary body, composed of individuals from all parts of the criminal justice system—the prisons, social services, public safety, the public. We gathered every month to address criminal justice issues. Scott Harshbarger was a member. We were also good friends. More of an insider now, I could represent clients and causes the old-fashioned way—by talking directly to the decision makers.

I spoke to him privately, cornering him at a break in the meeting. Levey is a troubling case, I said. It has profound political and legal implications for women's rights. Please look at the papers, I asked him. I'll send them to your office before they're filed. I don't want this to be a cause célèbre.

I peppered his office with calls, but he refused to dismiss the case. So I filed my briefs in court, and true to form, took to the airwaves.

———

True, society's protection of children was critical. But the Levey and Pellegrini cases were different, I argued. The only way that the state can protect the fetus is through the woman's body. The only way that the state could intervene on behalf of the fetus was to undermine the woman's autonomy.

For two hundred years, a pregnant woman and her fetus had been treated as a single entity. In 1884, Justice Oliver Wendell Holmes had to rule on a suit by a child against the town of Northampton because the mother fell on a defective highway and the fetus was harmed. Holmes held that an unborn child is part of the mother, that her damages are indistinguishable from the damages of the mother.

For sixty years that rule was followed. Courts belittled the very notion of treating mother and fetus as separate beings. It would lead to fetuses suing their mothers for the mother's failures during pregnancy, a result they regarded as outrageous. Even when courts and legislatures were extraordinarily protective of women, when women were seen "only" as mothers, when rules, laws, and statutes were designed to enhance that role and no other, there was no question that the pregnant woman and the fetus within her were to be treated as a single being. The state had no right to intervene to deal with her uterus if it had no right to deal with the rest of her.

In the 1950s, the laws began to change, but only for a very narrow purpose. Suddenly there were suits against doctors whose malpractice led to the birth of a disabled child, or against men who beat up their pregnant girlfriends, or against drivers whose cars negligently collided with the cars of pregnant women. But the rationale was clear: the pregnant woman and her fetus were on the same side. In those cases, their combined interests had been undermined by a third party—doctor, boyfriend, driver.

One court, writing thirty years later, was the most eloquent:

> Holding a third party liable for prenatal injuries furthers the interests of both the mother and the subsequently born child and does not interfere with the defendant's right to control her own life. Holding a mother liable for the unintentional infliction of prenatal injuries subjects to state scrutiny all the deci-

sions a woman must make in attempting to carry a pregnancy to term and infringes on her right to privacy and bodily autonomy. . . . Logic does not demand that a pregnant woman be treated in a court of law as a stranger to her developing fetus.

The moment before a child is born, it lies within the walls of its mother's body. To protect it, however much we may want to, requires acting on that body, working through that body, affecting that woman's rights. To prosecute each of these women, Levey and Pellegrini, the Commonwealth was obliged to intrude into her most private areas and use her newborn child as an adversary. The state cannot say in effect, "Well, ladies, you may have your brain and your arms and your legs, but once you get pregnant, we, the state, own your uterus."

Of course, no one suggested that it was good, or right, or appropriate, or correct to become pregnant and behave as did the women charged here. The issue was that however much the state wanted to intervene, it could not do so at this cost to a woman's autonomy. It was a familiar refrain: it would be far more efficient, for example, for law enforcement to be able to break down doors and search without warrants, but our constitutional democracy chooses a less-efficient approach—demanding probable cause and warrants—to maximize the privacy of its citizens.

Here was a troubling slippery slope, as law professors say—from avoiding cocaine and driving while drunk, to disobeying doctor's instructions, to mandating transfusions and caesarean sections to save fetuses. The seeds of such a progression were sown in a philosophy that made no distinctions between engaging in legal activity or illegal activity, nor drew fine lines between acts done by the mother pre-viability or those done post-viability. The rationale for state intervention was simple—anything that harmed the fetus.

There were already examples along that slope. Some courts, in the name of fetal rights, had ordered women to undergo surgical procedures, like caesarean sections, against their will. In one California case, a woman was prosecuted criminally for child abuse for failing to follow her doctor's directions. Given that she had had a history of miscarriages, the doctor suggested that she not engage in sex in her third trimester, but she did. When the child was stillborn, the woman found herself in prison. Later, in Massachusetts, a judge detained a pregnant woman, whose religion rejected medical intervention, to make certain that the birth was attended by medical personnel.

And whatever the legality of these policies, I argued, they made no sense. Public health specialists agree that anything that scares women away from seeking prenatal care is bad for babies. Smoking, ingesting alcohol, and snorting cocaine correlate with depression and, in fact, are coping behaviors. Interventions that help women deal with their feelings and reduce stress are the only way to go. And there was something cruel about penalizing pregnant women for their addictions when we turn them away from drug treatment facilities and stigmatize abortion. There was something unjust about blaming the victim and taking society off the hook for ensuring maternal health.

It worked. In the Pellegrini case, Judge Suzanne Delvecchio ruled that the relationship between the woman and the fetus within her was constitutionally protected. While the state has an interest in the developing fetus, it must carry out that interest in the most narrow means possible, in a way that minimally interferes with a woman's right to privacy, through educational programs, and maximizing the medical care and drug treatment centers available to pregnant women—not by throwing a woman in jail.

And in Levey, Harshbarger dropped the charges, ostensibly because the child died from the hospital's acts. The fact was that, even after the accident, Elizabeth Levey had arrived at the hospital with a live fetus within her. When the medical staff smelled alcohol on her breath, they ignored her, just as many critics were doing. So much for protecting her fetus.

The abortion rights debate was one that would not go away, and a woman's right to choose was in danger of dying of a thousand cuts. To me, it effectively defined the second wave of the women's movement—choosing when and even whether to be a mother. And as far as I knew, moving late into my thirties, I had chosen not.

CHAPTER SEVEN

Choosing Love and Work

We are eating dinner at the kitchen table, John Reinstein, my friend and co-conspirator of twelve years, and me.

"Steve Kirschbaum called me last week," he says.

"Oh," I say. "Tell me what that was about—but first pass the potatoes."

"There's a woman named Sissy Richardson in the school bus drivers' union."

"And?"

"I met her today."

"What's her problem?" I asked between bites of chicken.

"It's not her. It's her son, Ray. He was shot by the police."

"That's not good."

"Graylan Hagler has been poking around and thinks this is a bad shooting. He wants me to bring a civil rights suit against the police. I said I would look into it."

"OK."

"The problem is that the police arrested him."

"For what?"

"Assault on a police officer. They say that Ray pulled a gun on them, and that's why they shot him. The thing is, he was shot in the back, and the gun they found was yards away, closer to where the cops were standing."

"Well?"

"Well." He paused. "He's actually charged with assault with intent to murder the cops. He's facing serious time. He's in the hospital now, badly hurt, and Sissy says that they have no money for his defense."

"All right, already," I say. "When do we start?"

It would not be the first or the last case that we did together. And we had become more than just friends. Love, work, mashed potatoes—all mixed in. It couldn't have been any other way.

———

For most of my twenties and thirties, I was at best ambivalent about marriage. I was deeply skeptical that a woman could combine love and work—not my kind of work, not my ambitions. I had no models.

Dad put Mom on a pedestal, but not the one I wanted: She was the prettiest "girl" on Goerck Street, on the Lower East Side of New York City. They could watch sports together—they were rabid fans—but he did not want her to work outside the home, to drive, to venture far. Many of my male peers with challenging jobs had wives who stayed at home, or if they worked, their jobs were in the interstices of their husbands' careers, part time, or flexible. Someone's career had to yield, and it was always the woman's. I did not want to choose, but if I had to, it would be my work.

When I applied for a job with Chief Judge Luther M. Swygert, a federal appeals court judge, in 1970, he asked me if I planned to marry and have children. His first clerk was a woman. She had married and never used her training again after that. He didn't want this to happen again.

I had three choices—walk out, chide him for daring to ask such a sexist question ("chide" is a mild version for what I had in mind), or play along. I played along. "Oh, no, judge," I said, "I never plan to marry and have children. I will devote my life to work!"

Many years later, at the judge's eightieth birthday party, with all his law clerks and family present, I was asked to speak. I reminded him of that interview. Then I got down on my knees and said:

"Judge, I am thirty-eight and barren! Release me from my pledge!"

He roared with laughter. In the twelve years since my clerkship, he had had a succession of women clerks, including one with a newborn baby. For her, he closed off the law library so she could nurse in private.

In my twenties and thirties, "singlehood" had been yet another challenge. I remember the comment of Drucila Ramey, a Yale law student, at a women's consciousness-raising group.

"I did something radical today," she said.

"Yes?" we asked.

"I bought a pot holder! 'They' told me that it made no sense to buy pot holders, kitchen equipment . . . all sorts of things, until I was married. Well, I'm not. I am sick of burning my hands."

My "pot holder" was a beautiful two-family house on Mt. Auburn Street in Cambridge, which I bought with the settlement money from the suit against the Gulf Oil company. I wasn't about to wait until I was married.

Still, as time went on, this challenge was wearing thin. Part of the transitional generation, I was not entirely comfortable rejecting all the earlier models. After all, I had been a cheerleader, runner-up homecoming queen, but I also had to be valedictorian of Flushing High School. I was a feminist, but I always shaved my legs and wore makeup.

Anna Quindlen, in a 1999 commencement speech, spoke of this dilemma, which she had faced when she graduated from Barnard twenty-five years before, only a few years after I had left.

"You had to be perfect in every way," she said. "Being perfect was hard work, and the hell of it was, the rules of it changed. So that while I arrived at college in 1970 with a trunk full of perfect pleated kilts and perfect monogrammed sweaters, by Christmas vacation, I had another perfect uniform: overalls, turtlenecks, Doc Martens, and the perfect New York City Barnard College affect, part hyper intellectual, part ennui."

In fact, she adds, "[being perfect] really requires you mainly read the zeitgeist of wherever and whenever you happen to be, to assume the masks necessary to be the best of whatever the zeitgeist dictates or requires. Those requirements shift, sure, but when you're clever, you can read them and do the imitation required."

Maybe this particular part of the zeitgeist—being doggedly single and alone—somehow was not a point that I wanted to make for the rest of my life. Or maybe, by the 1980s, the zeitgeist was changing yet again. Or maybe I was just lonely.

In 1977 my mother died of a sudden heart attack at sixty-two. My father was aging rapidly; he suffered a heart attack in 1981 in his early sixties, and a near-fatal heart bypass operation in 1982. My sister, Roz—my great solace and closest friend—was as wrapped up in her family and her two small sons, Mark and Eric, as I was in my work.

I remember returning from a business trip to Europe. Meetings in London had been followed by a whirlwind visit to Paris to stay with an old pal who was living with a French lawyer. The plan was to meet their friends, hang out, and party. I loved to travel. I would go wherever I chose, meet whomever I wanted. After a stressful trial, on the day of the verdict, I would call my travel agent and say: Get me a ticket—Europe, Africa, Mexico—wherever. And I would go alone—happily, doggedly alone.

But on this trip, as the plane neared the United States, as I pictured my father meeting me at the airport, barely recovered from his near misses, my eyes began to fill up. The joy of seeing him was mixed with a sense of emptiness. This was my father meeting me, not a life mate. One day, there would be no one.

The life I was living—maniacal work, single adventures—was wearing thin.

But there was little time to pencil dates in around my crusades. Work was the functional equivalent of family. Gloria Steinem's words resonated: "I've been submerging myself not in the needs of husband and children, but in the needs of others nonetheless."

I had met John almost immediately after I arrived in Boston, after my clerkship in Chicago. I went to a legal panel meeting of the ACLU. I wanted to volunteer for public-interest civil liberties cases. We were introduced by one of my partners. He told John my name and then recounted my resume—law school, law review, clerking, and so on. John, true to form, was unimpressed.

Shortly after *Roe v. Wade* was decided in 1972, he called me about the doctors who wanted to continue to do abortions at a public hospital, the Hale Hospital in Haverhill. Although *Roe* had declared a right to choose abortions, a right that the state supposedly could not curtail, this public hospital somehow believed that it had the right to refuse to allow them.

He was standing on a street corner, Tremont and Park. I drove up in "Iffy," my battered Chevy. He was 6'2" tall and had bushy, dark brown hair, a brown mustache that always needed trimming, and yellow-hazel eyes. He spoke softly, as if each word was carefully considered and thoughtfully selected. There was no idle conversation. He had made the support of civil rights and civil liberties his life's work. Although he had had many options, he chose to work at the ACLU for a pittance.

He says the first thing I asked him was whether he was married. (He was.) I don't remember that at all. I recall asking him if he was Jewish. (He wasn't.) Perhaps it was the very same question. Although I would never have admitted it, I was screening him for, as Sadie would say (and I would vigorously deny), "marriageable material." Oh well, I said to myself, we will just be friends.

———

We worked well together. Our thinking, our habits, complemented each other. And it seemed like an emergency was always bringing us together. The first hearing in the Hale Hospital case involved a request for a preliminary injunction. It was critical that the facilities of public hospitals make abortions available. If this hospital no longer provided the service, and then if other public hospitals followed suit, women, particularly poor women, would have to travel greater distances, pay more, or worse, continue to resort to illegal abortion providers or even self-help. (We won.)

I hadn't anticipated the media interest. The federal district courtroom was filled with press. Cameras were lined up outside the entrance to the building.

"You argue," he said, although he was more experienced than I. "This is a woman's case." Never one to decline a chance to speak, I agreed.

And when the press pummeled us with questions, he said, "You deal with them." Never one to shy away from publicity, I agreed.

I had never met a man like that—one who pushed me forward, letting me take the glory, but shared the work. It was usually the reverse. You do the work; he takes the glory. I counted on our being friends for life.

Case after case followed. I had more stamina than he had. I would stay up all night to write briefs while he fell asleep in a chair. In the morning, he would wake up and I would collapse. He would painstakingly edit my 4:00 a.m. ramblings. Together, we made a formidable team. (It was like our command of French. I had book learning, six years of studying French at Flushing High School and Barnard College, an elaborate academic vocabulary, a perfect accent. He had lived in France for two years. He knew the idioms, the terms that were *au courant,* but he had a lousy accent. Together, we made a single French-speaking individual.)

In 1977, there was the Clamshell Alliance emergency, when 1,400 protesters were arrested after demonstrating at the Seabrook Nuclear Power Plant. We had to drop everything and get to Concord, New Hampshire, to get them out. We went up on Friday night and stayed until the demonstrators were released.

And the Clamshell case spawned another. Jan Schlichtmann, of *A Civil Action* fame, while acting as a lawyer for some of the demonstrators, discovered that one of his clients was an undercover agent spying on him and his defense. We sued the state officials responsible for violating the Sixth Amendment rights of the demonstrators.

In 1978, 1979, and 1980 there were more and more abortion emergencies as some public officials then, as now, tried to test the limits of *Roe:* the prisoner who needed an abortion, who could hardly shop around for the service; the poor women with cancer, or liver disease, whose doctor urged abortion and desperately needed Medicaid to cover it. These culminated in the sweeping 1981 victory in the Supreme Judicial Court of Massachusetts that found protection for the right to choose abortion in the Massachusetts constitution.

John even represented *me* once. One morning, the television stations reported a predawn law enforcement raid of Framingham State Prison. Susan Saxe, they said, who was still in prison there, was the head of a mob-dominated computer gambling ring. Extraordinary measures were needed at this minimum-security institution because of the rampant illegal activities. Prisoners would have no visitors, not even lawyers (although the press was given access so that they could film the ominous scene of police cars swooping down on the place).

True, Framingham was now coeducational, and some of the male inmates were imprisoned for mob-related activities. Also true that rather than make license plates, prisoners were learning twentieth-century computer skills. Still, I thought the security shutdown was bogus.

John sued to get me access to my client. Another emergency. By the time we got into court, late in the afternoon after the "raid," the state reported to the judge that lawyers would be let in the following day. Although we were concerned about any delay, the judge refused to act.

John advised me to wait. I didn't listen. I called every television and radio station, and all the print media, and announced that I was leaving for Framingham State Prison immediately. John was on call if I got into trouble.

We drove to the entrance of the prison, Byrna and I in Iffy, with a caravan of press cars and camera trucks following. I demanded to see my client, light bulbs flashing, cameras whirring. The guard called for his superior.

"You are not allowed to come in," he said.

"But lawyers must have access to their clients!" I insisted.

"Absolutely not," he said.

"Call the superintendent!" I demanded.

He refused.

"Very well then, I will be here tomorrow morning."

My point was made. There was no state of emergency—no guards surrounding the prison, no special security measures. It was an ordinary evening, except no lawyers were allowed in to see their clients. When I was at last able to speak to Susan, she said, true to form: "You had to know it was false. When did the mob become an equal opportunity employer?"

Happily, my lawyer was not too upset by my defiance. Minor charges were brought against Susan, but within months they were dismissed. And shortly after that, she was released.

Then I was subpoenaed to testify before a federal grand jury trying to find out who paid my fees to represent a client in state court. I refused to appear. John, in concert with bar associations and others, filed a brief protesting the inquiry. It was, he claimed, a violation of the attorney-client privilege and destructive of that relationship. This was another amicus curiae brief, the brief from a "friend of the court." A good friend, let it be said, not of the court, but of the lawyer.

In 1982, our friendship changed. Two years earlier, John's marriage of thirteen years had ended. He had weekend custody of his beautiful daughter, Sarah, then eight, a blond, blue-eyed child whom he doted on.

And me? I had just broken up with my latest love interest, who left me with a beagle named Samantha. (Assuming that there would be no actual offspring from me, I had named Samantha after my mother, Sadie, in the Jewish tradition.)

John heard all about my breakup, just as he had heard about a succession of failed relationships before that. Our stars were coming into alignment. We didn't have to go far to fall in love. I knew him; he knew me. I loved him, his work, his profound humanity, decency. I trusted him to let me be me; he loved me for who I was. There was no pretense. Ironically, he had his doubts about my commitment, still not married in my late thirties, seemingly unable to settle down. Trust would come, as love had.

We came from different worlds. Born in Washington, D.C., John was raised with his two brothers in a home filled with family heirlooms and pictures of his father's illustrious career. Jacques

Reinstein, a career State Department official, had worked for George Kennan on postwar reconstruction.

On his mother's side, John's blood was quite blue. His mother's family, with Scottish and French Huguenot roots, came to this country in the second or third wave after the *Mayflower*. One ancestor was a ship captain on Nantucket, another related to Frederick Law Olmstead of Emerald Necklace fame, another the mayor of Youngstown, Ohio, and on and on.

His grandfather on his father's side was Jewish. The Reinsteins, German Jews, raised horses for the Prussian army. (My family, I quipped, probably stole horses from the Prussian army.) He took off for the United States before the Nazis overtook Germany, and he married a Swiss Catholic woman soon after. As John tells it, since she was a formidable woman, it was clear that their offspring would be Catholic.

John went to parochial schools until his junior year, when his father was posted to the U.S. embassy in Paris. He spent two years in Paris and, quite the rake, tooled around the countryside in a used MG convertible.

My feelings were clinched when I met his mother, Rachel. She was seventy-five at the time. At seventy, disabled from heart disease, she divorced John's father and returned to the small town in New Hampshire where her family had a summer home. And then she did precisely what she had wanted to do all her life: She ran for office and served on the town's board of selectmen. She went to political conventions throughout the state and in D.C. And she traveled throughout Europe, making certain that airports had wheelchairs available. She spent every summer at the lake house of her youth. There were no recriminations, no feeling sorry for herself, no "might have beens." I felt certain that if she had been born when I was, she would have been a lawyer, or a senator. I loved her the minute I met her. She was the mother I had lost.

My father was a problem, though. John plainly was not Jewish enough (the religion is carried through one's mother). At breakfast one morning, I put bagels on the table. My father turned to John and—totally serious—started to explain what a "bagel" was. John listened patiently. But my father came around eventually.

It was impossible to ignore how well we fit, how much we loved each other. And given that I was in my late thirties, my father was just plain relieved to see me settling down, to take on a role that he could understand.

Not to say that John and I had no problems. An eight-year-old girl, for one. I wasn't quite ready for Sarah, and she wasn't quite ready for me. There was no peanut butter in my house, only four or five varieties of balsamic vinegar. No macaroni, no packaged cookies. I loved to cook complicated dishes from scratch with exotic ingredients—not quick enough or simple enough for a ravenous child. Worse, Sarah refused to talk to me at all. "Ask her to pass the ketchup," she would tell John, and he would ask me. "Ask her where the videotapes are," and he would. I felt like I was a Martian, or worse, a hag. Having the label "wicked stepmother" pinned to me was not exactly what I had bargained for.

Then one day, John was late to pick up Sarah at her soccer game, and he asked me to go. "How can I do it?" I asked. "She won't relate to me at all." "You'll figure something out," he said. So I brought Samantha, my adorable beagle. At the end of the game, Sarah and her friends ran to see the dog. "Whose is it?" they asked. "It's Sarah's," I said. We shared a glance, a breakthrough it seemed. And then she said, "How about ice cream? Or shopping?" Food and shopping—the twin pillars of our relationship as it developed over years and years.

Weekends now were for John and me—and Sarah.

———

Although life was changing, the enterprise—love and work— continued.

When the subject of his dinner entreaty, Ray Richardson, was charged with attempted murder of the police officers who had shot him, I represented the defendant with John sitting beside me. Ray was acquitted. Then Luis Beato, a Hispanic young man, was charged with assaulting officers whom he claimed had beaten him up. Again, I handled the criminal case (and won); John, now my husband, sued the police civilly (the case was settled). And I proudly sat beside him when he argued a search-and-seizure appeal before the U.S. Supreme Court. He would be at nearly every major court appearance of mine, his expression priceless. If I had to stay up all night working on a brief, he would make dinner. If it was his turn to blitz, we would switch roles. And we would play hard—hiking, biking, traveling, staying at a cabin on a secluded lake in New Hampshire. We competed only in the kitchen, where we both loved to cook.

But before the critical juncture, we formally asked Sarah for her permission. She granted it. It was a civil ceremony in our living room attended by my father, Moishe; my sister, Roz; her husband; her sons, Mark and Eric; John's mother, Rachel; Samantha, the dog; and Sarah, all dressed up, looking like an angel.

The justice of the peace was Joie Prevost Anzalone. I was representing her husband, Ted, a close aide to Mayor Kevin White.

When the gossip columnists reported this momentous story, it was under the caption "Taking Liberties."

CHAPTER EIGHT

Fighting at City Hall

All three of "my" men were in the courtroom for the closing argument in Ted Anzalone's extortion trial. Harvey Silverglate, my partner, sat beside me at counsel table. In the front row, next to Ted, was my father, beaming broadly. And next to him, shepherding Moishe around the courthouse, explaining what was going on, was John.

Ted Anzalone had served as assessing commissioner in the Kevin White administration, as the mayor's fund-raiser, and then as a manager of the Hynes Auditorium, the city's premier convention center. Firmly convinced that White was corrupt, U.S. attorney (and later governor) Bill Weld pursued everyone associated with the mayor in hopes of securing their "cooperation." Anzalone was the last in line, the highest official targeted at that time. After a lengthy and highly publicized investigation, Anzalone was indicted for extorting money—a campaign contribution for White—from a city contractor, supposedly in exchange for help with his city business. There were also two technical charges based on "causing" a bank to refrain from filing certain currency reports with the government when cash over $10,000 was deposited. The "causing" was accomplished by depositing amounts less than $10,000 at different times.

Now *here* was a client Dad could identify with! Nothing feminist about the case. No defense committee. No sex. Nothing revolutionary, or even violent. A white-collar case, with every newspaper in town focused on it. Once, when I was asked how I came to represent Ted Anzalone, I answered (with my father's perspective in mind): "Well, if I restricted my practice to lesbian feminist revolutionaries, I would starve."

———

In truth, Ted was Harvey's client, not mine. I was to step in only if there was a trial. While Harvey had been my partner, and one of the most important influences on my professional life for nearly twelve years, we rarely worked together. At the beginning of our partnership, we were kindred spirits. Harvey was the first-generation son of an immigrant family from the Lower East Side of Manhattan; he understood my battered Yiddish, my childhood stories about mahjong and pinochle games, because he had his own.

Our offices were on Lewis Wharf, in Boston's waterfront. The area nowadays is quite chic, but in the 1970s it was "in transition." I remember shopping for office furniture with Harvey when we started Silverglate, Shapiro, and Gertner. Always a mimic, I couldn't resist playing the part of the Jewish newlyweds to the poor salesclerk. "Hahv," I said, with a thick New York accent, "shouldn't we get the bedroom set and the credenza before we get the sofa? What about the plastic covers? Do they come with the chairs, or are they extra?"

And his work style was like mine—late evenings, little sleep. We went over the day's events at 1:00 a.m. at Moon Villa, a Chinese restaurant in downtown Boston, with the police officers and the "working women." Mainly, we shared a love of the law and a ferocity about civil liberties and civil rights. By the time of the Anzalone trial, we had moved to downtown Boston. The offices were still funkier than most, though. Harvey's had a nude picture of Allen Ginsberg, taken by his photographer wife, Elsa Dorfman. My office was decorated with political posters and a bed for Samantha, the dog.

Still, we had been growing apart for some time—in style,

in politics, even in legal strategies. He represented one client at a time, focusing passionately on him or her. With that single-mindedness, coupled with his courage and utter disdain for convention, his contributions were always unique—approaches that no one had ever heard of, tactics that no one would dare to try. But he would not—or could not—try jury cases himself, even as lead counsel. (He would do appeals, though.) Sometimes I thought that he simply had to be away from the day-to-day decisions of the trial so that he could think, as they say, "outside the box." Sometimes, less charitably perhaps, I thought it was to preserve his posture as the uncompromising advocate. Facing a jury, dealing with the day-to-day humdrum of court bureaucracies always meant compromise, always softened the edges of advocacy, which was something he was reluctant to do. But he would happily be the press spokesperson—he had been a journalist before he became a lawyer—where he could be brash and pure, rather than the workaday lawyer.

I had trouble focusing exclusively on a single case. Twelve years into the practice, I didn't have to prove anything to anyone anymore. It was *me*, my pathology—an endless fascination with the profession, the people, the issues. I could not say "no" to the interesting criminal case, the fascinating discrimination issue, the compelling amicus on a civil liberties issue. And I had begun to broaden my focus to bar activities, legislative testimony, and then-Governor Michael Dukakis's monthly Anti-Crime Council meeting. This was not about searching for clients; I had more than I could handle. This was about working on issues that I cared about, not just through litigation but by working with people who had the power to influence the lawmaking process (Michael Dukakis credits his Anti-Crime Council with "mellowing" me). Harvey loathed such meetings, the enforced civility and small talk, the socializing that necessarily came with it. He hated social events in general, and cocktail parties were the worst. Once I was negotiating with officials in the Dukakis administration, whom I had come to know from the Anti-Crime Council meetings, asking them to allow a defendant convicted of Medicaid fraud to continue to operate while his appeal was pending. At that moment, Harvey was on the front pages of the *Boston Globe* blasting the administration's close legislative allies for an allegedly corrupt real estate deal.

I was changing. My long hair was gone. It was no symbolic gesture—I was just tired of it. The miniskirts had been thrown out, too—although I continued to wear my red suits. And now I carried a real briefcase—indeed, four or five huge litigation bags with "NG" printed on them. Most important of all to my working relationship with my mentor and dear friend, after years of my own practice, I had a hard time being in the background.

To blunt the tensions between us, we changed the structure of the partnership. Tom Shapiro had left the firm, and new partners were brought in—Judy Mizner, Andy Good, Jean Baker, David Fine. But it wasn't enough.

Our relationship was not a problem before Anzalone was indicted. The grand jury investigation was Harvey's show. For the trial, we would switch seats; and although we would consult closely about strategy, I would be lead counsel, addressing the jury and examining the major witnesses.

In 1984, after months of investigation, rumors circulated that an indictment was imminent. A meeting was arranged with all the lawyers involved in the case in the Parkman House. A beautiful and stately mansion on Beacon Hill, the house was owned by the Parkman Trust and leased by the city for the mayor's use on special occasions. The participants were all former prosecutors or big-firm lawyers, most of whom specialized in white-collar work or defending political figures. They appeared supportive of Harvey, happy that he, not they, was catching the press's heat for criticizing the investigation.

But when an indictment was likely, their tone changed. *Boston Globe* columnist David Farrell, in a piece headlined "U.S. Attorney Tough, Tenacious," predicted that when Anzalone was indicted, when the defense no longer needed Harvey's "mouth," Anzalone would get "a top trial lawyer." The piece even went so far as to list names. But I was left out; once again, I was anonymous, like the potted plant of the Saxe days.

I had just come from a well-publicized victory in a robbery case. The defendant, John McGrath, who was missing an eye, had been positively identified by the robbery's victim, a Brink's guard. The *Globe* ran a picture of the guard on a hospital gurney, pointing to McGrath with the caption: "He's the one!" The case seemed hopeless. The government believed that the robber had made his getaway in a brown-and-white station wagon, which supposedly sped from the scene. McGrath had been found a few blocks away, near such a station wagon. But Byrna, in an extraordinary piece of investigative work, had found that there were two cars that matched the description of the alleged getaway car: One was driven by an innocent bystander, who happened to get caught in the crossfire after the robbery and found a bullet lodged in the trunk of his car. The other car was found near where my client had been arrested. McGrath was acquitted.

In spite of this victory and others, my name was not among those listed by the *Globe*. Indeed, some of the defense lawyers were planning to convince Ted Anzalone that he should shift to one of the more "traditional" trial lawyers.

In this group, Harvey and I were both outsiders. But Ted would not hear of abandoning us. With an indictment in hand, Harvey and I switched seats. Still, on the first day of the trial, the television news failed to notice.

The news broadcasts projected the text of my opening statement along with Harvey's face, as if he were the lawyer delivering it. "That was *me*, stupid," I yelled at the screen; it wasn't Harvey in drag. And there was Harvey, talking to the press about "our" strategy. I couldn't participate because I was preparing the next witness's examination. I was furious.

Even after a dozen years in the public eye, my own distinctive practice, and a succession of victories, the default position was clear: "they" assumed that Harvey was pulling the strings.

I vented everything to John. And maybe because he was there to listen and share, I didn't have to confront Harvey.

———•———

The government threw its best lawyers into this trial: U.S. Attorney Bill Weld assigned Mark Wolf, his second-in-command, a brilliant lawyer and dogged advocate. Also on the opposition team were Daniel Small and Bob Cordy, both experienced and talented trial lawyers.

We also spared no expense, but unlike the government attorneys, most of the resources came out of our pockets. There was Judy Mizner, now a partner in our firm, a relentless lawyer with an encyclopedic knowledge of the law and the ability to work twenty-four-hour days; Kathleen Sullivan, a Harvard Law graduate mentored by the brilliant legal strategist Professor Larry Tribe; Tom Viles, then a paralegal, planning ultimately to go to law school; Emmet Sheehan, our latest investigator, sometime babysitter for Harvey's son, folksinger, cook, and gumshoe.

There were countless dinners at Moon Villa in the wee hours of the morning. John understood.

———

The extortion charge was the hardest. It was the essence of political corruption, selling one's office to the highest bidder. The government claimed that in June 1979, Anzalone had conspired with George Collatos to extort $10,000—a campaign contribution, so-called—from the C. E. Maguire company through its president, John Slocum. According to the government's charges, Anzalone, acting through Collatos, threatened Slocum that his company would lose out on city contracts if he did not pay up. Collatos was a public official employed by the Boston Redevelopment Authority (BRA). C. E. Maguire provided engineering services to the government, and, significantly, had contracts with the BRA that were negotiated rather than competitively bid. They could be cancelled at any time without cause.

The second and third charges were technical. The government claimed that during the following year, in November and December of 1980, Anzalone converted $100,000 in cash into bank cashier's checks at the Haymarket Bank and Trust Company in such a way as to avoid creating a transaction that the bank had to report to the Internal Revenue Service (IRS). (The offense was called "structuring.") Rather than depositing the cash in one installment, which would have required the bank to file a government report because it was over $10,000, Anzalone broke the transactions up into smaller ones, each under $10,000, none of which had to be reported. But while Anzalone deposited the under-$10,000 checks into a stock brokerage account at Bear Stearns and Company in the names of White's mother and wife, the scheme had nothing to do with family investments, or so the government maintained. It had only one purpose: to hide money from the government illegally.

The third charge involved events in February 1981 surrounding a planned gala birthday party for White's wife, Katherine, scheduled for March 27. The government alleged that Anzalone took the cash that he received for the party, which was over $100,000, and thus reportable, and distributed the money in cash to associates, in amounts under $10,000, asking each of them to write checks for equal amounts. The checks would then be deposited into the "Katherine White Birthday Party account." After a great deal of adverse publicity—White soliciting funds from supporters, or worse, city employees, to throw a great bash for his wife—the party was cancelled. Anzalone then issued checks to contributors in the original amounts and took back the cash. Again, the government alleged that this was not at all about contributions to Katherine White's party and their return. Like the first charge, they claimed that this was a cover for illegal contributions.

———•———

Social psychologists speak of a halo effect: you know one bad thing about a person and its halo shifts to other things about which you may know very little. So prosecutors link weak charges to stronger ones. If evidence shows that the defendant clearly did this one bad thing, they hope that the jury will believe that he must have done the other one without their actually having to prove it. But our system rejects that reasoning. Every charge has to be proved independently, judged by the same rigorous standards.

To hear the government tell the story, the three charges were linked by three themes—"money, cash, and White." But consistency in "themes" was not enough. The proof had to show that this was part of the same scheme and the same plot, not three discrete events.

We filed a motion to sever the counts. Kathleen wrote the briefs and I did the oral argument. The three events did not involve the same sources of money. Kevin White's elderly mother reported that the Bear Stearns money was part of her savings, which Anzalone was to invest for her. The Katherine White birthday party money had come from supporters whose names the government knew by now, and Slocum, the contractor in the extortion charge, was not one of them. Finally, the timing was off; the birthday party, for instance, was more than two years after the alleged Slocum affair.

The judge, A. David Mazzone, agreed. There would be two trials, one involving the currency charges and the other for extortion.

———

The government chose to try the currency cases first; they thought they were the easiest. If Anzalone were convicted, it would be more difficult for him to testify in the extortion case because the early convictions could be introduced against him to challenge his credibility.

The Haymarket Bank charges and the birthday party involved a new law, a law requiring banks to report transactions involving currency—chiefly cash—to the government if they were valued at $10,000 or more. Nothing in the statute or the regulations suggested that an individual citizen had any obligation at all. We tried to show that Anzalone, like most ordinary citizens, had absolutely no idea that it was illegal for him to break up transactions over $10,000 into smaller ones, and in fact, had been advised precisely the opposite. There were no signs, no brochures, and no information about this on display at the bank. Ignorance of the law is not a usual defense, but here it was essential. The new law made what had previously been perfectly lawful suddenly illegal. The government had to prove that Anzalone intended to violate a *known* legal duty. The judge, however, declined to instruct the jury along these lines. Conviction on the Haymarket count seemed certain.

The birthday party charge was easier. The scheme was bizarre. Anzalone, they said, took the cash contributions that he had received for the party and gave it to some of his friends, in exchange for checks for the same amount that he then deposited. And after the party had been cancelled, Anzalone did just the reverse. He issued checks to the contributors in the same amounts.

Bizarre, to be sure, but hardly a secret plot to avoid the government knowing about the amounts involved. I told the jury: You don't rent the fanciest location in town—the Museum of Fine Arts—invite thousands of your nearest and dearest friends, and announce the party to the papers, all with the view of hiding the proceeds from the government.

What was the explanation? Candidly, we did not know. Maybe this was an effort to hide the names of contributors so that the *Globe* would not dog them. Maybe there were technical violations of the state campaign finance laws. But hiding money from the IRS via "the most publicized birthday party in the Western world"? Hardly.

On June 25, 1984, Anzalone was acquitted of the birthday party charges but, predictably, convicted of the other charges. We appealed.

John and I spent July with Sarah in Wellfleet, Massachusetts. I had never needed a formal summer vacation before. I would fly off during the year, when this or that trial ended. But now I wanted—no, needed—time with him, and especially with her. Installed in our rented beach house, we baked in the sun, biked, and cooked. I tried to slow down, but nevertheless I brought the boxes and the litigation bags with me.

At the end of July, my sister and I flew to Florida to close on a condominium for my father. After my mother's death and his own health problems, my father seemed unable to socialize with old friends or meet new ones. He was sinking more and more deeply into a depression, and we hoped that a new locale, one he had never shared with Sadie, would make a difference. In the whirl-wind of shopping and buying, my sister, a genius at such things, decorated the place so it would be ready for him the next winter. He had never had a home that modern, or that fancy.

Suddenly, money mattered to me. It allowed me to buy him the condominium and the furniture, to do what I could to lift his burdens. I could not wait for winter to come to see his face when he opened the door.

———

The extortion trial was set to start in September 1984, just two months after the previous trial ended. Jury selection—once again—was a special problem. How do we select a jury who had not followed the earlier cases, much less the prejudicial publicity that had preceded it? By now the formula was clear: the NJP, as much information as we could garner, as intense an inquiry as the judge would allow.

The BRA's George Collatos was the key. John Slocum, the contractor, agreed that there had never been anything more than pleasantries—hello, how are you, and so on—when he met with Anzalone and White and made his campaign contribution. The only question was what had been promised or threatened before those conversations. Collatos claimed that he had talked to Slocum, out of the presence of Anzalone and White. He had been the supposed "messenger." On his credibility rested the government's case.

By now, I had the craft—the art—of cross-examination down. And I had considerable ammunition. In February 1982, Collatos pleaded guilty to a scheme that looked a great deal like the Slocum scheme, shaking down a different contractor, claiming that he had "friends in high places" and could "fix" things with city officials. In fact, he had little or no influence over their dealings with the city. In fact, he had never even talked to anyone in the White adminis-tration about it. On the stand, he admitted that he was lying to the contractor about his supposed influence.

For that earlier extortion, Collatos was sentenced to serve

three years at the federal prison in Danbury, Connecticut. Within five months, he was compelled to testify before the grand jury investigating the White administration and given immunity from prosecution for his role in any offense that he disclosed. He testified, but the government believed that he was lying, so one month later, he was indicted for perjury.

Again, he pled guilty, his second offense in less than a year. At his sentencing, Cordy asked for a substantial sentence for the charge, six years, and made his intentions clear: "It is vital that Collatos receive a sufficiently severe sentence to dissuade him from continuing to commit perjury, notwithstanding whatever motivated him to lie previously." Cordy believed that he knew the truth. Collatos had to be lying. He was sentenced to two more years, but the judge left open the possibility of reducing the sentence if Collatos cooperated with the government.

In an extraordinary interview with the now-defunct *Boston Observer*, prior to the Anzalone trial, Collatos wrote:

> I saw the handwriting on the wall; they were going to keep squeezing me until I talked. Assistant U.S. Attorney Mark Wolf wrote the parole commission that I should be denied parole because I was suppressing evidence. . . . The mayor had abandoned me; I had no money left for lawyers; my family needed me. . . . So I decided to take [the judge] up on his order.

On March 3, 1983, Collatos drafted his own motion to have his sentence reduced to two years probation and offered his cooperation in exchange for immunity. Two assistants, he claimed, drove through a snowstorm the next day to meet with him. Within a week he was granted immunity, and by June 1983, the government supported a sentence reduction. He was ready to testify against Anzalone.

All this came out in a standard cross-examination; nothing should have surprised them. But we had more information than they knew we had.

Prior to Anzalone's first trial, he told us that Collatos had threatened to lie unless Anzalone got the mayor to pay him $200,000.

The mayor could cover up the transaction, Collatos suggested, by paying that amount for one of Collatos's thoroughbred horses. If he did not, Collatos would "burn" Anzalone and the mayor.

Here was the dilemma: Anzalone, himself a defendant, now had information about a crime. But if he went to the government, would they believe him? And more significant, would they pursue it—wiring Anzalone and taping Collatos's conversations, as only they had the legal authority to do? Would they, in short, take steps that could undermine their three-year campaign to get White?

A Silverglate brainstorm; since it is unlawful for private citizens to tape a Collatos-Anzalone meeting, then we will have an unimpeachable witness overhear it and get a stenographer to transcribe it. Our chief unimpeachable witness was John Wall, a former Justice Department prosecutor (he had prosecuted Dr. Benjamin Spock in the early 1970s for conspiring to violate the Selective Service laws by counseling antiwar draft dodgers) now in private practice. He would be accompanied by Tom Viles, our paralegal, and a court stenographer.

We chose La Bella's, the site of the initial Collatos-Anzalone encounter, for the meeting place. Wall described it as being like something out of a Dickens novel, with an ancient coffee urn, old books, and papers. Others were less charitable. Harvey said that "[y]ou wanted to wash [not only] your hands after you left but also your feet." Someone else said that it looked like a place out of Building #19, a local warehouse chain that sold random and impossibly cheap goods.

The trio went into the cellar of the shop through a trapdoor. The stenographer, whose boss had neglected to tell her the true nature of the assignment, came dressed in her best business suit and high heels. She took one look at the scene, banged her head on the low-hanging beams of the basement, and fled.

At 8:00 p.m., Collatos arrived. Listening for about an hour and ten minutes through the trapdoor, which was being held ajar by a stepladder, Viles and Wall took notes. They confirmed Anzalone's account of the earlier conversation—money from the mayor or else Collatos would lie.

———

Out of the blue, in the middle of Collatos's cross examination, I asked him about the encounter with Ted at La Bella's, making it clear I was reading from a memo and quoting his words chapter and verse. He denied it.

———

The next day, we told the prosecutor that we would call Tom Viles and John Wall as defense witnesses to testify to what they had overheard Collatos say in La Bella's. The government, as is their prerogative, sought to interview them. They found Wall in his office. He told them what he heard, and they left politely. They found Viles at his girlfriend's house in Cambridge. When he refused to talk to them, the federal agent informed him that his testimony could involve five federal crimes: perjury, extortion, bribery, obstruction of justice, and then added misprision of a felony. He asked, what is misprision of a felony? They replied, it's having knowledge about a federal crime and failing to report it. Frightened, Viles pled the Fifth and did not testify. Wall, on the other hand, was not intimidated: he testified to what he heard Collatos say.

———

The jury was out only a few days. The courtroom was packed, with Dad and John in the front row. The verdict? Not guilty.

That Saturday, the doorbell rang in our Cambridge home. It was a messenger with a dozen roses and a card:

> By all accounts of your colleagues in the profession and observers of the trial, your performance was outstanding.
> Congratulations.
>
> With gratitude,
> Kevin H. White

———

In the spring of 1985, the First Circuit Court of Appeals overturned Anzalone's only conviction, comparing his prosecution with prosecutions under the Soviet constitution. The Soviet constitution allows the state to criminalize behavior that is not described as illegal in the criminal code. Not so in this country, where criminal statutes must be clear from the outset. The statute and regulations under which Anzalone was convicted were not, and while "this court . . . is supportive of the law-enforcement goals of the government . . . we cannot engage in unprincipled interpretation of the law, lest we foment lawlessness instead of compliance."

———

It was over, but once again, what about "the truth"? Had we, true to the lawyer's role, ethically and ingeniously managed to squelch the "truth" about the White administration, the truth that years of a grand jury investigation had attempted to uncover? After Anzalone's acquittal, it was not at all clear how much "the truth" mattered to the prosecutors. Anzalone, who had no Fifth Amendment privilege against self-incrimination because he had been acquitted, was never asked to testify before a grand jury. He could easily have been compelled to tell everything he knew. But the government did not believe his "version"; I did not believe theirs.

The government did prosecute Collatos for perjury for the second time. He was convicted and imprisoned again.

Bill Weld left the U.S. Attorney's office and was elected governor of the Commonwealth of Massachusetts, then resoundingly reelected. Mark Wolf became an extraordinarily distinguished judge of the U.S. District Court, now a colleague and dear friend of mine. Bob Cordy is a well-respected justice on the Massachusetts Supreme Judicial Court, and Dan Small is a successful private practitioner.

Kevin White retired quietly, never to run for office again. Ted gave up his law practice because each and every one of his clients had been subpoenaed before a grand jury. He became a maintenance man, keeping up apartments jointly owned with his wife.

Tom Viles finished law school. Kathleen Sullivan went on to

be a renowned constitutional scholar, then dean of Stanford Law School, and then a named partner in a high-profile New York law firm. She is frequently mentioned as a possible nominee for the Supreme Court.

But Harvey and I never tried another case together. It was as if I had to leave home again—not Flushing, Queens, and Dad—but my first professional home. It was beyond cutting hair, trial strategy, the "more conventional home life." I had changed and would be changing still more.

———

I learned of the Court of Appeals decision about Anzalone over the car radio on my way to a doctor's appointment. I was thrilled, but a bit distracted. At thirty-nine, I was pregnant with Stephen Gertner Reinstein.

CHAPTER NINE

Work and Babies

I recognized this man immediately as he approached my bed. I hadn't had any sleep. Three days of labor, up all night, and I was an "older mother" to boot. Menopause and birth were running neck and neck.

But no matter how groggy I was, this was not the face I wanted to see.

I had approved seven of the eight obstetricians who might be on call when I was ready to deliver, but not him. I was explicit. I had cross-examined this man in a medical malpractice case. He was the defendant's expert; I was representing the plaintiff. I had challenged his medical qualifications.

But there had been a last-minute change, and now he, of all people, was about to cut me open. Actually, he was resisting it almost as much as I. Because he assumed that I was a mega-feminist wanting the most natural birth imaginable, he was determined to avoid a caesarean section at all costs. But after almost sixty hours of labor trying to deliver a baby that seemed not to want to leave my body, I was prepared for anything. I had to persuade him that I would not complain—or worse, sue—if he simply operated. "Operate! Operate! Enough, already. I promise I won't call the National Organization for Women!"

———•———

Funny, I loved being pregnant. Eating without guilt was unbeatable. And ironically, I loved trying cases with a big belly. After all the years of squeezing myself into what seemed to be a male role, literally and figuratively, there was something wonderful about being openly, irresistibly female.

During my first trimester, I represented a man who, along with his partner, was accused of insurance fraud. The claim was that the two of them had taken out an insurance policy on a third partner shortly before he was gunned down. The state could not make a murder charge stick but had convicted them of insurance fraud in an earlier trial, when the defendants were represented by another lawyer. Harvey handled the appeal and reversed the convictions. I would do the retrial representing one defendant; James St. Clair (who had represented President Nixon during the Watergate scandal) represented the other. Although I was only a few months pregnant and hardly "showed," I sported huge dresses. I worked out hand signals with the judge to let me sprint to the bathroom when I had to.

And later, when my pregnancy was more noticeable, I particularly loved to rub my belly and moan softly. It seemed only fair. Clarence Darrow was fabled to put a wire in his cigar (when you were allowed to smoke in court), so that the ash would linger and linger without falling off. The jury, they say, was transfixed. For all the years that men took advantage of their sexual stereotypes— the booming voices, the insider advantages, the presumption of competence—now I would take advantage of mine.

But I didn't do it for long. The fall before Stephen was born, I decided to take a year "off," as I described it, by teaching at Harvard Law School. (I suppose you have to be somewhat driven to characterize teaching at Harvard as time off.) Five months pregnant, I was lecturing 180 students about the rules of evidence, trying not to answer client calls or press inquiries. Trying to be an academic.

Stephen was due after the course ended. I had, I thought, timed it perfectly. Two weeks after my last class, at the beginning of the holiday break, he was born—and I was entranced.

True to form, I gave him Miranda warnings: "There are good

and bad things about having me as a mommy. The good thing is that I have waited a long time for you and will love you more than life. The bad thing is I work, and I love it too." He gurgled.

I recall once, long before marriage and children, in a study group I was a part of, arguing vehemently against any special relationship between mothers and children. It was all mythologizing, I thought, hype to socially construct motherhood and keep women tied to the home.

Then Stephen was born. John took a paternity leave. He had been at my side at the birth and would stick by me for two weeks. One morning, when I was still in bed, with Stephen nursing at my side, John announced that he would go into the office for a bit. It occurred to me that I could not. Whatever its source—nature, socially constructed roles—I was entangled and in love with this child. I could not venture far from him.

Still, I was surprised when everyone asked: Would I return to work now that I had a child? Return to work? This lawyer identity had been mine for over thirteen years. It was the mom part that was new.

I went back to teaching at Harvard in a month, and by the fall, I returned to practice. Within six months, I was pregnant again, now with Peter. (Needless to say, at my age, we had to work fast.)

A client charged with Medicaid fraud came in to see me when I was seven months into this second pregnancy. He had just been indicted; although I hardly looked the part of a lawyer and my son's birth was imminent, he wanted me to represent him and was determined to wait. The judge, Rya Zobel, the only woman on the federal bench at the time, agreed to put off all deadlines until after Peter was born. Meanwhile, with my client's help, I equipped my home with a fax machine, a computer, a copier, and every manner and means of technology then available. Less than two weeks later, my client drove Peter and me to his home to meet with him while his daughters babysat.

It was as if I had finally reaped the benefits of the movement that I had worked on for so long. Here were all the roles I had fought for—wife, mother, lawyer. But I had no illusions. Part of this was pure luck. After waiting so long, with an alarm on my biological clock about to go off, I was still able to have two wonderful, healthy children. Part of it was timing and circumstances. We managed to combine work and family because we had the income from two careers to support child-care help, a loving, live-in nanny.

And I could "do it all" without harm to my profession because I had carved out my own space. I had my own firm, an established reputation. I did not have to rely on the beneficence of others to give me permission to do what I wanted to do. Not so for other women: Susan Estrich relates a story from Paramount chief Sherry Lansing. Lansing told a reporter: "You can have two out of three. Take your choice: husband, kids, top job. If you pick kids, your chances of the top job go way down."

It was not always easy. At the twentieth reunion of the Barnard class of 1971, each woman was asked to stand up, introduce herself, and tell the group what she did. It was a standard icebreaker, but in this setting, for these women, it was laden with hidden meaning. One woman said, I have four children, and I supported my husband when his assignments required that we move from state to state, but I never finished my PhD. Another said, I have a PhD in biophysics, and I am a distinguished professor at x or y university, but I have never married or had children. And others, who had combined careers and family, lamented the cost to one or the other—I didn't spend enough time with my kids; or I didn't advance as far as I should have in my profession. I was last, and true to form, had to joke: "Well I have five PhDs, the last in astrophysics, ten children, and bake bread in my spare time." I could not imagine a group of male alumni reciting the same concerns. We were what Elizabeth Fishel called the "choice-rich" generation, the "opportunity-laden," "sky's the limit" generation. And this "choice-rich" generation, she notes, was at midlife, "calculating the distance between the choices she'd made and the ones she'd left untouched." No matter how it looked on the outside, on the inside, like the rest of my class, I worried if I was doing anything well anymore.

The world of work, like the world of home, looked different. It was predictable chaos. Once, in the middle of a cross-examination, I noticed rice cereal epaulets on my shoulders, clearly remnants from Stephen's last-minute snuggle. Or, running my hands absent-mindedly through my hair, I found clotted milk, the remains of Peter's sweet good-bye grope, tangled in my not-so-perfect coiffure. And I had the sniffles nonstop; a snotty face coming at you at 3:00 a.m. was always irresistible. (In fact, I was a petri dish for all their ailments. I was such a good mother that I tested their germs to understand what they were undergoing.) Sleep was out of the question. John couldn't function on four hours sleep, but, happily, I didn't need much. Trial adrenaline always came through.

Then, within only a few years of marriage, the family grew still more. Sarah moved into our new house in Brookline. She wanted to go to Brookline High School and be close to her baby brothers. When Rachel, John's mother, retired from her town's board of selectmen, she moved into the carriage house next door.

I felt like the guy in the old Alka Seltzer commercial: "I can't believe I ate the whole thing."

———•———

Dad was thrilled but, I think, skeptical that I could pull all this off, that John would "take" having a wife who worked, that the kids would turn out healthy and happy. And I don't know whether my mother would have understood either. She had known me only in my "doggedly" single stage. When she died, we were a mystery to each other.

I loved her with all my heart and soul, but I did not want to be her, so I thought. She was always at the beck and call of my father —and me. I had never even babysat as a teenager. Or cooked. Or cleaned. While my father extolled the traditional woman's role yet debated with me about politics every night, my mother made her point in a different way. If I offered to cook or clean up, she'd refuse. Go, she'd say, go study, do your work. It did not seem that she wanted me to be her, either.

Once, during a law school vacation, she insisted that I go to the apartment next door to visit a neighbor with a newborn grandchild. "Come, Nance," she said, taking me by the hand, and then grabbing a reprint of an article that I had written for the *Yale Law*

Journal. We rang the bell. Millie, the neighbor, came to the door saying: "Sadie, here's my grandchild!" My mother answered, "She's adorable! And here's Nancy's article!"

We spoke the week before she died in 1977. I was in a hot phone booth on Martha's Vineyard, just checking in as I was wont to do. The connection was terrible. "Nance," she said, "I think I finally understand you. I have been reading *A Different Woman*, by Jane Howard. Now, I understand everything." So I bought the book. I am not certain what she had read or what she focused on, but I found this. Howard, in describing being single and crafting a family of sorts, says:

> New links must be forged as old ones rust. Only children should be brought up close to other only children, so they will not someday have to reminisce alone. We who are unmarried, only children of another sort, must depend and cultivate our friendships until water acquires the consistency of blood, until we developed new networks as sustaining as orthodox families.

That was then; this was now. Now I had that family—Sarah, Stephen, Peter, Rachel, one dog, then two, a cat, a bird, two fish (named "Bush" and "Quayle" by Stephen). And in the twilight of the day, rattling around our house in Brookline, Massachusetts, making brisket of beef or cookies from the recipes that I had salvaged after Sadie's death, reciting her words to my babies, I *was* my mother, plain and simple. I could not be home in the afternoon as she had been to cheer every grade, console every disappointment. She never taught me to cook or babysit, but she taught me how to love. And loving these children with abandon was her greatest legacy.

CHAPTER TEN

A "Real" Feminist

Peter, my fourteen-month-old, was up all night before the closing. The trial of a woman accused of murdering her husband, who had beaten her, was two hours away in Springfield, Massachusetts. I spent every other night there, to minimize the time away from the boys. With absolutely no sleep, except a few minutes in the car, I was going on pure adrenaline.

I pace back and forth in the silent courtroom telling Lisa Grimshaw's story, a story so very far from my own:

She was the youngest of three sisters. The older two had been raised in comfort, but by the time Lisa was ten, her father was unemployed. Often drunk, he would fly into unpredictable rages. At first, the target was his wife, but soon it was Lisa. Alone with her father after school, the abuse turned sexual.

Remember the sound of her voice as she had described the pink bedspread on which he violated her. She seemed like a child, re-experiencing the pain.

At fourteen, she fled to Darryl Fredette. He was twenty-one, a batterer too, her face his favorite target. "I was the one who knocked out her front teeth!" he had crowed at trial. A son is born, Darryl Brandon Fredette, a boy so badly retarded that, within months, he was placed in foster care.

Then from Darryl to Tom Grimshaw. After moving to Miami,

129

Tom could not find work, and like Lisa's father, he began drinking and beating her, drinking and beating. She fled; he followed.

They reconciled. But when he found out that she was pregnant, he threatened to cut the baby out. Still, they stayed together. She loved him, she said.

Chad was born, this time, a normal son. They married and soon, much too soon, there were 911 calls, restraining orders, and finally, divorce. Now Tom's visits to Chad were an occasion to torture her. Remember her testimony? One incident more degrading than the next—forcing her to have sex by threatening her with scalding water, handcuffing her while she slept, raping her when she awoke. Wherever she moved, he stalked her, found her, beat her.

Five months before Tom's death, November 21, 1984, in the middle of the night, Lisa awoke to the sound of breaking glass. She had changed the locks to this new apartment, even nailed the windows shut, but Tom smashed them open. In the fight that followed, he knocked her front teeth out with a hammer—the second time her teeth were bashed at the hands of an abusive lover.

——•——

I pause. I bring a chair directly in front of the jury. I sit down, lean over as far as I can, and wrap my arms around my legs. This was as close to a fetal position as I could get, dressed as I was in court clothes and heels. For my closing, I will relive Lisa's story of the hours before Tom's death. I will transform myself into her.

June 3, 1985. Tom picked up Chad. They fought; she bargained: "You can have him now, but don't give me shit when I come to get him." When she returned, there was a struggle. Chad, only four, ran into the middle of the street. An oncoming car missed him by inches. Tom grabbed Lisa's keys and struck her with them. She scrambled away, grabbing spare keys and her young son.

Back in her apartment, safe for the time being, she drank and drank, sitting in a chair, staring at the apartment door.

And, as I recite these facts, I slowly rock back and forth, staring into space.

Every sound frightened her; Tom would surely break in at any minute. Then, taking on her voice, I say: *And this time, he will kill me or Chad. This time he will really do it.*

I shiver.

Two men, acquaintances really, came to the door after a night's drinking. Lisa had met Michael Bruyette at her job at Bo's Lounge in Chicopee. She was just twenty-three; he, nineteen. Michael Ashey, sixteen, hung out with Bruyette. Lisa complained about her husband's abuse. Bruyette, wooing her with his machismo, once threatened Tom on the phone. Lisa told Bruyette and Ashey what happened that night. Bruyette announced: "OK, that's it, let's go." In her alcoholic haze, she said, "OK."

Bruyette called the shots: Ashey's older brother, Ronald, would babysit for Chad. "You pick up Tom at work," Bruyette said. "We'll do the rest."

She met Tom as he was leaving the night shift. "I'm horny," she told him. They drove to a remote area. When they stopped, she said, "You walk on. I have to pee." Instead, she returned to her car, hands frozen to the wheel. The idea was to beat Tom, not kill him, but Bruyette and Ashey got carried away.

A very young woman, lurching from moment to moment, driven by her fear, her past, the abuse, the torture, believes that she has no choice but to fight back.

My voice breaks. I stop speaking, but rock slowly—my eyes closed.

Francis Bloom, an assistant DA in Springfield, Hamden County, stands up. He shouts. He paces. He is furious, his words dripping with contempt, as he counters:

Lisa was conniving and manipulative. A cold-blooded murderer. She had taken a nineteen-year-old and a sixteen-year-old, Bruyette and Ashey, "plied" them with sex in one case, alcohol in another, and promised them the proceeds of Tom's life insurance policy. She "lured" her husband to the boat ramp, in the middle of the night, where these two hired assassins were waiting behind a tree, knowing that they were going to splatter his brains all over the rocks.

Then he turns to the details: the officers who had found the body in the early morning hours, its battered condition, the contents of Tom Grimshaw's wallet tossed contemptuously in the dumpster en route from the Chicopee boat ramp, the brother's heartrending testimony when he described the last time he saw Tom. From what he could see of Tom and Lisa's marriage—and he saw them all the time—it was entirely normal.

Bloom recounts the testimony of Michael and Ronald Ashey in a rapid-fire narrative: Ronald, the older brother, who babysat for Chad while Lisa and Bruyette killed Chad's father, was charged as an accessory before the fact of first-degree murder. Michael, who had accompanied the others to the boat ramp, was charged as a co-conspirator.

Lisa promised them money from an insurance policy on her husband's life in return for the murder. Sure, she talked about her husband's brutality, not because it was true—but because she was manipulating them. Just as she was manipulating you.

Bloom pauses to glare at the jury.

When she told Bruyette and Ashey about the November 1984 hammer incident, she had added, "I want him dead." Bruyette was her special focus. She was sleeping with him, leading him on. Killing her husband was the return on her investment in these boys.

This was no spur-of-the-moment, no instant crime of passion. It was planned, and Lisa was the ringleader. Bruyette and Michael had picked up bats from Tom Grimshaw's house some time before the killing. She told them where to go. When she arrived at the boat ramp, she signaled them. Hardly sleepwalking, frozen, or dazed. And afterwards, when they left Tom moaning, grievously injured, she conspired about disposing of the body ("throw it in the river") and covering up the crime ("wash the car").

It was cold-blooded, first-degree murder, murder for hire, nothing more, nothing less.

———

From afar, this was an easy case for me—easier than the political corruption trials that I had recently finished, easier than the run-of-the-mill murder case. This was, after all, Gertner the feminist, representing a battered woman. True, Lisa set in motion the night's events, but should the law hold her responsible? Wasn't the killing committed in self-defense because of her state of mind, the psychological condition known as "battered woman syndrome," and therefore legally excused?

But it was not easy on many fronts—professional, political, and now personal. Should battered woman syndrome/self-defense excuse such an act entirely, with a not-guilty verdict, or should it mitigate the outcome with a finding of manslaughter, a lower sentence? What about other so-called syndromes that lead to killings—road rage, homosexual fear, "Twinkie" defenses? Or the "white fear" that a small white man, Bernard Goetz, claimed justified his shooting of four black teenagers on a New York subway? What about the "black rage" of any African American treated with contempt by our culture? If we exonerate one, do we exonerate them all?

I could not forget that a man, a father, had been killed. At this stage in my career, I could not pretend that the legal discourse framed all the complicated issues in this human drama.

But had I finally learned to just say whatever it took in court, what I didn't believe in, craft so totally trumping principle? No. But, sixteen years into the practice of law, I understood advocacy and its boundaries, complex reality and simple trial narratives. Trials, unlike one-sided grand jury investigations, are competing narratives, as Janet Malcolm once noted in *The Crime of Sheila McGough*—my version versus their version. Life, though, is chaotic; when you shoehorn it into neat stories, it is no longer, strictly speaking, the truth. Advocacy colors both sides. Lawyers are, after all, storytellers—even caricaturists—not reporters. And when the issues are complex, as in Lisa's case, the distance between a trial's stories and life's stories widens.

Still, there were limits to how far I was willing to go to separate legal argument and life—especially now that my time was more limited, my life more complex. These were not just the traditional ethical limits on lawyers. I had to believe in the cause, the person, the issues, or some combination. The label "a feminist case" was not enough. Why, then, this person and this case?

Many battered women plead guilty to manslaughter, however legitimate their defenses may be. Bargaining for a more-lenient sentence in exchange for avoiding a trial, their lawyers tell the judge a third narrative, the negotiated story, which is no more the complex "truth" than the trial narratives.

Once, representing a woman who killed her husband, I begged the prosecutor to let her tell her story to the grand jury. It was an unusual move; only the prosecutor appears before a grand jury, and because the proceeding is one-sided, few prosecutors fail to get an indictment if they want it. In this case, it was the Suffolk County District Attorney's Office, the same office that I had pilloried in the press after the Saxe case. A few days after my client testified, the DA's assistant notified me that the grand jury had "refused" to indict and added, "I assume that you will give the office some good ink." "Of course," I said, and I called the *Boston Globe*, giving them well-deserved credit for what they had done.

But "good ink" was not possible for Lisa. Her case had become a holy war.

Shortly after Tom's body was found, she was interviewed by the police. At first, she lied, but within perhaps twenty minutes, she confessed. No bargain, no lawyer. No one asked her about her life with Tom, just: "What happened June 5, 1985?" Michael Ashey, picked up shortly afterwards, confirmed her story. They both pinned the brutality on Bruyette, who had a considerable criminal record.

And Lisa went further, actively cooperating with the government from the outset. She testified at Ashey's transfer hearing, the session held to determine whether he should be charged as a juvenile or an adult. But the government ultimately didn't need her help to prosecute him. Because Ashey had turned eighteen between the time of his guilty plea in juvenile court and the time of his sentencing, the government lacked the authority to hold him. There would be no Ashey trial, no matter what his role had been in Tom's murder.

Then Lisa testified before the grand jury that indicted Bruyette. But because Bruyette pled guilty to second-degree murder, a life sentence but with the possibility of parole at fifteen years, there would be no trial for him either. Only Lisa's case continued—and with a vengeance.

Lisa's lawyer at the time advised her to wait. Rather than immediately negotiating for a manslaughter plea, which her cooperation might have warranted, he told her, for some reason: "Don't rock the boat." It was as if he expected that the passage of time would somehow make the plea negotiations for her easier. Not so. For nearly three years, she was locked up in an overcrowded pretrial detention facility. She could not see her young son because her sister, who had temporary custody, refused to allow it. It was while she was there, in pain and alone, that she decided to take charge of her own defense. Lisa learned about battered woman syndrome from a counselor at the detention facility. On her own, she sought state funds to retain Dr. Lenore Walker, a very-high-profile psychologist credited with originating the concept of battered woman syndrome. Walker confirmed the diagnosis.

In short order, Lisa's case became a cause célèbre for feminists concerned about domestic violence. The direct services coordinator at a local women's shelter in Springfield, Gail Kielson, mortgaged her home to post $35,000 for Lisa's bail. The Women's Bail Fund Project put up another $15,000. Amidst a hail of publicity, Lisa was released.

If a manslaughter deal had been available before, it was gone now. The only offer was second-degree murder, the same as Bruyette. She refused. Being docile had not worked, and now she was determined to fight.

———

In February 1986, a year and a half after the crime, and before she managed to make bail, Lisa had called me from the pretrial detention facility in Framingham, Massachusetts: Would I represent her? No, I said. I had just given birth to Stephen and was teaching full-time at Harvard Law School.

A few months later, Lisa wrote again, and a month after that, her mother did. Stephen was now six months old, we had a full-time nanny, but the last thing I wanted was a difficult murder trial, ninety miles west of Boston.

Lisa persisted, calling me again in the fall of 1987. My step-daughter, Sarah, then thirteen, was living with us, and Peter was due in December.

"No," I said, again. I planned to return to work after a short maternity leave, but the idea was to focus on a monthlong Medicaid fraud case. A white-collar case, this was one that for once was interesting, even compelling—and for which I would be paid market rates. The members of my firm—even as newly constituted—had started to fight about money, who was contributing what, who wasn't pulling his or her share. And now that I had three children to support, these issues started to matter.

"Not a problem," Lisa said. The trial would wait for me.

I caved in. I agreed to seek appointment as her lawyer. It wasn't the challenge of the case, although there was plenty of that. Battered woman syndrome had never before been admitted as a valid defense in Massachusetts, and this could well be the most difficult case of all to try to win on it: a killing that took place hours after the last encounter with the batterer. And it wasn't that I still needed to "show 'them' I could do it all." Surely, I had proved enough to the ubiquitous "they" for one lifetime. It was very simple: Lisa needed help. I knew I could help her. I had followed the issue of domestic violence for years. I had gathered materials, attended panels, and taught about it.

Reluctantly, I agreed to commute back and forth to Springfield every other day, staying overnight in between to maximize the time with my babies. I wasn't sure if it was the "right" thing to do; Sadie, my mother, surely would not have approved. I knew only that it was what I had to do.

John supported me. When I shared Lisa's problem with him—the usual dinner "meeting," now more chaotic than ever—he understood why I felt that I had to take the case. I know I counted on that.

We had a warm, attentive nanny, Lydia Santiago, on one front, and a talented and committed staff on the other. It included Sharon Beckman, a former paralegal at the firm, who had completed a brilliant law school career culminating in a clerkship for the U.S. Supreme Court; Ann Blessing and Pia Sass, my paralegals and drivers; the NJP (again); and Emmet Sheehan, now my investigator. (Byrna had left as my work evolved away from the "political" cases in which she had been interested to a somewhat more traditional criminal practice. She would use her considerable skills to start her own investigative firm.)

———

Criminal law in the early 1970s and 1980s, while pretending to universality, in practice measured the defendant's culpability by the yardstick of a "reasonable man." The facts that could lower the degree of murder, or even excuse the crime entirely, were described in terms of situations that men might encounter. The standards seemed neutral enough: First-degree murder—a killing with premeditation and malice. Second-degree—a killing with malice alone. Manslaughter—a killing with neither. But somehow the examples of the lesser offenses were invariably male—the barroom brawl that went too far, or the killing provoked by seeing your wife in bed with another man.

Self-defense was even more problematic. The defendant had to have "a reasonable ground to believe and actually did believe that he was in imminent danger of death or serious bodily harm," that he had no means of escape, that he had "availed himself of all proper means to avoid physical combat," before resorting to deadly force, and then, he could use no more force than was "reasonably" necessary. These subjective beliefs, however, had to be measured objectively; the unit of measurement, again, was the reasonable man.

But the law didn't take into account that the reasonable man was sometimes a woman. Socialized not to fight, often smaller than her assailant, a woman perceives a threat as imminent and deadly long before and long after a similarly situated man might. She would conclude that she could not escape, that she had to kill, when a man facing the same threat might well believe that he could subdue his assailant with physical force or intimidation. And when weapons were involved—typically weapons that the woman was not accustomed to—the response might be excessive. The law's admonition to use only that amount of force necessary to subdue your attacker simply resonated differently for women.

There was Zakia Lamrini, a streetwalker charged with stabbing a "john" thirty-six times. He was 6'2"; she was 4'11". They were in his car, in a secluded spot outside the city. He tried to get her to do something that she did not want to do. When she refused, he attacked her. She stabbed him once, then twice, then again and again. Each time, he seemed to come after her, invulnerable. In fact, she had grievously injured him on the first or second blow. First-degree murder, said the jury, a result later reversed. Then Zakia pled to manslaughter and was sentenced to eight years.

Or take the case of Donna Pitcher, a homeless twenty-year-old who had moved in with a middle-aged admirer. One evening, angered by her flirtation with a younger man, he threatened her with a gun. She grabbed it and fired over and over again. Like Zakia, when the first shot did not stop him, when he continued to walk towards her (or, more likely, staggered), she believed he was unstoppable. This time, there was a negotiated guilty plea to manslaughter and a sentence of four to seven years.

Still, compared to Lisa's case, these were straightforward. The jury had only to take a snapshot of the night of the murder—who did what to whom. It did not have to delve into the relationship between the women and their victims, or too deeply into their psyches. The only leap, and it was not much, was to ask the jury to take the perspective of the reasonable woman.

But it was not such an easy leap when the killing followed the threat by an hour or two, or even more, and when the killer and the victim had been embroiled in a violent pas de deux for years. A reasonable woman who had never been beaten might believe that the danger was over when the threatening man walked away or put down his weapon. The reasonable battered woman would not.

Battered woman syndrome has been defined as a subclass of post-traumatic stress disorder (PTSD), a syndrome that began to be widely discussed in the late 1970s for its prevalence among Vietnam veterans. The stress of being attacked had taken its toll on otherwise entirely normal men. When they tried to resume their lives, they saw the Vietcong at every turn, threats around every corner. Likewise, these normal battered women, subject to abnormal stresses—sexual abuse, torture—experienced symptoms more like embattled veterans than wives or lovers.

Of course, these were not justifiable killings. Returning veterans who had faced the trauma of war or battered women had no legal right to kill because of the treatment they had received. That was pure vigilantism. But the syndrome was the key to their state of mind. Various degrees of murder required different states of mind, as did the defenses to murder, including self-defense. The fact that a woman was suffering from this psychological syndrome was critical to mitigate her culpability or even exonerate her.

———

The first challenge was to convince the judge to permit Dr. Lenore Walker to testify. Dr. Walker would describe Lisa's symptoms: she had flashbacks to previous beatings, so real that they threw her into a disassociative state, fully believing that another beating was imminent. The testimony would corroborate Lisa's statement that she had acted in the belief that she had no choice, that her life or that of her child was in immediate jeopardy. And further, I wanted to introduce evidence that Lisa had in fact been abused by Tom, as well as by Fredette, her ex, and her father. She had not lied to Dr. Walker; she had suffered the kind of trauma that triggered battered woman syndrome.

Bloom vehemently opposed. This was not remotely a self-defense case, he insisted. Battered woman syndrome, if it were true at all, was completely irrelevant. Ten hours had passed between the threat and the killing. It had taken planning for her to get Tom to the Chicopee boat ramp that night and to get away undetected. Others had carried out the job at Lisa's direction. And no matter what we said we were doing when we "maligned" the victim— which was corroborating Lisa's state of mind—what we were really telling the jury is that the bastard deserved to die, not because of anything he did at that moment, but what he had been doing to Lisa long before.

As to the evidence of beatings from Lisa's father and from Darryl Fredette, Bloom had a particularly colorful argument for keeping it out of the trial. "It's like if you and I were going out with the same woman, and we beat the hell out of her over and over again while wearing red top hats. She goes out later with a guy who wears a red top hat. Is she justified in using battered woman syndrome as a defense in his killing?" Without saying so, what Bloom was doing was spoofing Bernard Goetz's defense. When Goetz had shot several black teenagers on a subway, he claimed—unsuccessfully—that it was not because of any imminent threat from them, but because of Goetz's "history" of having been threatened by black people, his "state of mind" that he needed to kill or he would be killed.

The truth is, the issues that Bloom was raising were not so far-fetched. I understood that my arguments were breaking new ground, perhaps with troubling implications. But whatever concerns I felt as a sometime legal scholar and teacher, I had different ethical obligations when it came to this client. The woman whom I was charged to defend faced life imprisonment.

I said: Lisa had a right to mount a defense. Her testimony would satisfy all the elements of self-defense—that she feared imminent danger; that she believed, not unreasonably, that she had no choice but to respond with deadly force; that she had, up until that point, availed herself of all means to avoid violence. The jury could reject the defense, but she had to be allowed to raise the issues.

And if she had a right to claim self-defense, then it followed that she had a right to retain an expert to explain that claim. Without Dr. Walker's testimony, Lisa's would be incomprehensible, like watching a 3-D movie without the special glasses.

Moreover, this was not just testimony about any old "red top hat." Lisa was not predicting random violence from a figure she did not know. Nor, like Goetz, were her fears based on nothing more than racial stereotypes. She was reasonably expecting violence from her husband, who, in the past, had acted violently.

Finally, battered woman syndrome was an authentic syndrome, recognized by psychologists. Not so with Goetz's psychological profile or Bloom's "top hat" syndrome.

I thought: Should antisocial behavior be excused, or even mitigated, just because some psychiatrist or psychologist blesses it? Should psychologists or psychiatrists be the gatekeepers, separating true self-defense claims from bogus ones? And psychologists' opinions aside, surely there were certain claims that are beyond the pale, that we do not consider legitimate no matter how many experts weigh in, claims such as a cultural defense that legitimizes domestic violence, or severe methods of child discipline.

I said: This is not a "slippery slope." Battered woman syndrome was different than any cultural defense or bogus syndrome. Years of study suggested its importance in understanding the mens rea of women driven to kill their husbands. Besides, the ultimate issue was one for the jury: were Lisa's perceptions objectively reasonable under the circumstances? Juries could be trusted to deal with these issues, to define the limits. Indeed, they were pragmatic and often skeptical, especially when the killing was far from "traditional" self-defense. The syndrome rarely exonerated the perpetrator. If it proved effective at all, it was in reducing murder to manslaughter.

The judge allowed Dr. Walker's testimony. I could argue self-defense based on battered woman syndrome, and I could introduce the evidence of prior abuse.

—

Springfield, Massachusetts, had been flooded with publicity about Lisa, both favorable and unfavorable. First, there was the "murder for hire" variety, just after Tom's body was discovered and during the early proceedings with Ashey and Bruyette. But later, upon Lisa's release from jail and her public statements, the themes changed to domestic violence and its horrors. I needed to pick a jury carefully, one that would, at the very least, not be tainted by the earlier stories nor reject the battered woman defense out of hand. I turned again to the NJP. Elissa Krauss, who had been indispensable in the Saxe case, was busy; she recommended Sue Stacey, who worked in the NJP's Minnesota office.

Again we pursued an elaborate jury selection process, which I had come to regard as essential when representing unpopular people or causes. It had now become one of my signatures as a trial lawyer. We would first marshal every shred of evidence suggesting how the negative publicity had tainted the pool: the circulation figures for the newspapers, the reach of the television signals from Springfield stations. Because neither Springfield papers nor Springfield television signals reached very far into Berkshire County, the judge ordered the jury to be selected from this rural county and bused to Springfield for the trial, and they would be sequestered for the duration.

When asked about whether they were or ever had been victims of domestic violence or whether they knew anyone who had been, 15 percent of the prospective jurors answered "yes." We suspected an even higher number.

Again, we had an extraordinary jury. The most committed of all was the foreman, Robert Lohbauer. He had a master's degree in counseling and taught special education, working with troubled youths. We hoped that, in his life, in his work, he had met young people like Lisa.

—•—

The government's case was straightforward: the police officers who found the body; the emotional testimony of Tom's brother; the Ashey brothers, who claimed that the proceeds of an insurance policy were dangled in front of them; Lisa's behavior after the crime. Our case was equally direct: cross-examining the co-conspirators (the standard "Aha!" cross), who had an incentive to please the government; then Lisa's testimony. While I rarely wanted the defendant to take the stand, this case required it. If we hoped that the jury would understand her thoughts, they had to hear her words.

Lisa testified for hours. She was a beautiful woman, with angular features that made her look alternately stunning and etched with pain. She testified in a monotone, sometimes composed but often dissolving into tears. To her supporters, the testimony was deeply moving. To Bloom, it was all an act.

I was uneasy. Once before, with Zakia Lamrini, the client who stabbed an abusive "john," I had assumed that the jury was sharing my own abiding empathy for the woman. And that mistake led me to misjudge the jury, which convicted her of first-degree murder (a result I was later able to get overturned on appeal).

We had to deal with the claim that Tom had life insurance, which Lisa supposedly would use to pay her collaborators. Lisa insisted that there was no policy. Tom had stopped paying the premiums some time before his death. Why would Lisa risk dangling the policy before some "assassins," as the government described them, when she knew the policy was worthless? In fact, Lisa reported that she had never mentioned such a policy to Bruyette and Ashey, but that she had found out after Tom's death that her mother, Shirley Becker, had. Fleeing from her own husband, Shirley had lived with Lisa during the time preceding Tom's killing, and she knew both Michael Ashey and Bruyette. They would drop by, waiting for Lisa to return from work, and would brag and brag about what they would do to Tom. Ms. Becker, perhaps kidding, perhaps goading them, conceded that she had told them about the insurance policy, daring them: "I don't think you guys are man enough to do anything."

But Ms. Becker would not testify. She faced the charge of accessory before the fact of murder. I urged Bloom not to prosecute her. Typically, the government immunizes its witnesses in exchange for their testimony, but Bloom would not even consider it because Becker's testimony would undermine his case. In extraordinary cases, a court can order immunity where critical exculpatory evidence, not available from another source, was involved, because the defendant's right to a fair trial trumped the government's interest in controlling its own investigation. This was such a case, I argued. Bloom had known from the outset that Ms. Becker was present at conversations leading up to Tom's killing, and he had not taken steps to prosecute her. At an earlier court appearance, he had even assured Lisa's lawyer that the government was not interested in Ms. Becker. But when we called Ms. Becker to the stand, Bloom exploded, threatening prosecution. Obviously, his decision was not about the public interest; it was about squelching a defense.

The judge denied our request for immunity for Shirley Becker, and she refused to testify. Lisa's testimony was all we had. Would it be enough?

Inadvertently, Bloom came to the rescue. Not content to argue that battered woman syndrome should not be applied to a killing that happened hours after the last threat, Bloom denied that Lisa had been battered at all. Because of his assertions, we were permitted to replay every episode of domestic violence, detail by detail, episodes that otherwise might have been ruled superfluous.

There were restraining orders, a criminal complaint against Tom, work orders of locks changed, dental records of teeth repaired, social service records about the "many secrets" of the Becker family, reports that during the Darryl Fredette relationship, Lisa would appear for appointments with black eyes. Then, after TV coverage of the case, two surprise witnesses surfaced.

Judy Wheelock, Lisa's downstairs neighbor, called. Ann Blessing and I went to her home. It was a new experience for me. She had two small children, a bit older than Stephen and Peter, and I talked to her as I never had talked before to a witness, as a mother, swapping stories. At her kitchen table, we talked about our babies, what we were feeding them, what they were doing. I watched hers and ached for mine. Lisa could well have been sitting there with us, drinking coffee, talking about Chad. Judy had been Tom's friend, too, and she was initially reluctant to get involved, but now she agreed to help us. She could confirm that Tom had stalked Lisa after they separated, the loud arguments, the police visits. She had seen Lisa's bruises.

Then a woman named Joanne Vercellone, whom we hadn't heard of, called out of the blue. She had only just met Lisa at work. One day, she had accompanied Lisa to her apartment to pick up some clothes. Tom, waiting in the parking lot, came up to Lisa and punched her in the face—just like that, as if it were something he had every right to do.

The government rebutted with witnesses of their own. Brenda Duclos, Lisa's sister, testified that she had never noticed anything during Lisa's marriage to Tom. Moreover, she had never seen her father hit Lisa. Oh yes, he was a strict disciplinarian; there were rules that all the girls had to follow. But Lisa rebelled; she was nothing but a rotten, spoiled kid. At most, Brenda said, Lisa was "spanked" if she disobeyed a rule. There was a difference between "hitting" and "spanking," she insisted. Not only did Lisa invent her father's abuse, she invented Tom's.

A lawyer usually can't wait to cross-examine such a witness, the sister who turns against one of her own with a vengeance. Brenda's anger toward Lisa, and toward me as her surrogate, was palpable. At one point, she referred to the prosecutor as "Fran," Bloom's first name. ("Fran?" I countered sarcastically. "Who's Fran?") In fact, Brenda was not in a position to see much of what Lisa experienced growing up. Brenda was in her teens when she moved out. Nor did she "hang" much with Lisa and Tom. And what was the difference between "hitting" and "spanking," after all?

I began, *You said you never saw your father hit Lisa, is that right?*

On direct, she had simply said no, but now she said:

Not unless she was being disciplined.

Oh, and just what was "discipline"? I thought.

You have two children of your own, is that right? I asked.

Yes I do.

You are a strict disciplinarian?

I wouldn't say strict, I do spank my children.

What's your definition of spanking them?

When they're doing something they are not supposed to, they have been corrected, one, two, three times, then they deserve a spank.

With a fist?

Open hand.

I repeated, now sounding incredulous:

You do that *to your children?*

I most certainly do, she said, barely concealing her contempt for me.

Then I turned to the subject of her father.

Just like you are, your father was a disciplinarian, is that right?

Yes.

And if you disobeyed the rules, you could be hit?

You could be punished.

And the punishment would include hitting?

Sometimes.

And he would get very angry when the rules were disobeyed?

At times.

In fact, he would go into a rage?

Possibly at times.

And those times when he would go into a rage, he might hit whoever did the disobeying, is that right?

A possibility, yes.

But . . . the times he hit any of you, the four of you, you don't consider that becoming violent.

No.

Then back to her parenting. If she and her father were alike, she would be conceding that she too flew into rages. If he were different, she would be conceding that he could well have been abusive.

You don't consider your father a violent man because what he did is what you do?

No.

Was he the same kind of parent that you are?

I wouldn't say that.

Was he a stricter parent than you?

Yes.

He hit the children more than you do?

Yes.

Now I moved on to her relationship with Lisa. After Tom died, Brenda hired a lawyer, became Chad's guardian, and tried to block Lisa's access to Chad. She sought control of Tom's money, ostensibly on Chad's behalf. She succeeded in getting $387 per month for Chad. And although her husband worked as a machinist and she was a waitress, it was Chad's money that allowed her family to move to a larger house.

If you lose Chad, you also lose the money you're getting for him?

That would make sense, yes.

You don't want to see him go?

Of course not. I've had him for four years. I treat him like my own . . .

Treating him like your own, you spank him too?
Most certainly.
You act as a strict disciplinarian?
I act as a parent.
You have hit him?
I have spanked him.
With an open fist?
Open hand.
How many times a week do you hit him?
I don't keep count.

No more questions. Lisa was right—she had been abused as a child. Her sister was prepared to deny it because she couldn't tell the difference between discipline and abuse.

Next came Darryl Fredette, Lisa's ex. Sure, he hit Lisa, but she "gave as good as she got." Sure, he hit her in the mouth just once, loosening her front tooth, but he was no wife abuser. Bloom wanted the jury to believe that when Lisa said Tom knocked her teeth out in November 1984, she was either making it up or it was just an accident; her teeth were loose because of Fredette, not Tom.

Days before the killing, Fredette and Lisa met. Fredette testified that Lisa told him that she was splitting up with Tom and, after showing Fredette some of Tom's charge cards, that she was going to take him for everything he had. Far from being frightened of Fredette, she slept with him.

So, Bloom continued, Lisa was willful and promiscuous (as if the only women who could go through battered woman syndrome were the long-suffering, loyal ones, not like Zakia the hooker or Lisa, the rebel). Her life was messy and troubled.

On cross-examination, Fredette conceded that he had started seeing Lisa when he was married to someone else. In fact, Lisa was not sixteen or seventeen, she was more like fifteen. He was sleeping with a minor. And the relationship was violent, by anyone's definition. But he denied that when she ran to her social workers, it was to avoid him and his brutality.

I moved to his criminal record. The law in this area is arcane. The jury may use the convictions on a witness's record only for the purpose of evaluating the witness's credibility. The syllogism is this: if he was convicted of a crime, then perhaps the witness is predisposed to lie. But the jury is not allowed to assume that just because the witness committed a crime, he was likely to commit other crimes or was generally a bad person.

And so I asked the standard, canned question: are you the same Darryl Fredette who was convicted of such-and-such? But I paused for dramatic effect, and faced the jury. I slowly read the content of the records, convictions for assaulting and beating people—including Fredette's first ex-wife. The subtext was clear: it was not only that the jury should not trust his testimony because he had numerous felony convictions, the acceptable use of prior convictions. Fredette confirmed Lisa's account of his violence. He was a proven batterer, long before he met Lisa.

The prosecutor's final rebuttal witness was Roland (Chico) Tetreault, a friend of Tom's. He witnessed the November 1984 argument when Tom broke into Lisa's Springfield apartment and allegedly smashed her teeth. No, he insisted, Tom did not hurt Lisa. Rather, Tom had hit him, Chico, with a hammer. More troubling for our defense, he claimed that the next time he ran into Lisa, months before the killing, Lisa said that "she was thinking about doing something crazy about Tom."

Tom and Lisa, he would say, in response to my cross, had a "normal" relationship. He would see them argue once in a while, although never "violently." But "violence," as he defined it, did not include slapping each other, because, yes, he had seen them slap each other. And no, he had not heard Lisa's account to the police of her injuries in November 1984 after Tom broke in. And Lisa's teeth, they had been knocked out in the 1970s, before the 1984 "hammer" incident. But on second thought, "something had happened to her teeth again and they fell out or something," but it was not in November 1984. And Lisa's comment when he met her months before Tom's death was not about doing something "crazy" about Tom. When asked about their relationship, Lisa said simply that "she was thinking about doing something about it."

These witnesses had provided me with my closing.

———

I spoke first, again linking Lisa to me.

The government talked about what happened on June 5. But I want to talk about Lisa's mind, what she intended, what she felt. I want you to put yourself in her shoes. . . . In most cases, that is easy. But in this case, it is not.

For you and me, the world is predictable. I don't expect the husband I love to hit me. And when I call the police, I expect them to stop him.

For Lisa, it is not.

Violence came and went without warning. It came from people she loved, from her caretakers, fathers, boyfriends, husbands. She called the police, went to court; nothing worked. The result: she saw danger lurking when you or I would not.

But don't take her word for it. Because this is a world so alien to all of us, we needed a guide, Dr. Lenore Walker, a psychiatrist. Dr. Walker, who has seen many women like Lisa, who testified from one end of this country to the other, told you about the syndrome that afflicted Lisa, battered woman syndrome. She told you how it affected what she saw and how she behaved.

The government will try to tell you Dr. Walker has it all wrong. There was no abuse. This was a normal world, with normal relationships between Lisa and her father, between Lisa and Darryl, and then Lisa and Tom. We can only shudder about what their ideas of normal are—where wives nail windows shut, change the locks, husbands attack with hammers, teeth are knocked out, children are hit. And what they described was probably the tip of the iceberg. Domestic violence does not take place in the open, on the streets of Springfield, in the square in Pittsfield, the highways of Lee. Lisa was battered and bruised, and it shaped her response that June night.

And then I sat down in a chair squarely in front of the jury and leaned into a fetal position. Rocking back and forth, I described that night, ending with these words:

Can you be so certain that Lisa was not lurching from flashback to flashback, in an alcoholic, frightened fog? Is it so clear that this killing was not colored by the cruel and abusive world she found herself in? How can you be sure at all, and especially, beyond a reasonable doubt?

Then Bloom:

He described the murder scene in detail, the bloody body, the weapon used. His reiterates the insurance policy claim, her "manipulation" of Bruyette and Ashey.

Battered woman syndrome? Hardly. Do you even believe she was beaten up by anyone? And do you believe that it had anything at all to do with what happened that night?

While the "usual" battered woman would stay with the body, filled with remorse, this woman covered up the crime for twenty-four hours. Then, not at all pained that she had destroyed her son's father, her husband, she slept with his murderer, Bruyette, that very evening and took him to a mall the next day.

Remember when she finally told the truth to the police the day after the murder? She didn't mention any battering, any fancy syndrome.

Battered woman syndrome? Ridiculous! She needed this stuff to try to con her way out of this. To allow this type of conduct would so cheapen human life that it would decrease the humanity of all of us.

I go back to Brookline, totally spent. Harvey is getting annoyed at the amount of time out of the office this case is taking; I have a ton of messages from him about office matters and other cases that he thinks I am ignoring. He's right. I am. There is not much I can do until the trial is over.

John is supportive, but also a bit overwhelmed. Sarah, now a teenager and asserting her independence, is completely withdrawn. Although she chose to live with us, she's pressing to eat her meals in her own room. She has nearly stopped talking to me—again. Stephen is in preschool for a few hours a day and not having an easy time of it. Peter, a toddler, is getting into everything. Samantha, the dog, is old and frequently incontinent. Rachel, John's mother, is diagnosed with cancer and may need to move in with us after her operation. Funny, though, the chaos at home is less stressful than the trial. I can wrap myself in it and forget the violence, the rage of Lisa's life.

Days pass. The jury returns a verdict of manslaughter. Lohbauer tells the papers that he argued for acquittal but could not persuade the others. Lisa was crushed. I, on the other hand, was relieved that my client had avoided first-degree murder.

Bloom accused me of manipulating the jury. My empathy for Lisa, that closing, was nothing more than part of my craft, another sleazy defense lawyer's ploy, crocodile tears.

True, that closing had become part of my craft, another of my trial signatures. Look at me if you have trouble looking at Lisa. Empathize with me if you have trouble empathizing with her. It was a woman's closing, passionate and emotional.

But the empathy was real, even if it was housed in the same human being who understood the complexity of the legal arguments that she was making. I represented Lisa, not society. I was an advocate, not an academic, and surely not a judge. I feared a first-degree murder conviction for this troubled and tortured woman far more than I feared the implications of runaway battered woman syndrome defenses.

I had persuaded Lisa to let the judge instruct the jury on manslaughter, not to go for broke—first-degree murder or acquittal. Now the focus could be where it belonged: what sentence fit this crime?

———

Bloom argued for the maximum. He seemed affronted that Lisa tried to defend herself.

"I have had women," he said, "in the time I have worked here, that have killed their husbands or the person they were living with, and we have done investigations, and it was very clear that those people were battered." But these women were different: "All . . . of those women pled guilty, received a probationary sentence, and walked out of court."

Lisa Grimshaw dared plead not guilty, dared to fight, and worse, to garner publicity. In Bloom's estimation, "[T]his case was made into a three-ring circus, probably starting a year ago," all to manipulate the court.

Then he moved to character assassination: her lifestyle, the biker bars she frequented. He still insisted that there was no evidence of physical abuse.

I argued—no, begged—for leniency. There are several tragedies here—the death of a young man, a child who would grow up without a father, and the tragedy that was Lisa Grimshaw's life. Sentencing, I said, cannot resolve them. I argued for time served, the three years that Lisa had already spent in prison. Lisa's record since she had been released on bail was exemplary. She got Chad back and resurrected their relationship. She was spending her time as an advocate in a battered women's shelter; scores of women had written about their gratitude for her contributions. Never in sixteen years of practice, I said, had I ever seen this kind of outpouring. She had a steady residence, meaningful work, and a productive life in the community.

And, I reminded the judge, Lisa cooperated with the authorities, participated in every hearing they wanted her to participate in, with no strings attached. There were guidelines in Massachusetts, under which her sentence should be two and a half to eight years.

Finally, I pointed to members of the jury who had returned for the sentencing hearing, a sure sign of support for the defendant. Lohbauer even wrote a note to the judge:

> I feel strongly that this is not the same woman whose actions in 1985 I could not find totally defensible. As an educator/counselor, I must argue for a view of human nature that embraces growth and change. Lisa's own testimony convinced me that she has changed and has the capacity and courage for continued growth as a wider range of life options are presented to her—options she could not have imagined or recognized in 1985.
>
> It is with these thoughts in mind that I earnestly request that you be merciful. She has suffered in ways that you and I, as men, can never fully comprehend.

The judge took a break. When we returned, Bloom rose for one last parting shot: "Judge," he said, "I want you to know that

Lisa Grimshaw was laughing in the hallway, then we come back in and she's almost crying. It's all a con job," he insisted. I hadn't noticed her laughing in the hallway. What I had seen is how hard she had hugged me after my closing argument, at best smiling wanly to break through the terrible anxiety that had gripped her in the courtroom.

Without a word of explanation, the judge directs the clerk to read the sentence:

"Lisa Becker Grimshaw, hearken to the sentence the Court has awarded against you, charging the crime of manslaughter, the Court now orders you to be sentenced to the Massachusetts Correctional Institution for not less than fifteen years, and not more than twenty years."

Nearly the maximum. Twice the national average for manslaughter. Inconceivable for a first-time offender, especially one with a history of sexual and physical violence.

Lohbauer was quoted in the paper: "If I knew then what I know now, I would have held out for an acquittal."

———

All appeals failed. Indeed, the Supreme Judicial Court thought Lisa got a better trial than she deserved. It was openly skeptical of the admissibility of battered woman syndrome in this case.

Lisa's only hope was for commutation. For the first time I can remember, I had run out of cards. I had never before given up on a client. I wasn't certain whether it was the new complexity of my life or my concerns about this case, my very real doubts about being able to do better for Lisa.

A new group of lawyers took over, ably led by Professor Abbe Smith at Harvard Law School. The same community that had risen to Lisa's defense at the trial came forward again. But the best evidence that Lisa deserved a break was Lisa herself. She didn't crumble after the verdict. Forced to return to jail after eleven months of freedom, she worked on her own case and helped other women affected by domestic violence.

In 1985, when the crime occurred, this was a "murder for hire" story. No one seemed to be interested in the whys and wherefores. Four years later, in no small measure because of Lisa's efforts, this was a "battered women's case," dramatizing the horrors of domestic violence. By 1992, Lisa's story was featured in *Fighting for our Lives,* an Academy Award–winning documentary about "The Framingham Eight," eight women imprisoned in Framingham State Prison for killing their abusive lovers. Then Governor Weld commuted the sentences of four of the women who had not been able to present evidence of battered woman syndrome. Lisa's was not one of them. Through my efforts, she had been able to raise and fully litigate the issue—all to no avail. But the state parole board, initially dividing on gender lines, finally voted for her release on early parole in 1995, after she had served a total of seven years. The foreman of the jury, Robert Lohbauer, again made an impassioned plea on her behalf.

Women across Massachusetts celebrated her release. I was asked to speak about the case on multiple occasions and was applauded for my role in it. The applause didn't last long, though.

CHAPTER ELEVEN

A "So-Called" Feminist

"We question why attorney Nancy Gertner was invited to participate in this forum," the circular begins. "We demand that so-called
'women's rights' attorneys like Nancy Gertner be held accountable
for their role in decisions that hurt women." This is a flyer distributed by a group called "White Women Against Racism and Violence Against Women."

I see it right before I am supposed to speak. I am at a forum
run by the Civil Liberties Union of Massachusetts (CLUM). My
job is to talk about the Supreme Court's decisions involving fetal
rights and the workplace. The Court had recently addressed the
question of how far an employer may go to restrict women's access
to certain jobs because of their potential to harm reproduction. I
have been here many times before. I love the work, the setting, the
people. I have followed the decision, reviewed the case law, determined the impact that this case will have on the Women's Rights
Project of CLUM.

But here, one year after Grimshaw, I was a "so-called"
women's-rights attorney.

The reason was "Paul" (I think that fairness requires masking
the identity of my client as well as his accuser). I had represented
him because I believed that he was innocent. Not just legally innocent. Not just "the government's case is weak" or "I think I can win

this case." Not even the "establish important new precedents" kind of innocent. I thought he hadn't raped anyone. When I looked at him, I suddenly saw my baby sons, Stephen and Peter.

This is not supposed to matter to a lawyer—real innocence or guilt. With few exceptions, lawyers are supposed to take any case, argue either side. The "hired gun" is the pejorative side of the picture; serving all people equally is the beneficent.

I agreed with that principle in most criminal cases, except where a man was accused of rape.

———

It began with a call from a former roommate of mine. She said that the son of her piano teacher was in trouble, accused of rape at a Boston-area university. Would I see him? Because the caller was a very close friend, I agreed. I hastened to add that I did not handle these kinds of cases—she must understand that—but that I would make certain that he was well represented.

I met Paul on the fourteenth floor of our "downtown" office at 89 Broad Street. I had to wait for him to climb the stairs. He was intensely claustrophobic, so taking the elevator was out of the question. At seventeen, he was very small for his age. He seemed childlike, barely an adolescent, neurotically talking all the time. His goal was to be a musician like his mother and father; he hoped to conduct orchestras. It had been, he said, his first sexual encounter.

I was too busy for this, I said. I had virtually back-to-back murder cases, sex discrimination cases, abortion rights litigation, a family. Besides, I had never taken a rape case. My excuses went on and on. But I believed him. It seemed clear that if the woman had so much as laughed at him—let alone said no— he would have been mortified. Any cue, any hint of her displeasure would have fractured his resolve. He was that timid, that tentative. The attack, especially as she described it, was not credible.

He nervously recounted the facts. Anne (not her real name either) and he were both freshmen, and they were very close friends. They had socialized before, and most significantly, *after* the supposed rape on April 19, 1988. She spent the days before her encounter with Paul with her real boyfriend, someone she had dated since high school. When he left, Anne had had dinner with Paul and a woman friend to share her concerns about her boyfriend. It seemed that he did not want to attend a Boston-area college. After dinner, she invited Paul to her room. They started to have sex, but he had to leave. He was in a musical performance that evening. They agreed that he would return after the concert.

When Paul returned, they "made love," he said. Anne said that he forced himself on her. Paul was 5' tall, weighing about 100 pounds. She was 5'4" and weighed 140 pounds. Before Paul came into her room, she claimed, she had consumed one drink of Southern Comfort (a plastic cup, one half to three quarters full), which she got from a neighbor, but Paul reported that the neighbor told a different story. The neighbor said Anne had taken a very small amount from the Southern Comfort bottle—and that the drinking may well have been on a different night. The neighbor reported that Anne came over to her dorm room for a visit in the middle of Paul's sexual overtures, but she had never mentioned what was supposedly happening in her own room, or seemed in any way reluctant to return. Afterward, Anne told a friend that she had been raped, but she swore that friend to silence.

A short time later, Anne invited Paul to her parents' home in Connecticut for the weekend. She went out of her way to make certain that he got the proper directions, that he would come as planned. He stayed for two nights. Later, she told police that this was a test—to see if he would repeat what he had done.

In January 1989, nine months after the alleged attack, Anne was admitted to a local hospital, having taken a large number of cold pills. She explained that she was depressed because her old boyfriend had finally broken up with her. The records of her hospitalization, which the prosecutor had inadvertently disclosed to the defense, never mentioned Paul, never suggested that anyone had raped her. Then, an anonymous caller reported to Anne's father that she told "some people" that she had been raped. Her father pressed her for the name; "Paul," she said. To another student at or near that time, she mentioned a different male classmate.

Of course, none of these facts guaranteed that Paul was innocent. A woman could delay the accusation of rape because she was embarrassed—but it could also suggest a contrivance. A man of small physical stature could be able to rape a larger woman—or not. Socializing with the alleged assailant, inviting him to her parents' home for the weekend, could reflect the denial of a painful memory—or it could suggest that the rape did not happen. And inconsistent stories could mean that she was nervous about the details—or that the rape accusation was made up.

Nor did Paul's background matter. Both of his parents were classical musicians, well-educated, well-spoken, and ardent feminists. When they talked about sex with him as an adolescent, they made certain to talk about respecting women. They were determined that he understand the woman's perspective. And they were overprotective—just as I would likely be with my boys, and as my parents had been of me. Of course, all of this made the claim more and more unlikely to me, but it was not necessarily exonerating.

———

Still, I ducked the case. Obviously, if a man accused of this crime could not find a decent lawyer, I would relent. It was an easy cop-out because in Boston, that was unlikely. I would happily recommend another lawyer. I never urged other lawyers to follow my lead and decline these kinds of cases. It was not a campaign. It was only what I had to do.

After the Saxe case, my phone rang off the hook with calls from men detained at the Charles Street jail, accused of rape. There was suddenly a new exception to the old rule: "Beware of women criminal defense lawyers." Now they realized that a woman lawyer could go before the jury and, by her very presence, communicate: "If I believe him, so should you."

That was the problem. I feared that the men seeking my help were not really looking for my skills; there were plenty of others more than capable of doing the job. What these defendants wanted was my symbolism, my legitimacy, my very gender to vouch for them. It was one thing to use my brains at the service of a defendant; it was another thing to use my personhood. I would reserve that for the cases that meant more to me.

In her book *The Journalist and the Murderer,* Janet Malcolm surmises that to be a good trial lawyer, you have to be a good hater. I wasn't in general, and especially not here. I didn't hate Anne; in fact, I could easily find myself sympathizing with her. I feared that either I would temper my advocacy, to Paul's detriment, or if I did not, if I were as zealous as I could be at Anne's expense, I would be sick to my stomach afterward. Either I would not be very good at defending him or I would be *too* good at it. Anyhow, because I committed myself so completely to the cases I took, I needed to choose my crusades. This was not one of them.

Rape was a different category of crime, as Susan Brownmiller had said in the 1970s, and Susan Estrich in the 1980s. Women, I among them, felt uniquely vulnerable to it. I remember taking the subway back from Barnard one early Friday evening. I had just received wonderful news about a project; I felt powerful, independent, exuberant about my future. I was uncharacteristically dressed up, in a suit, high heels. Suddenly, a group of kids, perhaps twelve or thirteen years old, approached. One ran up to me, grabbed at my breasts, and ran away. The group erupted in laughter. In that moment, by that seemingly trivial gesture, I was reduced to my anatomy. True, men of slight stature, younger men, could be similarly victimized. But this kind of male-on-female attack resonated with other messages, a culture that announced loud and clear: no matter how high and mighty you get, you are "just" a woman, that your physical vulnerability trumped everything.

In the 1970s, I was a vocal critic of the rape laws. Throughout the history of the prosecution of this offense, there were two popular, dynamically opposed camps: those who decried the unredressed, unprosecuted sexual assault of a woman, and those who railed against the false accusation of a man. For most of our history, the law seemed to be concerned only about the latter. A woman rape victim was treated with a disrespect to which no other crime victim was subject.

Until the 1980s, an accusation of rape had to be corroborated by "independent evidence" in most states, something other than a woman's word. The rationale, often quite explicit, was that women lie. This belief, as Susan Estrich described in *Real Rape*, "equally reflected the ... seventeenth-century distrust of women and the twentieth-century view of women as confused and complicit in their sexual relationships." In the real world, a woman's word may well have been all there was, the classic "he said, she said." Other states required a "fresh complaint"; unless a woman complained of being raped at the first opportunity, her accusations were not worthy of being believed. It was a throwback to chivalry, the notion that a truly chaste woman would proclaim loudly that she had been violated the first chance she got. In the real world, a woman who had been raped wanted to deny the crime, shower, pretend it had not happened—hardly announce it. The woman's past, and especially her prior sexual history, was also fair game. For instance, in a respected 1973 manual for defense attorneys called *Crimes of Violence: Rape and Other Sex Crimes,* F. Lee Bailey and Henry B. Rothblatt urged lawyers to aggressively cross-examine the accuser—probing into personal matters, using any ammunition they had: "If you can totally destroy her character or reputation, as with proof of specific ... immoral acts, ... launch your attack." The only limit: don't make her cry.

The definition of the crime itself was an anachronism. It focused on the victim's conduct—whether she had resisted "to the utmost"—rather than the defendant's conduct. Only with clear physical evidence of resistance could the victim demonstrate that she had not consented, something no other crime victim had to prove. To the extent that the defendant's conduct was examined at all, force was required before the man's actions would be called "rape," not deception or drugging or simple coercion. In the real world, it did not take "utmost resistance" by the woman to signal her horror at being violated. Nor was violence the only way to force a woman into having sex against her will. In fact, we were all taught that resistance was not only futile; it was dangerous. The clear message by parents, schools, and communities to girls and women in the 1960s and 1970s was to "let him have his way," rather than risk much greater injury or possibly death. But once we did that, under the law, we could not claim we were raped.

The aim of much-needed reform movements in the early 1980s was clear. Get the law to treat this crime like any other; be no more skeptical about this victim than about any other victim in any other setting. No one blamed the victim of a robbery for flashing cash openly before it happened; no one required corroboration for an assault, or "fresh complaint" for larceny, or "utmost resistance" for a battery. The mere threat of violence, drugging, coercion, or even deceit should have been enough to label the nonconsensual sex "rape." It was not.

So I worked on "rape shield" laws, testifying before the state legislature, giving interviews to the press, participating in panels, whatever I could. Introducing a victim's reputation for licentious-ness or evidence of her prior sexual encounters with other men to suggest consent to rape was preposterous. It was no more legiti-mate in the late twentieth century, in the midst of a feminist revo-lution, than submerging witnesses in water to determine if they were telling the truth during the Salem witch trials (if you sur-vived, you were vindicated—but few did).

By the 1980s, rape shield statutes were passed around the coun-try. They prohibited the introduction of prior sexual experience or reputation evidence at trial, except in what appeared to be carefully controlled circumstances. In theory, the defense lawyer could no longer engage in a wholesale exposure of the woman's sexual past, as F. Lee Bailey had advocated. Prior sexual history could be intro-duced only where necessary to establish the relationship between the defendant and the victim (that is, specific sexual conduct with the defendant) or evidence of recent sexual conduct that al-legedly was the cause of a characteristic of the victim (like the presence of someone else's sperm). Just because a woman was no longer a virgin, or because she had had sexual experience, or even that she had a reputation for "unchastity" (whatever that meant) did not equal consent to sex at any time with anyone.

But this reform was not enough. The law, still reflecting so-ciety's old-fashioned views about sex and women, did not cover "date rape." So long as violence, and not simply unwanted sex, was the linchpin of the crime, only aggressive encounters involving weapons or violence, typically between strangers, would be prosecuted. What Susan Estrich called "simple rape," unconsented-to sex without violence or weapons, was ignored. My parents would have understood; they had taught me that meeting someone at a bar or wearing a miniskirt "invited" rape. "Boys will be boys," Moishe would intone, but women had to be responsible. Women had to control themselves; men were incapable of doing so. In the same Barnard freshman "hygiene" class in which we read Betty Friedan's *The Feminine Mystique,* we were taught how to get in and out of cars so as not to allow men to look up our skirts, lest we provoke their uncontrollable urges. Undaunted, or more appropriately, unwilling to let my fears control my life, I traveled the world alone and single. I had to persuade more than one "liberated man" that "no meant no," no matter what I was wearing, no matter where we had met, no matter how much I dated or how much I believed in sexual equality. It was more than legal or legislative reform; to women of my generation, to me, it was personal.

Finally, by the late 1980s, most rape statutes were changed formally. Now rape was defined as sex performed against a woman's will, without her consent, and now it included date rape. But although the words were right, the practice lagged. Even without formal "corroboration" requirements, many—largely male—prosecutors would not proceed on a date rape charge without independent proof. Even if they believed the woman, they would decline to prosecute, predicting that jurors would be skeptical. And their predictions, at least at that time, were not off the mark.

Trial narratives reflect the social and cultural milieu. Lawyers representing men accused of rape harked back to the old strategies because they were more helpful to their cause. If not directly in their questioning, then indirectly in their tone of voice, they communicated their lack of respect for the victim. Blame the victim, attack her reputation, question her motives; these themes continued to have an audience—the media, as well as juries of people of all ages. It was like Prohibition. We had announced our repulsion about rape in the strongest possible terms, but we were still ambivalent about date rape prosecutions. Social mores change at their own pace. With the sole exception of interracial accusations of rape (meaning a black man raping a white woman, of course), which were successful even when false, the myth of the false accusation of rape continued to trump concerns about unprosecuted crimes—or so it seemed.

Harvey and I argued and argued on these points. Rape, he insisted, was the only crime in which innocence was no defense. He pulled every clipping about men accused of rape in situations in which the woman's words or gestures were, at best, equivocal. I had to agree that there were ambiguous situations—she did not say yes or no—but I insisted that the burden of ambiguity should fall on the man. In other crimes—battery, for example—one person was not allowed to touch another without his or her consent. Unless the signals were clear, the man was to err on the side of no touching, no sex.

Of course, I knew rape was more complicated than that. Sexual encounters were not like an unauthorized operation (which the law called a battery). There were no pre-sex "informed consent" forms, no witness signatures, no clear lines. Worse still, sexual cues in the 1980s were different than they had been even in my youth, and they were changing rapidly. Racial or ethnic or even class boundaries complicated communication still further. How fair was it to use the criminal law to effect social change, especially where sexual encounters were concerned?

I was paralyzed, so I steered clear of all criminal prosecutions for rape. I would bring civil actions for rape. In a civil case, the woman—not the Commonwealth of Massachusetts—is the plaintiff. She seeks damages for her pain, not the imprisonment of the offender. As the plaintiff, she and her lawyer, not the state's representatives, control the litigation. The defendants were different—not only the rapist could be accused, but also the owners of premises charged with maintaining security. The standard of proof was lower, a fair preponderance of the evidence—not the standard for a criminal case, beyond a reasonable doubt. Using criminal law to enforce new social expectations was unfair; criminal law was supposed to give people notice in advance of what conduct would be prohibited, not criminalize that conduct after the fact. But on the civil side, it was not at all unusual to use the law to help shift social standards. We did it with laws prohibiting discrimination and regulating the environment. If we were wrong about the civil accusation, only money changed hands.

The civil cases were straightforward. Most settled. No press. Confidential. The cost of doing business had to include the cost of protecting all of us.

———

No, I had never represented a man in a rape charge before, I told Paul, and whatever I felt about him, I did not want to start. I referred him to one of my partners, Andy Good, an extraordinary lawyer. Surely Andy could make the case go away. The woman would recant. Or, if she didn't, Tom Reilly, the Middlesex County DA, and David Meier, the assistant DA, would agree not to bring charges. And if they did not, the grand jury would see the weakness of the case and refuse to indict.

But I profoundly misjudged the changing times—indeed, the very effectiveness of the movement of which I was a part. The media, pressured by a new generation of feminist lawyers and scholars, had begun to highlight the victim's plight. There were movies and books and articles on date rape, urging prosecutors, judges, and in effect, juries to look differently at the woman's accusations. And slowly, slowly, the draconian traditions of rape prosecutions had begun to erode.

Anne did not recant. The DA stuck to his guns. And the grand jury indicted. And although I had turned the case over to Andy and got absorbed in my other cases—the usual fare, murder and sex discrimination—I followed its twists and turns.

Andy and I agreed that Paul should testify before the grand jury, an unusual move for a defendant. The grand jury was entirely controlled by the prosecutor. He asked the questions he wanted. There was no cross-examination. In the state system, a defense lawyer could stand there—but he could say nothing. Andy went with Paul.

A member of the jury, who I later found out was a producer of a local TV news program, told the group that he knew I was Paul's attorney. Because I was a feminist, he assumed that there "must be more to the case." Even as I tried to stand in the background, my association with Paul somehow legitimized his defense, the kind of "profiling" that I had tried to avoid all my professional life. Gertner is on the case; he must be innocent, or at least, he will be well-represented. The grand jury, therefore, didn't have to take full responsibility for screening the charges, as they were supposed to do. In fact, although many on the grand jury believed that this young man would never be convicted, they agreed to indict—by one vote.

I was in the middle of trying a sex discrimination case on behalf of Teresa Contardo, a stockbroker. Andy and I barely talked. The weekend before Paul's trial, there was a television program about date rape, one of many that finally sympathized with the woman's point of view, at last decrying the traditional biases against the victim. Andy feared that this program could prejudice potential jurors against Paul. He decided to waive jury trial and have a bench trial before a judge instead. I wasn't consulted.

So weak was the government's case that during David Meier's closing argument, the trial judge peppered him with questions suggesting reasonable doubt. He had "some problems," he announced, with the inferences that the prosecutor asked him to draw—the victim's invitation to her parents' home after the incident, the circumstances of the accusation, the discrepancy in physical stature and the physical improbability of her account, the delay in reporting. Everyone in the courtroom assumed that the result was going to be a "not guilty" verdict.

Then the judge left the bench, only to return with a simple pronouncement: "Guilty." In a stunning concession, he compared his performance—unfavorably—with what a jury would have done. "The special genius of jurors," he said, "is that they recognize that this particular incident . . . is the most important dispute that will ever come before them for resolution." In contrast, "The major limitation that I had . . . is that the Court, unfortunately, sees these cases come on a conveyor belt. And the Court can never be, in my judgment, a fact finder that a jury can be."

Justice on a conveyer belt? Extraordinary! It is not supposed to matter if this was the judge's first rape case or his last. It was as if he were admitting that he was too tired to do his job, too tired to resist the public pressure that would surely follow an acquittal in this changed atmosphere. "There we go again," a leading feminist would be quoted as saying in the *Boston Globe* and *Boston Herald*. "Judge Acquits Rapist," the headlines would scream. The victim's family would express their deep disappointment at the outcome. Perhaps a columnist or two would attack the judge; he was, after all, a man, probably anti-woman and into coddling rapists. On the other hand, no public outcry would follow a conviction. Paul would be known only in terms of the offense of which he was convicted. "Convicted rapist gets his just desserts," the media would announce. The pain of Paul's family would be ignored. The comments of his defense lawyers about evidence, or worse, innocence, would be dismissed as "lawyerspeak."

———•———

When Andy called to tell me the verdict, I was appalled. I agreed to meet Paul's family at my home, not the office. My husband, John, Stephen, and Peter were there. Paul's family begged me to participate. This was no longer a case; it was a nightmare. I would do whatever I could.

I did the sentencing argument, and it is fair to say that I harangued the judge for hours. It was like a filibuster; I feared that the minute I sat down, Paul would be taken away. Don't send Paul to prison, I argued. He had no criminal record, an exemplary background. Witnesses had come from one end of the country to the other to testify about his childhood, his religious education, his mental state. He was deeply neurotic, profoundly claustrophobic. He would go crazy in prison. And he was slight, an easy target for other inmates. Jail was not necessary here. His bright future was in shambles.

I concluded, nearly shouting (or so they tell me): "Feminism did not demand this man's incarceration; no 'ism' called for the punishment of an innocent man!"

The judge felt "compelled"—yet again—to sentence Paul to prison. It was not a long sentence, for sure. He was sentenced to fifteen years at Concord Reformatory, ninety-five days to be served, the remainder suspended, and a lengthy probation with community service. But for Paul, a simple elevator ride or a plane trip was harrowing. In a beneficent gesture, the judge stayed the execution of the sentence for five and a half months, until June 1990, so as not to interfere with the completion of the school year. It was useless; Paul had already been kicked out of college.

In my despair, I wrote in my diary that I felt like I had witnessed the new "fascism" of the women's movement, a complete turnaround from years past. There seemed to be an ideological line in the sand that no one would cross. The prosecutor seemed to be compelled to go ahead. He could not disbelieve a woman who claimed rape; that had, after all, been the unfortunate historical pattern. The grand jury seemed compelled to indict, despite their misgivings. And most horrifying of all, the judge, with life tenure, could not distinguish this case from others on the conveyor belt.

———

The case weighed heavily on me throughout the winter of 1989 and the spring of 1990. As I enjoyed my boys, the *Peter Pan* performance after Christmas, the ceremony of signing Stephen up for kindergarten, I thought of Paul. We investigated the case some more, re-interviewing old witnesses, tracking down new ones.

As June approached, and Paul's imprisonment was imminent, it was clear that I would have to argue for bail pending the appeal of his case.

In the Massachusetts appeals court, in the lobby of Judge Edith Fine, I argued for bail. Judge Fine, now deceased, was an exemplary judge. Opposing me was another woman lawyer, Wendy Murphy, then an assistant DA. The three of us spanned three decades of the women's movement: Wendy was ten years younger than I, Judge Fine, ten years older. In the Middlesex County District Attorney's Office, Wendy specialized in sexual assault cases. After leaving the District Attorney's Office, she dedicated her practice to stopping violence against women. While I had an enormous amount of respect for her decision to represent women victims, I was troubled by the positions she was taking, not just as a criminal defense lawyer but as a feminist. Indeed, some time later, Wendy, now a regular commentator on Fox News, went so far as to call all women who worked on the defense side in rape cases—apparently including me—"boy toys," traitors to the cause. Still later, she would insist on cable TV that the Duke lacrosse players accused of raping a black woman were guilty even after the rape charges were dropped and the North Carolina attorney-general declared that they were innocent.

Violence against women was a symptom of women's inequality, not the cause of it. I would decry it, represent battered women, women victimized by sexual violence, but I would not give up work on economic discrimination, reproductive rights, the broader pastiche of issues that made women an easy mark for subordination. Nor did I believe that no woman would ever make a false accusation of rape, as Murphy has said; or that even when a woman said yes, the law should always be skeptical so long as women were still powerless relative to men, as Andrea Dworkin and Catherine MacKinnon suggested. The criminal law should not swing from one gender stereotype—women always lie, no means yes—to another—women never lie, yes means no. Life, politics, culture, and, notably, sex are far more complex.

It was not at all clear where Judge Fine stood in this debate or, more significantly, what impact her feelings would have on her decision. Judge Fine had graduated from Barnard College in the 1950s, had been one of five women at Harvard Law School, and had been an early Peace Corps Volunteer. She had been on the bench—as a superior court judge, and then the appeals court—for almost twenty years. Because of the historical under-prosecution of date rape, would she be unwilling to release Paul pending appeal, and in so doing, dignify our challenges to his conviction? Would she be concerned that it would "send the wrong message": again a woman was attacked, again a woman disbelieved? Or would she recognize that the Sturm und Drang of feminism was irrelevant here? The only issue was this man, this woman, and what had happened between them. You don't "send messages" when to do so might mean perpetuating an injustice, sending an innocent man to jail.

The lobby setting, somewhat less formal, combined with the gender of the participants took the edges off our arguments. There would be no bombast, no great sweeps of rhetoric. All the standards for bail were met, I argued: there was no risk of "further acts of criminality" while the appeal was pending; nor was there any risk of flight. The appeal was hardly frivolous; there were a number of substantial legal issues. Finally, I insisted, the case had the aroma of innocence.

Wendy focused on the fact that this was a jury-waived trial. It was primarily a credibility contest, and the trial judge, who was in a better position to judge than the court of appeals, did not believe Paul. And he found that the evidence met the highest standard that the law can impose: guilt beyond a reasonable doubt. Reversal was unlikely, she claimed.

Judge Fine was not impressed with my presentation, but she agreed to stay the execution of Paul's sentence at least until the trial judge decided one last motion still pending before him. When the trial judge denied the motion the very next day, I geared up to appeal what I expected to be Judge Fine's denial of bail. Less than a week later, without explanation, Judge Fine granted bail pending appeal.

Much later, I learned that Judge Fine told a friend that she was considering a stay of sentence in a rape case that she found very troubling. Although she strongly believed the defendant to be innocent, she did not think there was anything she could do. All that was supposed to matter at the appellate stage were trial errors and omissions, whether the legal rules had been followed. However extraordinary it may sound to lay ears, the U.S. Supreme Court has said over and over again that in most cases, actual innocence is irrelevant. If the procedures were followed, the *i*'s dotted and the *t*'s crossed, we are supposed to accept the outcome; verdicts, we are told, must have finality.

But while jurors and judges should not be second-guessed ad infinitum, ultimately the purpose of these timeworn procedures is to effect justice. And therefore, Judge Fine allowed Paul to remain free pending appeal.

———

Paul and his parents were very concerned. Apart from my bail victory, none of my predictions about his case had come true— charges would never be brought, he would never be indicted, the case for acquittal was strong. So Paul's family went around town shopping for a new lawyer.

Maybe they also sensed the chaos in my firm. Because Harvey and I had been such close friends, such kindred spirits, now every squabble seemed to escalate into personal battles, almost like domestic disputes. Truly vitriolic memos were flying back and forth—about my parking tickets, about his annoying memos that "neatness counts," who was working harder, and on and on. The staff was taking sides. We had loaded so much into the firm—our love for each other, our shared values, in what was a true professional marriage—but the partnership didn't change even as our lives did. I was linked to his crusades, from which I felt more and more estranged; and he was linked to mine, more and more reluctantly. I had begun to look for space to start my own firm.

One of the lawyers that Paul's family consulted referred them to Tom Dwyer, a former Suffolk County assistant DA, now a partner in a small "boutique" law firm, Dwyer and Collora. I knew Tom well. He was in the Suffolk DA's office when I tried the Saxe case, and he had been part of the team defending Mayor Kevin White while Harvey and I represented Ted Anzalone. His partner, Mike Collora, was a former federal prosecutor. The firm, Dwyer and Collora, was the polar opposite of ours. It was not "political" in the same way. It was not organized to promote any particular position or defend particular kinds of people. While Tom worked for Democratic Party candidates, the partners were not expected to share any philosophy or unite for any given cause. Their clients were largely defendants accused of white-collar offenses or businesspeople in commercial litigation. The firm did well financially—not the kind of "feast or famine" that Harvey and I regularly experienced. In short, it was a real "downtown" firm—no posters, no doggy beds, no Allen Ginsburg photographs.

When Paul's family met with Tom, he asked them who had been representing them up until now. They said "Nancy Gertner." Tom told them that they were crazy to change lawyers, that they had the best in Boston. Paul's family related the story to me. I called Tom and told him to put his money where his mouth was. Could I join his firm?

A traditional firm, where no one was expected to agree with

one another, would be almost a relief. I could continue to do the work I wanted to do, so long as I also brought in money. Bringing in money was not a problem. I was handling "paying" white-collar cases, sex discrimination cases, sexual harassment, and malpractice cases. More and more executives (women and men) were consulting with me on their situations. I could pair fee-generating cases with my "causes" and so long as I controlled the mix, it would be enough—not as much as I could have made, but enough for me.

Tom was extraordinary. Within a month, he drafted a partnership agreement, set up the office, sent out announcements and a press release and orchestrated a huge celebration to welcome me on the firm's waterfront deck. Harvey and Andy came—Harvey reluctantly, because this was, after all, a party. On one level, we were all relieved. Now our long and deep friendship could continue. And Dwyer & Collora became Dwyer, Collora, & Gertner (DC&G for short).

———

I worked on Paul's case at DC&G. Judy Mizner, my former partner in Harvey's and my firm and a talented, dogged criminal defense lawyer, helped scour the record of the case and the law. Now I planned to make certain that this was an explicitly feminist brief. Just because the legal system has moved away from the view that all rape accusations are contrived, we said, does not mean that it must move to a view that none are. Just because it has stopped singling out rape victims for especially harsh treatment does not mean that they should be singled out for blanket accommodation. This conviction was not just technically imperfect—it was a true injustice.

The first argument, and the major one, broke no new ground. The judge had wrongly limited Andy's cross-examination of the accuser. Andy tried to question her about whether she told her parents that Paul was the rapist to keep them from learning that she had had casual sex with him. To show the depths of her concerns about her parents' reactions to premarital sex, Andy questioned her about the fact that she had even kept from them her two-year-long intimate relationship with her high-school beau. And he also tried to show why she would target Paul: her relationship with Paul had gotten around campus; the friend that she had allegedly told about the rape had mocked her for her interest in this small, somewhat eccentric young man. When she was in the hospital and an anonymous caller said something about an assault, she needed to come up with a story quickly. With no explanation, only a perfunctory "sustained" when the prosecutor objected, the judge excluded the questions.

To the Supreme Judicial Court, which at that point had only one woman member, Justice Ruth Abrams, I argued that this cross-examination was not the gratuitous badgering of a woman, a la Messrs. Bailey and Rothblatt. It was not a return to the bad old days before the rape shield statute. Andy's questioning was not intended simply to make her uncomfortable or expose her as "unchaste" or "loose." Although sexual mores had changed, it was not unreasonable to suggest that this daughter cared about parental disapproval and would take steps—even extreme steps—to avoid it.

Judge Abrams would have none of it: "Isn't that just another version of the typical sexist generalizations about women?" she insisted, and my heart sank.

The final argument in the brief, after we had challenged nearly every ruling in the case, was a throwaway. We did not expect to win it. We sought the records of Anne's encounters with a social worker and then a psychiatrist in New York. A set of records from the local hospital had been produced inadvertently at trial by the prosecutor; they contained no mention of anything like a sexual assault, or even Paul's name.

If Anne had first made accusations about Paul to her neighbor, we would have been able to interview that neighbor. Although no longer required by prosecutors to bring charges, evidence of the complainant's words and her affect at the time that she claimed to have been assaulted were still relevant. What if the New York records, like the local hospital's records, did not mention rape at all, or Paul, or spoke only of her boyfriend? What if she did describe the events, but in such a way that did not suggest rape, and it was actually the psychiatrist who put the word "rape" in her mouth? What if the records suggested that her account was directly related to concerns about her parents' disapproval of premarital sex? What if she talked about her ex-boyfriend's jealousy and the need to hide her date with Paul from him?

Because the listener was a psychiatrist, and the answers privileged, we could not ask these questions. I understood the reasons. If she had been raped, she would be in dire need of counseling. If her words to her counselor could become fodder for the likes of Bailey-Rothblatt, she would not speak, and if she didn't speak, she wouldn't heal. In my civil cases, I had blocked inquiries like the one that I was making.

But this was a criminal case; the defendant was presumed innocent. The prosecutor's argument, preventing access to the records, assumed the opposite, that there was nothing in the records that would cast doubt on this accusation. Worse yet, it also assumed that all criminal defense lawyers were rabid and overzealous, that the records request was gratuitous, like the fishing expeditions for unchaste behavior or mental instability of the past. To balance these concerns, the judge was supposed to review the records, out of the presence of both parties, to determine if there was a legitimate need for them as part of the defendant's constitutional right to a defense. It was called an "in camera" review. If that need outweighed the victim's interest in maintaining her privacy, the records were to be turned over. The procedure, the prosecutors claimed, protected all sides.

I was skeptical. In Paul's trial, the judge had refused to allow any access to the New York records, and when Judge Fine finally ordered their review while the case was on appeal, it was a perfunctory review at best. A judge reviewing such records is rarely an adequate protector of the defendant's rights in general. He could only know the victim's side of the balance. Her interests were clear: don't tell anyone about anything. The defendant's were more complicated. The young woman's bias could stem from a complex entanglement of relationships and feelings about which the judge would know nothing. The judge had to decipher hospital scrawls and put them in a larger context. Judges, good, bad, or indifferent, were not up to this task.

And this was especially so with the trial judge in Paul's case. I was blunt. This trial judge could not possibly have read anything.

He had rejected Andy's request for access to the records during the trial. And when Judge Fine ordered a post-trial in camera review, he was sitting in the county adjacent to the one in which the trial was held and where the records were located. In fact, as of 4:00 p.m. the day before his decision, so the clerk told me, the files were still in Cambridge, Massachusetts, while he was in Dedham, a few towns away. At 9:00 a.m., when I called the Dedham clerk's office, the trial judge had just received Judge Fine's order staying the sentence until he rendered his decision on the record and denied all pending motions on the spot.

I said, "How could that be? You told me he didn't even have the records."

The clerk answered, "I won't comment on that." So much for a careful, in camera judicial review.

On May 1, 1991, the Supreme Judicial Court, to my great surprise, reversed the conviction based on the limitations on cross-examination. Then, anticipating a second trial, the court addressed the psychiatric records issue: all of the complainant's psychiatric and therapy records should be available to the defense—period. There would be no prior judicial review. What's more, defense lawyers no longer had to make any showing to get the records. This decision could easily be interpreted—as many judges did— as saying that psychiatric records would be routinely turned over whether there was a "legitimate need" for them or not. All of us on the defense team were stunned.

The DA agreed not to retry the case. Paul was free. While my former partner, Andy Good, was quoted in the *Globe* as rejoicing, I announced that it was "a step back for rape victims." I was described as "perhaps the first lawyer to complain that she got more than she asked for."

This decision—yet again—created a special rule for women complainants in rape cases. One privilege was totally dismantled, the psychotherapist-patient privilege, with respect to one crime, rape, and one type of victim, a woman. While the decision suggested that such records would be available in all cases, as a practical matter, they were sought only when a woman cries rape. The message was clear. Now defense lawyers would be allowed, without limitation, to fish around in a woman's therapy records. The tactic was an old one, as Susan Estrich said: Prove that the woman "is either 'a nut or a slut' or both."

Two feelings—seemingly contradictory—coexisted in me. I did not regret representing Paul, not for an instant. Nor did I regret my decision to turn down other rape cases. In fact, Paul's case proved my point. Advocacy is unlimited. Once you are enlisted to represent someone, you must do everything you can that is lawful to secure his liberty. You cannot control the outcome, the court's reasoning, the impact on other cases. That's why I wanted to control the first decision—whether to take the case at all.

———

Just what I feared could happen did happen. By the late 1970s, it was very unusual for the Supreme Judicial Court to reverse a rape conviction. The pendulum had indeed shifted. Even weak cases were affirmed. And it appeared especially difficult to claim error concerning the procedure for reviewing psychiatric records—the in camera judicial review—because that approach was in place across the country. The U.S. Supreme Court had affirmed it. What had been different in Paul's case? I believed—perhaps immodestly—that I had made a difference exactly because I could not be caricatured as a rabid criminal defense lawyer, or painted with the Bailey-Rothblatt brush.

The angry demonstrators at the CLUM forum were right. I had hurt the cause. When the issue came up again, I was asked by NOW to write an amicus brief to effect a compromise between the rules before Paul's case and the new rule. I was in the middle of trying a vehicular homicide case on Martha's Vineyard when the brief was due. I stayed up all night to complete it; during the day, I tried (and won) the homicide case.

Less than a week after the brief was filed, NOW was besieged with calls and faxes from rape crisis centers, women's groups, and other feminist attorneys—an orchestrated campaign urging them to withdraw the brief. It was, they said, "too moderate," not sufficiently protective of women. The NOW Legal Defense Fund agreed.

I was then being considered for a judgeship on the federal

bench. The press reported the withdrawal of the brief as if NOW's action had something to do with my application, that somehow I was afraid to come forward on the issue. The *Massachusetts Lawyers Weekly*, in an article headlined "Nancy Withdrew Mystery," published on August 30, 1993, reported that the "usually outspoken Nancy Gertner appears to be lying uncharacteristically low now that she seems headed for a seat on the U.S. District Court."

Laying low? Me? Hardly. I had *volunteered* to remain in this debate. I had never pulled my punches before; I would not do so now. The Supreme Judicial Court, like courts all over the country, continued to debate this issue—how to balance a defendant's rights to defend himself with the privacy of the woman complainant, how to keep from re-victimizing the woman by exposing her private thoughts without jeopardizing the defendant's right to a fair trial.

Over the next fifteen years, the Supreme Judicial Court struggled with the standard for access to a victim's psychiatric records. A measure of the complexity of the issue was how much the pendulum swung back and forth, in case after case, more or less protective of the victim, more or less protective of the defendant. In the most recent decision, in 2006, the Supreme Judicial Court came up with yet another protocol, requiring that before the defense could access privileged records, the lawyer must show that the records are relevant, material, and necessary. And if she did, her access to the records would be pursuant to a court order limiting further disclosure without court approval.

————

What distinguishes our country from others is the value that we place on liberty. As part of that commitment, we prosecute individuals, not categories. The man charged with rape is an individual, not the generic "male capable of raping." The victim is likewise a human being, not a "woman who did not consent."

I have great faith that the criminal justice system is capable of treating individuals as individuals—so long as it has all the facts. Precisely because trials tell stories, because we fight the culture wars in court, the decision makers must have all the information. How does one address the degrading innuendoes of criminal defense lawyers about women, the anachronistic attitudes of jurors, prosecutors, even judges? "Head on" is the answer—in closing arguments to a jury, in public speeches, in op-ed articles.

Obviously, there are limits. Certain arguments are beyond the pale, certain evidence that we as a society have completely rejected because it appeals to racism, or, in the case of rape, it equates lack of chastity with invitation to sexual assault.

But beyond these—where we all agree—there must be room for debate. When I represented Lisa Grimshaw, the goal was to tell everything. What on the surface seemed to be a cold-blooded murder was far more complex when you considered her psyche, what had happened to her at the hands of the "victim," or indeed, during the rest of her life. Some of my sisters in the women's movement wanted rape accusations to be treated differently. Here, we should limit the information that the jury gets, close the spigot.

Rape was different, I agreed in my soul. But the criminal law is different too, the potential loss of liberty especially compelling. Rape is unique, but so is freedom.

I was a feminist and a criminal defense lawyer, a woman's rights advocate, a mother of sons. I understood what advocacy demands, the insular world of the trial lawyer. But I would not ignore the larger issues. I would remain a critic even after I had become an insider.

The rape debate was no longer an abstraction; it was about real people—the women I knew and had represented, Paul, and, ultimately, Stephen and Peter and me.

I saw Paul again in my lobby after I had become a judge. He was, as usual, a sweet and gentle soul. Even though he had been deeply scarred by the prosecution, he was about to marry.

I don't know where the complainant is. I have no doubt that she is in pain, too. She may believe that Paul is responsible for her pain. Perhaps, in a larger sense, he is, even if their encounter had been completely consensual. What is clear to me is that he had committed no crime.

CHAPTER TWELVE

Sexual Harassment Pays;
Sex Discrimination Doesn't

Teresa Contardo's trial, in the fall of 1989, had been my excuse for ducking Paul's case. This was, after all, my specialty—representing a professional woman suing a national brokerage firm for employment discrimination—which was about as far from a rape case as could be imagined. But at the risk of overstatement, I will submit that there were more similarities between the two than met the eye.

Even the judge agreed that the Boston office of Merrill Lynch was like a "locker room," especially in 1972 when its first female broker, Teresa Contardo, began work. There was the usual fare—pornographic pictures left on her desk, conversations laced with sexual innuendoes, a flood of sexist jokes, usually at her expense. But the parties were the most memorable. In the boardroom, during working hours, with management present, the male brokers would celebrate a birthday, a retirement, or whatever, with spouses excluded. Nothing could be wrong with that—workers gathering together, being collegial, lightening up a stressful day. But then a birthday cake would be wheeled in, elaborate, frosted, multicolored . . . in the shape of a gigantic penis. Or entertainment would be ordered—so-called exotic dancers, paid to writhe over the "birthday boy." Management did not deny that these things happened. "No problem," they said, as long as the door to the conference room was closed, so long as nothing was on "public view."

Teresa was not about to complain. She had sued once—to get the job in the first place—and she didn't want to sue again. Merrill Lynch had rejected her when she first applied, no doubt because of her reaction to their written employment test, which included such classic questions as "What qualities appeal to you in a woman?" and "If you have a dispute with your wife, who has the last word?" They relented and finally offered her the job while the case was pending. Once she was on board, the "parties," the pictures, the jokes were minor irritants. She'd show them she could swim with the sharks.

I knew that approach. It was not until the late 1970s that the courts recognized sexual harassment as a form of gender discrimination prohibited by the civil rights laws. Before then, the focus of litigation was on tearing down the obvious signs, or their functional equivalent, that said, "No women need apply." The idea was to prevent the exclusion of women from jobs because of stereotypes about what *most* women could or could not do. If any woman was up to the task—even one—she should be permitted to do it. In theory, it was about equal treatment: women and men who were similarly situated were supposed to be treated the same. In practice, it meant treating women the same as men insofar as they behaved like men.

At this time, the early 1970s, Teresa, like me, *did* behave like a man—to a point. Both young, childless, and very ambitious, Teresa could be a stockbroker; I, a lawyer. We claimed no special advantages or special vulnerabilities. We would put in whatever time the job demanded, day and night if necessary. It's not that we believed that men were so satisfied in the dog-eat-dog world of business or law that we wanted to emulate them. In fact, I remember someone asking in my Yale consciousness-raising group whether sexual equality was going to mean being equally alienated, equally aggressive. But we couldn't begin to talk about transforming the workplace to make it more human—we might say "family-friendly" today—until we had become a full-fledged part of it. We simply accepted the premise that the workplace would reflect the needs of its incumbents, who then were all male. Male humor—read "sexual harassment"—was only the tip of the iceberg.

In 1967, after I had graduated from Barnard, I was working for a well-respected Columbia sociology professor, ten years older than I, who was newly remarried with a baby. I was living at home for the summer before starting graduate school. The professor was slated to testify before Congress on an important issue. I was helping prepare his testimony. One day, he said to me: "Where will you tell your parents that you are staying in D.C., since you'll be staying with me, of course." We had had no relationship whatsoever apart from our professional relationship. I knew of his reputation for "hitting on" Barnard interns, but I had not noticed any overtures to me. I was stunned by how matter-of-fact his tone was, more in the nature of an entitlement than a romantic advance. "No," I stammered, less confidently then I would have wished. He was furious. Suddenly, my work appeared less than adequate to him. I was horrified, but I was not his student, not in his field, not beholden to him in any way. So I could ignore his feelings—or try to; not so for many of his other interns.

In 1979, I was trying a murder case before a well-respected male judge. One time, after the prosecutor had left the judge's chambers and we were alone, he looked up at me from his large desk and told me how much he liked my "build." I smiled as if I was flattered. (Needless to say, I was not.) When a prosecutor in another case said that he would rather chase me around the desk than negotiate with me, I mocked him. "Ooo," I squealed. "When do we start?" He backed off. I was troubled, even angered, by all this, but I was also aware of my power, my ability to control these encounters. By this time, I had my own firm and status in my profession. I could spoof it—and hope to make him feel foolish—or laugh it off. But other women, whom I represented, were not so professionally secure, not so lucky.

In 1989, I sued Browning-Ferris Industries, a large trash company based in Nashville, Tennessee, on behalf of one of their female sales representatives. She reported that a middle manager "joked" with a woman subordinate by standing in her doorway, turning his back to her—and "mooning" her. Another manager gave an employee that he was dating special status and pay, above other, better-qualified employees. My client described the sexualized terms of address whenever the bosses were unhappy with a woman's work—calling her a "cunt" or "bitch." When the women complained, the company responded: "This is a *trash* company, after all!" "Boys will be boys" was the subtext. But it wasn't the sexual harassment that triggered the women's complaints. It was when the "boys" fired all the women dispatchers because they believed that male truckers shouldn't be ordered around by women. The "boys" lost.

In 1990, a coach at a local college regularly flirted with his female students. It wasn't sexual harassment, he claimed. Sexual harassment, he said, only meant "intercourse." Everything else— sexual comments, dating students—was fair game. And of course, there was nothing wrong with his naming the women's soccer teams—"Muffdivers" and "Peckerheads." It was like the 1950s; if you didn't go "all the way," it wasn't a problem. He was disciplined by the college, and then he had the temerity to sue them for violating *his* rights. I represented the college. He lost.

At about the same time, a young Harvard Law School graduate told me about her boss in a Los Angeles entertainment law firm, who required that she attend parties with the "stars" the firm worked with and also insisted that she come to his home to review drafts of contracts. When she did, he would appear in his underwear, beckoning her. When we called other young women who had left the firm after working with this partner, assuming that they would be reluctant to cooperate with us, they said, "What do you want to know about? The sex or the drugs?" The case settled.

But the worst was Susan Tarasckewicz's case. Susan was a baggage handler at Boston's Logan Airport who found sexual graffiti on her locker and endured an unending stream of sexual epithets. While I told her that there are risks to bringing a charge while staying on the job, neither of us had any idea how serious the risks were. She decided to wait. Two months later, she was found dead in her car—the newspapers linking her murder either to her sex discrimination complaints or a wider probe of criminal activities on the job. The murder has never been solved.

———

"This was *not* about sexual harassment," the former Merrill Lynch employee Teresa Contardo insisted. "I realized this is not a perfect world and I just wanted to show them what I could do and be fairly compensated for it." She was from working-class Everett, Massachusetts, not so different from the Lower East Side of Manhattan or Flushing, Queens. She knew what she wanted, she told the judge—a house on the beach, with someone else cleaning it. So she worked six days a week, from 7:45 a.m. until late evening.

In those days, each broker had a "book," a loose-leaf binder with pages listing a customer's accounts. If she worked hard, Teresa thought, she would get the customers, her book would expand, and the commissions would follow. She wouldn't have to "please" the boss—or do more than just please him—to get her due. So long as the playing field was level, so long as the company just counted up the numbers, she could excel.

But the playing field was not level. Ten years into the job, in the mid-1980s, when her production levels were among the highest in the office, Teresa was assigned to share an office with a male broker and what she learned—or perhaps confirmed—was the final coup de grâce.

She knew that she had been excluded from some company outings, where important new customers were entertained. One memo, inviting everyone to the golf outing, for example, was addressed "To all AEs [account executives/brokers] except Teresa." She knew that the company owned Celtics tickets and a box at Sullivan Stadium, then home field of the New England Patriots, to which others—the men—were regularly invited and encouraged to bring clients. She could count on the fingers of one hand—two times—when she was able to offer her customers such coveted perks.

She knew that special investments were offered occasionally to customers who met certain income requirements, requirements that her clients could have met. But then she discovered that there had been many such offers, about which all brokers were supposed to have been notified. Instead, word typically went out to a select few—all male.

And she knew that she had missed out on all the accounts

reassigned from the "book" of retiring brokers. These reassignments provided instant customers, and in the case of retiring senior brokers, usually substantial ones. The office manager, a male, distributed the accounts; there was no discussion, no meeting. Brokers learned about the distribution after the manager took the pages from the retiring broker's "book" of accounts and placed them on the desk of the brokers to which they were reassigned. Whatever the standards, somehow Teresa, and the few other women who joined the office after her, came up short. Men who were familiar with the former broker's customers received preference, but when she knew the customers, she did not get their accounts. Junior men received substantial accounts to help them get a start; when she was junior, she had not been awarded any. High-producing men received substantial accounts to reward them; when her production levels soared, she received nothing.

In 1984, when three brokers resigned, she waited expectantly. On the day of the distribution, she received almost no accounts, and no lucrative ones. And just prior to that, she learned, for the first time, that her male suitemate was receiving substantial additional compensation for being a "product coordinator." She had the same title. She got nothing for it.

That was the last straw. She quit. Penis cakes and exotic dancers did not do it; unequal treatment—clear, job-specific discrimination—did.

———•———

Teresa had been represented by two other lawyers before I entered the case. (She had tried to retain me earlier, but again, I was having babies.) They were moving too slowly for her taste, and so she sought me out, again and again.

Just before the trial started, Anita Diamant, a writer for the *Boston Globe*, started to follow me around for an article in their Sunday magazine. It was to be called "The Defense Never Rests." She was in my classes, in court, in my home. She reviewed my earlier cases, from Saxe to Anzalone, and met the family. She planned to attend the Contardo trial; I wasn't so certain I wanted her to.

On the eve of trial, I was worried. What were the damages? With money apparently the only way our society measures worth, how could we show what she would have earned had she received the same advantages that the men did? How do you quantify access to the Celtics tickets, the golf outing, or the Patriots box? How do you predict the number of high-income customers that she would have had if she had had access to the special investments or the reassigned big customers that Merrill Lynch distributed to the male brokers? How do you measure all the intangible benefits that flowed to the men, not the women, on the job?

The reassignment claim was the key. If we could show that but for discrimination, she would have had x or y share of the retired brokers' accounts, we could measure their value. Statistics would prove it—cold, clear data. But the company's records were abysmal. Teresa's previous lawyers had tried and tried to get access to them. Curiously enough, the only records that were remotely complete were the records of the few women brokers who had tried to steer their "books" to the other women.

The company of course, was well-prepared. It was ready to exploit the deficiencies in record, deficiencies that, we alleged, their inadequate recordkeeping had created.

Two weeks before the trial began, I changed my strategy.

———

We were before Judge Walter Skinner, a judge for whom I had—and have—enormous respect. (Jury trials were not then available in federal employment discrimination cases.) My opponent tried the case that Teresa's previous lawyers had started, the statistical case, the case about the reassignment of accounts. He had extensive charts and elaborate diagrams, impressive testimony sorting out which account went to whom, when, and why. This client asked for this male broker; this one involved special expertise, etc. He had expert statisticians with fancy credentials. And he was exhaustive, leaving no stone unturned. Too exhaustive: at one point, while a witness droned on about account numbers and customers, Judge Skinner, stood up, turned to him, and said, "I have to take a break. You are driving me into a coma."

I told a different story. It was a narrative whose starting point, indeed, its central metaphor, was penis cakes and strippers. My opponent talked numbers. I talked sex.

No, I could not make a statistical case; the reassignment claim was largely anecdotal. Nor could I show the precise amount of income that this or that investment offering would yield. But I could paint a picture, about a cup slowly filling up until it was overflowing, about a thousand small cuts that finally made a mortal wound. It started with that employment test, then the so-called "parties," the numbers of broken promises of equal treatment, through the discovery of each and every advantage accruing only to the men. No, Merrill Lynch did not fire her, but they undermined her until she had to leave. It was a "constructive discharge," in legal parlance.

True, despite the odds, as Merrill Lynch's lawyer took pains to remind the judge, she was paid very well. She was earning a great deal *for a single woman* was the message: what more did she want? Equity was the answer. "I have no choice. I can't stand working here anymore. This is enormously painful. I have to get out," she said.

Judge Skinner agreed. There had been discrimination. In fact, while I called the office "A Tale of Two Cities," one for the men and another for the women, he did one better. It was more like "Great Expectations," or, from Teresa's point of view, "Bleak House." But he denied the constructive discharge claim. "Constructive discharge" involved conditions in which a reasonable person (not a reasonable woman) in the employee's position felt forced to resign because the working conditions were intolerable. And intolerable working conditions somehow did not include "the mere fact of discrimination," as one federal court after another had said. Plaintiffs were not supposed to quit when they believed that they were being discriminated against, let the damages mount while they are unemployed or earning less in another job, and then run to the courts. Rather, they had a duty to "mitigate damages"—in this case, by staying and suing. You somehow had to be prepared to run the risk that an already unwelcome atmosphere would become worse with litigation.

Nonetheless, although Judge Skinner awarded Teresa just $1,

"nominal" damages, for the discrimination, he awarded $250,000 in punitive damages. Reportedly one of the largest punitive damage awards ever handed down in a sex discrimination case, it was a measure of the court's indignation at how blatantly the company had disregarded the law, and in 1986, it amounted to very real money.

We held a press conference at the Boston State House, with Evelyn Murphy, the first woman lieutenant governor, Teresa, and me. The audience was filled with other women stockbrokers, women professionals, activists. The money that the judge had awarded was nowhere near what Teresa had sought, but it had made the point. And she, fully vindicated, went on to have a successful career.

———

When the "men only signs" were taken down from the workplaces, both literally and figuratively, in the 1970s and 1980s, the economic landscape did not change dramatically. Sexual segregation of the workplace continued. Women continued to be channeled into lower-paying, lower-status jobs. To some, it was just a problem of underenforcement of the laws. To others, the persistent patterns suggested limits in the theory of equality. Equality theory failed to recognize real differences between men and women, whether they were biological or socially constructed. When women were not like men—when they got pregnant, when they were the child rearers, when they were sexually harassed—equality theory seemed to validate unequal treatment, often wildly out of proportion to the actual differences. There were silly decisions: discrimination against pregnant women, the Supreme Court said in a 1976 decision, was not gender discrimination; there are, after all, two relevant classes, "pregnant women" and "non-pregnant" persons. While the first group is exclusively female, the second includes members of both sexes. Likewise, some courts in the early 1970s held that sexual harassment was not gender discrimination covered by the civil rights laws. Men can be harassed just as easily as women. The norm was male; women were measured by it. If they deviated from the norm, differential treatment was justified.

When, beginning in 1976, the courts finally acknowledged that sexual harassment was a kind of sex discrimination, it was heralded as an advance, a new and more sophisticated approach to the problem of gender inequality. Women and men were not similarly situated with respect to sexual harassment. Women, generally less powerful than their male bosses, and, given the prevailing norms, sexually and often socially powerless, were uniquely vulnerable. Study after study suggested that when men were the object of sexual overtures, they were flattered. Women in comparable situations were disgusted. To pretend that there was a single equal standard under the circumstances would only exacerbate the harm; "naming" the differences, as Sara Lawrence-Lightfoot suggested in her 1994 book *I've Known Rivers: Lives of Loss and Liberation* (referring to the work of Katie Cannon, a philosopher and theologian) was critical.

My sexual harassment workload tripled after Teresa's case. At the beginning, just a whiff of an accusation was enough to prompt a settlement offer. The "oh shit" letters were successful beyond my wildest dreams. In fact, the cases were a source of substantial revenue for my new firm. Tom, in particular, was determined to invest in these cases, even advertise them as one of "our" specialties. (Harvey, on the other hand, had entirely different concerns; the desire to avoid sexual harassment lawsuits was leading to speech codes in businesses and campuses, which he vilified.)

While sometimes we had problems proving the claim, more often the behavior was blatant. Coworkers would corroborate it, or there would be physical evidence (letters, photographs, or sexist graffiti). Sometimes, the woman just got lucky.

When Jane Smith (not her real name) was working for a large, well-known company, her boss summoned her into his office, ordered her to her knees, and demanded that she perform fellatio. She was horrified. "What are you saying? How dare you?" But her job was not secure, and she desperately needed it. Humiliated and disgusted, fighting back tears, she complied.

I did not know what to believe. It was an astonishing accusation. A prominent male manager, married, with a family, behaving like the lord of the manor, "droit du seigneur," demanding access to the female worker of his choice. This was the ultimate "he said, she said." Still, I gave her the standard advice: if she stayed on the job and complained, the risks were incalculable. Sure, the law was supposed to protect against retaliation, but it was hardly a guarantee. And if she left, she would have to prove "constructive discharge." She would wait.

She called periodically, whenever she believed that she could not take it any longer. We talked. We met for lunch, or I had dinner with her and her husband. I comforted her as much as I could, but my advice was no better than "Don't take these risks unless the odds of success are better." I wasn't at all certain what we were waiting for.

One day, she asked for an appointment with me. There was news. The company was laying off people, and she was among them. Each employee was asked to sign a form, releasing the company from any claims that they might have against it in exchange for severance pay.

Now, there was a different cost-benefit equation. She was about to lose her job in any case. She had little to lose. Don't sign the release, I advised. Just take the money, if they will give it to you. Let's see what happens.

About a week later, I was in New Bedford, taking a deposition in another case—ironically, my first representing an employer against sex discrimination charges. (I had always received calls from employers seeking counsel and listened carefully—there was no categorical rule, just a preference for the plaintiff's side. I was chastened after Paul's case; I no longer believed that one side had the monopoly on truth.)

A secretary interrupted the deposition; I had an emergency call. I excused myself and took the phone. A very prominent management lawyer was on the line. "Nancy," he said, "I have a very important case for you."

"Oh," I said. "Sounds interesting."

"It involves representing a very high-status man accused of sex harassment. Do you do that?"

"Oh, yes," I said, confidently, although I had only started working on "that side." "Tell me more about it to make certain that I don't have a conflict."

"Well," he said, "I think this company official is about to be accused of sex harassment and, just between you and me, I think he did it." Then he named the company—and I told him to stop. It was Jane Smith's. I was representing her, I told him. There was silence on the other end of the phone. The case settled for a substantial sum a few weeks later.

———

This was getting too easy. At a time when courts were applying stricter and stricter standards of proof in the "ordinary" employment case, such as a claim of gender bias in promotion or hiring, when it was getting harder and harder for such claims to even get to trial, sexual harassment law was becoming more and more expansive.

"Harassment" could not have been more vaguely defined. There were no firm rules, no bright lines. The standard was broad, not "Did she consent to the conduct?" or was it "voluntary"—a form of the rape model—but was it "unwelcome." As the Supreme Court said in an early case, *Meritor Savings Bank v. Vinson*, in 1986: "[T]he fact that sex-related conduct was 'voluntary' in the sense that the complainant was not forced to participate against her will is not a defense to a sexual harassment suit. The correct inquiry is whether [the victim] by her conduct indicated that the alleged sexual advances were unwelcome, not whether her actual participation . . . was voluntary." The analysis was contextual: "In some instances, a woman may have the responsibility for telling the man directly that his comments or conduct is unwelcome. In other instances, however, a woman's consistent failure to respond to suggestive comments or gestures may be sufficient to communicate that the man's conduct is unwelcome."

This appreciation of the context, of the significance of socially constructed differences, was apparent nowhere else in discrimination law. Court after court rejected comparable-worth claims—claims that the difference between the wages for a woman's job and

those of a man's job were not justified by the real differences between the two, that the jobs were comparable and should be paid
comparable wages. The only claims that would survive were the
standard "equal pay for equal work" claims, when her job was,
strictly speaking, "equal or substantially equal to" a man's. Not
many jobs qualified, nor did "equal pay for equal work" address
sex-segregated jobs, where women doing similar jobs as men on
a different shift or in a different setting were paid substantially
less. Constructive discharge doctrine stalled, as in Teresa's case.
Women were not able to convince judges that the atmosphere in
the workplace had forced them to leave, except perhaps when alleging sexual harassment. Cases involving higher-level jobs, the
glass-ceiling claims, and the academic-discrimination claims were
made more and more difficult. The procedural requirements—the
time within which you could bring the suit, how carefully the complaint had to be framed—were getting more onerous. Courts were
requiring "direct evidence" of discrimination, the employer who,
like the perpetrator in the old *Perry Mason* series, would finally
break down and announce, "I can't stand it anymore! I fired her
because she was a woman!" Unlikely.

Something was very curious here. The same judges who were
skeptical of employment claims in general endorsed sexual harassment theories with enthusiasm. Legislators from both the right
and the left of the political spectrum, otherwise insensitive to
gender issues, spoke gravely of sexual harassment problems that
women were having. What was wrong with this picture? It was not
a renewed respect for feminism, a more subtle view of its role in
impeding women's participation in the workforce. It was chivalry.
It was as if the legislators and judges were saying: I don't want my
daughter, mother, aunt, or sister exposed to that kind of talk, that
kind of language, that kind of treatment.

Given the narrow focus, there were bound to be unintended
consequences. Susan Estrich, paraphrasing Katie Roiphe, wrote
in *Sex and Power* in 2000 that "feminist law reformers, instead
of making women feel more powerful, have done just the opposite. . . . [R]eformers are responsible for turning [the next] generation into passive victims who would rather march with candles or

file complaints than take responsibility for their lives and stand up for themselves." Janet Halley of Harvard Law School argued that sexual harassment law had changed the social construction of work, changing women's expectations of how they should be treated, creating a generation of women who don't know how to say "Shut up!" or "Stop that."

I saw it too, in the faces of women who wanted me to represent them the minute their boss used profanity in their presence or told an off-color joke. "Did you tell him your feelings?" I would ask. "No," they would say. Law, complaints, and courts were replacing human interaction. Victimhood, as Roiphe described it, had become a permanent feminist tactic.

It was never clear to me what was "cause" and what was "effect"—whether sexual harassment is a symptom of women's lack of progress in the workplace, or its cause; whether when women are subordinated in the workplace, sexual harassment follows, or whether women seen as sexual objects are discriminated against more easily. All that was clear was that the political and legal focus on sexual harassment threatened to obscure all other—perhaps more profound—discrimination issues.

———•———

Teresa's case was over in 1990. By then, she had moved on to what she thought was a more-welcoming atmosphere, at Smith Barney (then Salomon Smith Barney). In 1997, 900 women sued Merrill Lynch in a class action that alleged, among other things, just what Teresa had alleged, discrimination in the distribution of the accounts of departing brokers. But just the year before, a class-action lawsuit was brought against Smith Barney, this time for gender discrimination, paying women lower wages, pregnancy discrimination, and denying leave time for the birth of a child.

Significantly, most of the publicity in the Smith Barney case focused on one claim. In the basement of one office, in Garden City, New York, in 1991, there was a "Boom Boom Room." There, crude talk and Bloody Marys mixed in a garbage can were served beneath a toilet strung from the ceiling. It was a "fraternity house" atmosphere, reported one paper. When a woman complained, she was told, "Sorry, we just don't see anything wrong." It sounded familiar.

Both cases settled in 1999. Two years later, the *Wall Street Journal* reported a demonstration at Merrill Lynch's stockholders meeting. Female brokers marched to protest the company's handling of the settlement process. One riled-up shareholder stood up and said, "I saw these women here last year, and I don't want to see these women here next year."

The penis cakes and Boom-Boom Rooms were gone, but the Smith Barney case came nearly a decade after Teresa's. It was extraordinary that such behavior had been going on at all. Still, at least some women were playing a high-stakes game now—gloves off, taking no prisoners. That was an improvement.

CHAPTER THIRTEEN

Glass Ceilings at the School of Law

In 1991, Bill Clinton announced he was running for president. While I had not been active in politics at all—and surely not presidential politics—Hillary asked if I would help with fund-raising. We had stayed in touch intermittently over the past several years—when she came to Wellesley reunions, at bar conferences, at Yale events when we ran into each other. We shared talk about children, and even political ruminations. I didn't know Bill well or think he had a prayer. Fund-raising was hardly my forte, either. But I agreed to help out as a sign of our friendship and my feelings for her. I started to attend regular fund-raising breakfasts with Hillary and sometimes Bill, and I spoke at pep rallies, a different venue for me. I managed to drum up support in New England, not a shameful showing for a neophyte.

Tom Dwyer couldn't get over it. Here he had labored in the trenches of many political campaigns, and in my first, the man I supported won the presidency of the United States.

Life at home was changing. Stephen was in kindergarten; Peter in preschool, Sarah in college. On their school vacations, we would schlep them everywhere—Hawaii, the Caribbean—active vacations, biking, hiking, and snorkeling, with their middle-aged parents determined not to lose a step. And we spent summers with John's mother, Rachel, in New Hampshire.

John was going on twenty years with the ACLU, loving the work, as passionate as ever. And my life at work continued at the same pace—murder and mayhem, sexual harassment and discrimination, lucrative and not-so-lucrative cases, and now—improbably—presidential politics.

—•—

Introducing me at a panel on sex discrimination in 1990, the moderator said: "While most people should be introduced in terms of the colleges they had attended, or honorary degrees they have amassed, Nancy Gertner should be introduced in terms of the colleges she has sued." They were Harvard (the Sociology and Law departments), Brown (Anthropology, Economics), the University of New Hampshire (English), Dartmouth (Sociology), the University of Massachusetts (Sociology), Tufts (Art History, Physical Education), Northwestern (Sociology), and on and on.

It is not that the universities were the most powerful defendants I had taken on. I had represented women suing law firms and challenging major corporations. Nor were they the most controversial. I had sued the Superior Court of Massachusetts for not assigning me murder cases, then all the judges of the U.S. District Court for Massachusetts for discriminating against a woman clerk, and, later, the Boston School Committee to enforce the employment goals for black faculty in the controversial Boston school desegregation case. Nor was it just that I identified with the plaintiffs. In an especially close fit, for example, I represented women challenging General Electric's maternity leave policy while pregnant with Peter.

But the academic discrimination cases were different. Here, I could track what my life would have been like if I had followed my first instincts, if there had been no Saxe case, no early victories, if I had become a full-time law professor rather than sandwiching part-time teaching into my law practice. These women were me, my models, my friends. What they had experienced I knew—or could well imagine—up close and personal. They were also insiders with outsider consciousness.

I write about these cases, near the end of this book, even though they defined my career from the beginning. I do so because the one that was closest of all to me was the last.

———•———

Clare Dalton was hired as an assistant professor at Harvard Law School on July 1, 1981. It was not an easy time to be at Harvard. A group of junior, untenured faculty, identified with the Critical Legal Studies (CLS) movement, sought to challenge the very premises of legal education—what was taught, how it was taught, and most important, by whom. Identified as leftists, they pressed for the hiring of a more diverse faculty, including those who would share their critical perspective. The law school was so split that one article called it "Beirut on the Charles." Clare was a member of CLS.

Clare was to be considered for tenure in 1984–85, but rather than awarding it at that time, the faculty voted to extend her appointment as an assistant professor for an additional two-year term, in part to give her a chance to finish a scholarly book on Justice Oliver Wendell Holmes. It had been a controversial decision at the time, and some thought it forecast future problems. She finished the book; it was accepted for publication and got extraordinary reviews. Her future at Harvard seemed secure.

The following year, 1985–86, I was a visiting professor at Harvard Law School, my year "off" from practice that I spent awaiting Stephen's arrival. As a visitor, I was affected only indirectly by the faculty's fights. I would overhear faculty members discussing the writings of junior faculty. One might say "brilliant"; another would say "shit." With every word I tried to put on paper, I thought: Where is this on the brilliant-shit continuum?

Clare and I were running into one another constantly. She taught at Harvard when she was pregnant with her second son. I was doing the same thing with my first. She had two sons; in a few years, so would I. Even with its problems, she adored the intellectual give-and-take at the law school, as did I. And her academic life seemed easier to combine with a family than my advocate's. I began to seriously consider—again—leaving practice for academia. We became fast friends.

The next year, 1986–87, Clare came up for tenure review, along with five male candidates. When the year began, the faculty and administration, acutely aware of the split within the school, "clarified" the tenure standards. Concerned that the faculty had imposed far more rigorous standards than ever before in the preceding year, resulting in the rejection of two men, they agreed to return to their "usual" standard, which was "the demonstration of promise of excellence in scholarship by means of substantial scholarly achievement"—whatever that meant. And to keep political divisions within the faculty from affecting the tenure decision-making process, the dean, Jim Vorenberg, and the president of Harvard, Derek Bok, agreed to make "greater use of outside experts' advice" rather than rely entirely on the opinions of its own faculty. In fact, Bok intimated that he would intervene if "divisions within the faculty might unjustifiably block well-qualified candidates from receiving the two thirds vote," a requirement that the faculty had implemented for appointments. In such cases, he would convene an ad hoc committee, apart from the faculty, to help him decide whether the appointment should go through. We were confident that Clare's record would stand up to the new tests.

All five men received tenure; Clare did not. On May 6, 1987, the faculty voted 29–20 in favor of Clare's tenure, falling four votes short of a two thirds majority. When she called, I rushed to her office.

She seemed shell-shocked. I'd seen that expression before. The truth is that it is hard for high-achieving women to believe that they have been discriminated against. They don't rush to claim bias, to blame others for their own inadequacy, as the critics say. They reach that conclusion last, not first. While they might believe that there is discrimination "out there," they are confident that their worth will be recognized, as it has been in the past.

The next day, Clare set up a meeting with friends on the faculty in her Cambridge home. I was a natural participant, both as a lawyer and as a close friend. I knew everyone. Several were part of my reading group from years before. I dropped Stephen off with

John after taking him to "Gymboree," the toddler gym class, and rushed to Clare's.

The conversation was chaotic. Most needed to vent their outrage—How did this happen? Who was responsible?—rather than engage in anything like a lawyerly debriefing. Trying to focus the conversation was, as they say, like "herding cats." It was not at all clear what Clare wanted to do, or what she should do.

On May 28, 1987, seventeen law professors, in an extraordinary move, wrote to the dean criticizing the faculty vote and calling for Bok to review the case. They charged the faculty with gender discrimination that had distorted both the process that the faculty followed and the result that it had reached.

On October 29, 1987, now back in practice, I filed a claim against Harvard Law School for sex discrimination on Clare's behalf with the Massachusetts Commission Against Discrimination (MCAD). It seemed as strong a case of sex discrimination as I had ever seen. She had met each and every requirement for tenure that had been imposed on her. Her work product was exemplary by the standards of nearly all the experts to which it had been submitted, inside and outside of Harvard Law School. When her treatment was compared to that of the men who had received tenure that year, the outcome was even more suspect. No one—not that year, not ever in Harvard's history—had been subject to the kind of scrutiny with which her work was reviewed. And there was direct evidence of sex discrimination, not only against Clare but against other women, too—comments made by the participants before and during the meeting itself.

Finally, Harvard's record of tenuring women faculty was abysmal. Only 10 percent of the faculty were women. Among rejected female candidates in the past were such luminaries as future Supreme Court Justice Ruth Bader Ginsburg and MacArthur "genius grant" recipient Professor Sylvia Law.

———

Academic discrimination is harder to prove than discrimination in any other setting. First, there is the illusion of due process—

a committee structure and reams of documentation—which, from afar, looks like the optimally deliberative process. Determinations are made by a collective. The group, not the individuals within it, comes to a decision, much like a jury in a trial. And the process is supposedly transparent, with written recommendations and committee reports. It is the reverse of decision making on the shop floor, with one boss in control, often making snap judgments, flying by the seat of his pants. Then, there is the illusion of "merit," that academic merit is objective and easily identifiable. And finally, there is the illusion that our legal system—its decision makers, its standards—can deal adequately with sex discrimination even in the rarified setting of the academy.

In fact, the committee structure is no guarantee of fairness. There are leaders and followers, those who feel competent to evaluate the work at hand and those who will defer. When art historian Barbara White sued Tufts for sex discrimination for denying her tenure, Tufts convened a committee that logically included Professor Ivan Galantic, the chair of the Art History Department. But he was the only tenured member of the department and the only one on the committee who knew anything about the subject. The "collective" thus boiled down to one man, and that man was a problem. Long before White's tenure hearing, students had complained about sexist comments that Galantic had made during class. He had, for example, barred women from wearing pants in his class because it was not "ladylike." He had written a letter to the school administration asking for more money to hire a "male" (his word) faculty member, and shortly thereafter, he did. He confessed to Suzanne Butler, the Equal Employment Opportunity Commission (EEOC) investigator, that he believed that there were too many women in fine arts. The EEOC brought suit; I represented White; we won. Tufts was enjoined from discharging her.

Once, when suing the University of New Hampshire on Annette Kolodney's behalf, I questioned a member of Kolodney's tenure committee. Prior to the deposition, I had spoken to his students at length. With their permission, I recounted what the students had said about his sexist attitude and inappropriate comments about their appearance or marital status. He looked up, threw his coffee cup at me (happily, he missed), and stormed out, screaming, "I suppose you will turn all *my* women against me!" With the coffee dripping down the wall, I told the court reporter to make note of the professor's departure and conduct.

My clients insisted that tenure standards were hardly objective. Joan Smith, suing Dartmouth College, came to believe that merit, rather than existing independently, was "conferred" by the institution on the men, but not the women. Men were given more of the research funds, plum teaching assignments, committee credentials, and so on. It was surely easier to do significant research if you have the best labs, the right equipment, and access to funds. It was a variation of Teresa Contardo's travails—the subtle and not-so-subtle advantages granted to males, but not females.

I heard a familiar refrain from my clients: You speak during a common discussion. The remark is ignored, and indeed the conversation continues among the male participants as if nothing had happened. (In fact, Justice Ruth Ginsburg recounted a similar story to Joan Biskupic of *USA Today,* only the conversations that she described occurred during case conferences of the Supreme Court.)

If the words are actually heard, gender colors their evaluation. Between 1975 and 2000, numerous psychological studies confirmed that gender unconsciously affects the way that employers evaluate women's work. In one 1975 study, fictitious summaries of resumes of PhDs in psychology were circulated to heads of psychology departments and asked at what rank they should be hired. Some resumes had women's names and others had men's names. The resumes of the men were ranked at the associate professor level, while the exact same resumes with women's names on them were ranked at the assistant professor level. More recent studies, including one by Jerry Kang of UCLA and Mahzarin Banaji of Harvard, describe how implicit gender and racial prejudice influences supposedly unbiased and objective evaluations of women and minorities. Bias—conscious or unconscious—in fact may not be the best way to characterize the problem. It may be a more fundamental problem of cognition—judging women by a set of stereotypes, a "picture in our head" provided by culture and mass media. Ann Seidman's case was a classic. One participant said simply that he "just couldn't see" Ann as the Henry R. Luce Chair in Comparative Development at Brown (even though she was well qualified for it), any more than he could see himself as biased (even though he was).

One cross-examination was particularly instructive. After demonstrating statistically significant differences between the salaries of men and women faculty at Tufts University, I asked the dean in the White case:

"So . . . if there are differences between the salary of men and women, [they] can be explained either because women are discriminated against or because they are inferior."

"It is not my testimony that they are discriminated against, and it is not my testimony that they are inferior."

True, but he had earlier said that any and all differences derive from "quality of mind."

"What exactly does that mean?" I asked, reminding him of his earlier testimony.

"The strength and intellectual force and ability to be a good scholar," he answered.

Oh, I see.

If the woman is aggressive—or worse, if she professes controversial views—the problem is exacerbated. In a case against Westfield State College, the hearing officer accepted the fact that Professor Marilyn Denny, otherwise qualified, was rejected because of her strong personality. He never examined what that meant, whether it was simply a code for an old gender stereotype. In another of my cases, Dr. Joy Hochstadt, a brilliant scientist, was dismissed from the Worcester Foundation for Experimental Biology in part because she used profanity when she was complaining about gender discrimination in the setting of her salary. We lost. The "bitch" stereotype is always out there, ready to be launched if we go "too far."

All this adds up to what sociologist Virginia Valian calls the "accumulation of advantage and disadvantage" in *Why So Slow? The Advancement of Women*:

[L]like interest on capital, advantages accrue, and . . . like interest on debt, disadvantages also accumulate. Very small differences in treatment can, as they pile up, result in large disparities in salary, promotion, and prestige . . . the disadvantage of not being heard, comments overlooked, the disadvantage of initial impressions, walking into a room, not being seen as a serious professional.

The Tufts salary study tried to quantify the extent of the gender factor. The expert opined that in the late 1970s, it cost a faculty member at Tufts roughly $1,500 a year if she was female. And law schools were not much better. While by the 1990s, women had made significant strides in entering the profession—49 percent of first-year law students and 27 percent of all lawyers were female—in legal academia, women were congregated in lower-ranking, lower-paying, lower-prestige positions.

The problem is that all of this may occur with the best of intentions, by well-meaning faculty who profess to be egalitarian, even feminist.

Perhaps the most crippling illusion of all for my clients was that, notwithstanding the complexity of discrimination, "the law" can address it. "Sue!" everyone said. "Do it for your sisters!"

After a while, I jumped off that bandwagon. I advised most women faculty not to go forward, no matter how strongly I believed that they had been discriminated against. When Title VII, the law dealing with employment discrimination, was applied to universities in 1972, it had little support in the courts. Liberal judges, wed to the idea of academic freedom, were profoundly uncomfortable second-guessing the judgment of professors. Conservative judges were skeptical about gender discrimination laws in general. And there was the problem of competency, or at least the belief that it was a problem: where do judges come off deciding who is qualified in literature, or physics, or math? (To be sure, judges decided equally complex matters, like who violated whose patent, but somehow this seemed different.) When the remedy was tenure—lifetime employment—judges were especially timid. It came as no surprise that the elite institutions—like Harvard— were the last to be challenged.

The cost of litigation was astronomical; the university's resources, compared to the woman's, seemed endless. Each case was bound to take a considerable amount of time. An old friend from Yale, Janet Lever, delayed suing Northwestern to give the internal review processes of the school an opportunity to work, at the advice of the provost. At the eleventh hour, and after Lever spent a considerable amount of money, the university claimed that the time that she spent waiting for that internal review caused her to miss the filing deadline—their complicity notwithstanding. Northwestern won, the court sounding almost relieved that it did not have to deal with the piles of documents.

If the woman actually got her day in court, the legal standards made little sense. Legal precedents tell stories—what Linda Krieger calls the law's "core" stories, with "commonly recognized plots, symbols, themes, and characters." They tell us who wins and who loses, what the paradigms of discrimination are.

The main paradigm for academic discrimination cases derived from the theory of "disparate treatment," that a woman was disadvantaged "because of" her gender. The problem was that there seemed to be two, and only two, "core stories"—someone intentionally discriminated against you because of your gender, or you were not discriminated against at all. Either you found a villain or the law found no problem. The winning scenario implied that if you asked the decision makers why you were denied tenure—and if they were truthful—they would say: "Easy. It's because you are a woman!"

The villain model may have made sense in the 1960s when the law was passed. Bias against women and minorities was blatant then, some of which I recorded in my "Sexist Tidbits" file. Sometimes, even in the 1990s, the villains were clear, like the men in the Tennessee trash company, Browning-Ferris Industries, whose sexual harassment of the women was ignored by the company because "boys will be boys."

In fact, the villain model may have deeper roots. We want to believe that discrimination is just a glitch in the market, a problem caused by a malevolent individual rather than something cultural, institutional, or ingrained. Once the villains have been reformed, the market will be fair. The meritocracy will rule. But if bias is unconscious or built into the governing stereotypes, the discrimination is harder to ascribe to one bad apple, and the law seems to offer no recourse.

How does one prove intentional discrimination? What professor, in his right mind, would openly admit: "I am denying you tenure because you are a woman." What about all the coded expressions, like her writing was "charming," or she is "aggressive." What about comments on her appearance, her marital status, or the length of time it took to get her PhD, when she was busy having a family? Some courts have held that comments like this are not even direct evidence of discrimination. They may or may not connote gender stereotyping. It depends on the context.

Compare the treatment of racist comments. When a boss uses a racial epithet or even a racist generalization, a court is more likely to label it direct evidence of racial discrimination. Anyone who talks like that at any time can be assumed to be biased in his or her employment decisions. There is no concept like "it depends upon the context." While there are exceptions, we know racism when we see it.

The fact is that we are more ambivalent about sex discrimination. Sexist comments are regularly excused as not serious, a casual observation, a "stray remark" unrelated to the job, life, culture, or what have you.

Circumstantial proof of discrimination is somewhat easier to find, but even that model is difficult to apply to academic situations. The court asks three questions to determine if there is enough evidence to proceed to trial, or whether summary judgment should be granted, meaning there will be no jury trial: Does the woman qualify for the job? (The plaintiff must show evidence of this point.) Does the employer have a legitimate, nondiscriminatory reason for denying her the job? (The defendant merely has to "articulate" this.) If the employer does state such a reason, can the plaintiff prove that the reason offered was not the "real reason," that it was a pretext for discrimination? The theory is that the phonier the reason, the more likely it is that the discriminator is hiding an illegal motive.

To be sure, every academic defendant can come up with a credible reason for their candidate's rejection. Some fault can be found with everyone. The proffered reason may even be the "real reason" for the candidate's rejection, but implicitly encode bias.

The critical question is this: is this reason not only true, and supported by the data, but is it applied to similarly situated men? Dawn Hooker, whom I represented, was turned down for tenure at Tufts because she did not have a PhD, a perfectly plausible requirement—except that this was tenure in the *Physical Education* Department! None of the men—the coaches—had a PhD either. (They were "upgrading" the department, they said; employers typically "upgrade" just as a woman comes along.) The testimony would have been funny if there were not real consequences. Hooker won.

——

Despite all of this, and all my reservations, Clare's case seemed as strong as any I had brought. I could tell the "core story" of intentional discrimination, even if I knew that the reality might well be far more complex.

No judge had to worry about second-guessing Harvard professors. After all, a majority of the faculty had voted for her, even though it was not the required two-thirds majority. Her book had been accepted for publication by the two university presses to which it was submitted. Her "outside" file, the evaluations of experts outside Harvard Law School, which was supposed to have been the focus of attention, was exceptional—including scholars in her field (torts and legal history) on both sides of the Atlantic. In fact, the dean described it as the "best outside file" he had ever seen. The evaluation of the outside reviewers was confirmed by the overwhelming number of experts on the Harvard faculty and the opinion of the majority of the appointments committee.

And while it is sometimes difficult to compare a woman to similarly situated men when an institution tenures one or two people every four or five years, in this year, 1986–87, Harvard had given five men tenure despite serious concerns about their productivity, the quality of their scholarship, and their teaching skills. In several cases, members of the faculty who had reservations about the qualifications of one of the five men expressly deferred to the opinions of the outside experts, something they were unwilling to do for Clare. Nor could the differences in treatment be explained entirely by other factors, namely political discrimination. While Clare had been identified with CLS, at least one of the male candidates, possibly two, were also so identified.

And the collective decision-making process dissolved, as it had in the White case and the Kolodney case. A junior faculty member who opposed Clare wrote an eighty-seven-page invective designed to discredit virtually every aspect of Clare's research and analysis. He went so far as to check original sources and pore over volumes of material. His enterprise was characterized by the seventeen faculty members on the committee who charged gender discrimination as "calculated not to reach balanced conclusions as to the worth of Professor Dalton's work but to state the strongest possible case against her accomplishments, devot[ing] untold hours of time and untold quantities of energy to the destruction of the Dalton book." One faculty member described it as a "relentlessly hostile memoranda [*sic*]" which, if it became precedent, "would frustrate any future tenure appointment. Anyone's work could be trashed by a resourceful opponent determined to spend the time doing it." While his critique was rejected by the outside experts, it was accepted by a substantial number of those who opposed Clare, most of whom had no expertise in her field.

It could not be denied that Clare's work had been scrutinized more than any male candidate, a benchmark of discrimination. Unhappy with Clare's overwhelming support by renowned outside reviewers, Clare's opponents kept on digging until they came up with something—anything—disqualifying.

———

Even though we had filed a discrimination complaint before the MCAD, something we had to do before we went directly to court, we still urged Harvard president Derek Bok to review the file. I was optimistic. I knew him from an earlier case. I had consulted with Professor Theda Skocpol, an extremely accomplished and talented sociology professor. When her tenure appointment with the Sociology Department was at risk, Bok seemed to be genuinely concerned about gender discrimination. And within a short time, Theda became a tenured member of the Sociology Department.

Bok finally appointed an ad hoc committee. He selected prestigious senior faculty from Harvard and Yale; Archibald Cox, Loeb University Professor Emeritus and former Solicitor-General of the United States; Judge Robert Keeton of the Federal District Court of Massachusetts; and a former Harvard Law School professor; Anthony Kronman, chair of the Appointments Committee of the Yale Law School; Chief Justice Ellen Peters of the Connecticut Supreme Court and former faculty member at Yale Law School; and Harry Wellington, professor and former dean of the Yale Law School. But they were given Clare's files and only her files, not the files of the men. And they were encouraged to use their own standards—however rigorous they were or how inconsistent they were with the standards that Harvard had applied to the other male tenure candidates. Professor Cox, in fact, said that the standard that he imposed was one from twenty years ago, before faculty quality had "deteriorated."

It seemed unlikely that the former members of the Harvard faculty would reverse their colleagues' vote. It seemed unlikely that members of the Yale faculty would say that a woman apparently rejected for tenure at Harvard would nevertheless qualify at Yale. Indeed, some members had participated in negative decisions involving Clare on other occasions or expressed hostility to the theories which she espoused.

I called this "the intergalactic tenure committee." They were not asked: "Is Clare Dalton qualified for tenure at Harvard Law School based on the standards actually applied at the school, namely to the five other men?" They were asked—in effect—"Is she the best candidate in the universe?"

Still, this committee had complicated Clare's case. The core story now seemed to require that we cast aspersions on these icons of the legal profession and, in the simplistic themes of the court, show them to be discriminators and/or liars.

———

Clare concentrated on rebuilding her life. She got a tenured appointment at Northeastern University Law School. She urged me to put the case on hold until she could decide what she wanted to do. No depositions, no investigations. We asked the MCAD to defer its investigation. The case was effectively frozen at the preliminary stage.

I pursued my other cases and my new political interests. Clare, her husband, Robert Reich, and I ran into one another at Clinton events. Reich had been a roommate of Bill's at Oxford, where they both went before Yale Law School. We appeared on TV talk shows as FOH's or FOB's (friends of Hillary's or of Bill's). In April 1992, I held a reception for Hillary at my Brookline home, inviting clients, friends, and colleagues. (The boys shook her hand, although Peter had his wrist in a cast. When Hillary asked how he hurt it, he announced loudly: "My mother broke it!" Terrific. An accusation of child abuse. In fact, I had grabbed his wrist when he fell from the tightrope that he decided to walk on.) Clare's file was put away.

———

Four years later, out of the blue, on May 21, 1992, Clare received word that the MCAD had referred her case to the Cambridge Human Rights Commission. The MCAD had a work-sharing agreement with the CHRC. If the CHRC found probable cause to believe that there was discrimination, the MCAD would give its findings "substantial weight." She was asked if she wanted to pursue the case.

"Of course," she said.

Harvard had never answered the complaint before the case was deferred. And when they did in 1992, all they said was: "Harvard's position is that it did not discriminate against Ms. Dalton on the basis of gender." Period. I wrote a lengthy rebuttal.

The CHRC found probable cause, adopting each and every one of the statements that we had made. The MCAD adopted the CHRC's findings. Now the agency would try to conciliate—settle—the complaint or, failing that, proceed to a public hearing.

No settlement was possible. Clare was ready.

Harvard's first tack was to try to nullify the faculty's decision. Everything that had happened before the Harvard faculty that year—the five men who had received tenure, the eighty-six-page diatribe, the comments of the faculty—was somehow irrelevant to the proceedings. Harvard claimed that it all had been superseded by the "intergalactic" tenure committee's actions and Bok's review.

We took depositions of Bok's committee. Harvard was represented by an extraordinary and accomplished woman lawyer, Joan Lukey of Hale and Dorr. Generally, when one deposes witnesses from the "other side," the witnesses are either neutral or overtly hostile, like the professor who threw his coffee cup at me. This was different. The depositions were eminently cordial. In fact, I had an easier time than Joan. Ironically, I was in the "old boy network" in a sense, meeting with my former professors at Yale or current colleagues at Harvard. Joan, a graduate of Boston College Law School, was not.

I believed we could still show that Bok's review, rather than wiping out the discrimination, exacerbated it, imposing an even higher standard on Clare—one that was not remotely applied to the men.

———

While Harvard had rejected Justice Ginsburg, Professor Sylvia Law, and others, by the time of the CHRC proceeding, it had offered tenure to Professor Martha Minow and Professor Susan Estrich, extraordinarily brilliant scholars. Because 1987 was the second time that Clare came up for tenure while others in her class had already been reviewed, they claimed that it was not appropriate to look at a single academic year, 1986–87. If we looked at the class of people who started with her, two of the women (Minow and Estrich) were tenured, and one man was denied. See, they were saying, some women made it—feminists to boot! How bad could we be?

But the Minow and Estrich cases were not relevant, we countered. After all, Harvard had made a great ceremony of reevaluating the rules for tenure for the 1986–87 year. It was entirely reasonable to look at men reviewed by the very same decision makers—the 1986–87 faculty—and by the very same standards.

As always, I wanted the "smoking gun," the testimony of faculty members about inappropriate comments during the tenure proceeding, the functional equivalent of Galantic's old-world attitudes toward women. Harvard tried to block my conducting further interviews of the faculty without their counsel attending, but the CHRC permitted it.

The disaffected faculty members (and there were quite a few of those) were hardly reticent. There were rumors that the faculty members who opposed Clare decided not to attend the tenure hearings of the male candidates; they made sure to attend just hers. One told a colleague that he did not attend the meetings involving certain male candidates to avoid taking inconsistent positions with respect to Clare. At least one faculty member who criticized Clare's work admitted to me that the work of some of the male candidates was "trivial" and "inconsequential." Certain professors, it appeared, always voted against women candidates. One professor told me that he thought that some of those who had opposed Clare were behaving like "spurned lovers." These kinds of comments, though troubling, surely, were not at all conclusive, and some were not even admissible.

And I knew that this was not the whole picture. The "core" story, the villain model, was not adequate. Clare understood this as well. In an article that she wrote for the *Boston Globe,* she drew a composite profile of her opponents. The dissenter to Clare's tenure, in this profile, had no women or few women in his law school classes and surely had not had any as teachers. His experiences of women were derived from his experiences with his wife, daughter, mother, and secretary, "having to do with their taking care of him, and making him feel good about himself." This woman colleague, Clare Dalton, "isn't like anyone else in his life." Nothing about her work makes him feel good about himself. She refers to authors that he never read and is critical of the men that he admires. When they served together on a committee, she wasn't a "good listener." When she came up for promotion, she "carried a high burden of proof." It wasn't his field. Two of the six reviewers were women, and one woman was so enthusiastic about Clare that he felt he had to ignore her because women stick together. On the other hand, the other woman, who was lukewarm, he was inclined to respect. When, shortly before the vote, that junior faculty member wrote an eighty-six-page memo, even though this wasn't the junior faculty member's field either, he felt "that [the junior faculty member] was helping him clarify and articulate his own doubts."

Bob, Clare's husband, was characteristically more direct in a piece he wrote for the *Boston Globe*:

> She had not played at being a good daughter to the older and more traditional men on the faculty, giggling at their jokes and massaging their egos. Nor had she pretended to be one of them, speaking loudly and talking tough. They had no category for her, and to that extent she had threatened them, made them uncomfortable. So that when it came time for them to try to see the world from her perspective, they chose not to.

———

By the time the hearing was set to begin, it was 1993. Six years had passed. Everyone had "moved on."

I had just recently arrived at Dwyer, Collora, & Gertner, and I wasn't not at all sure how full-scale war against Harvard would be funded, by whom, and how much of a "hit" my new firm was prepared to take. I just pressed on, assuming that I would somehow figure this out if I had to.

Harvard had changed, too. The five male candidates were now colleagues. A relative calm had settled over the law school. Whether or not it was true that they had received tenure with equivalent or weaker portfolios than Clare Dalton, it was far more difficult to attack them than before. The delay had taken the edge off the case. I was not so certain about the smoking gun.

For Harvard, the prospect of rehashing the "Beirut" years, as the newspapers had labeled them, was disconcerting. Thirty or forty witnesses were on each witness list—nearly every faculty member and administrative officer at Harvard Law, in addition to distinguished scholars. The MCAD was not a court and was not bound by traditional evidentiary rules. Whatever the outcome in Clare's case, there would be an airing of dirty linen like none before.

On the eve of trial, Joan Lukey and I met at the Charles Hotel to try to mediate the claim. The Charles is a posh hotel in the middle of Harvard Square. The mediator was another woman, now a distinguished federal district court judge. Clare was there as well; Harvard's general counsel, Margaret Marshall, later the Chief Justice on the Supreme Judicial Court, was a phone call away. Consider this scene, now over twenty years from where I started: all women—lawyers, mediators, clients. We labored for nearly eight hours.

Finally, Harvard agreed to pay $260,000 to the domestic violence program at Northeastern, which Clare had founded in 1990 and still ran. She would be paid as the executive director from the budget of the new Domestic Violence Institute. Harvard admitted no fault.

The settlement was unusual and innovative, but more importantly, it granted legitimacy to Clare's pain. Because there was no gag order, on September 21, 1993, we issued a press release:

> The Harvard Law School and Northeastern University School of Law announced today joint sponsorship of a newly formed Domestic Violence Institute. The Institute, conceived by Professor Clare Dalton of Northeastern University School of Law, was agreed to in connection with the settlement of a lawsuit filed by Professor Dalton against Harvard Law School for gender discrimination. The Institute will significantly expand the work of the domestic violence clinic established at Northeastern University School of Law by Professor Dalton in 1990.

Clare told the Associated Press: "This is a price that Harvard is paying for gender discrimination. Harvard's money is being put into resources for women who suffer the most egregious form of gender discrimination." Clare called the settlement a "vindication," noting that it "gives me the professional opportunities that mean the most to me at this time in my career." The papers cited my pre-hearing documents, that there was an "institutional history of discrimination against women faculty." One professor characterized this as the "first breach in the wall of silence which surrounds the sexist employment practices at America's elite schools."

Harvard was furious. No, there had been no gag order, they complained, but surely there had been a gentlemen's agreement— that we would keep away from the press. Somehow, I had missed that. Pressed to respond, the law school said that the settlement was "forward-looking," "wonderful," "good for the community"— and had been hotly contested.

As usual, I was ambivalent about giving up the fight. Clare's tenure denial had reverberated in the academic world, read by some women as a warning not to engage in provocative work.

But she was my dear friend and better rid of all of this. Discrimination law and litigation was a square peg in a round hole for the women who needed it most. It didn't fit the complexity of bias, especially not in the academy. The costs were extraordinary, personal, and financial. The "law cure" that seemed to have worked so well in my other cases was far less satisfying here, and was becoming less and less effective over time. It was as if with respect to gender—and even race—the courts simply wanted to believe that the war was over, or if it were not, that legal tools were not the way to end it. I was not so sure.

Still, it was better to end the case; we—Clare and I—were both distracted and ready to move on.

Many years later, I was in Budapest giving a lecture. A Jewish student in my class asked me to dinner at her house. In her parents' backyard, I asked how it felt to be Jewish in a post-communist Hungary. Her mother quickly told me to keep my voice down— the neighbors did not "know." I was appalled. And when we went inside the stuffy apartment, we fought. Her parents kept money and an extra passport under their beds, believing that their neighbors' hatred of Jews would never change, that one day they would have to flee again; the law could never change people's attitudes or meaningfully affect their behavior. I could not have disagreed more. Although not as much as I had wanted, or as fast, I had seen great changes in this country brought about by law, statutes, cases, trials. It was what I had spent my life doing.

———•———

Bill Clinton had just become president. Bob Reich, like many of my Yale colleagues, had joined the administration as secretary of labor. Clare was taking a leave from Northeastern and, with her two teenage sons, moving to D.C. As for me, I was restless. Clare's case cured me of my academic temptations. Hillary's old offer—Come to Washington!—beckoned. But I couldn't do much about it. I was in the middle of a very celebrated case that had begun with a brutal murder in 1989. A celebrated murder case following a celebrated discrimination case, an old—if odd—pattern.

CHAPTER FOURTEEN

Murder and Racism

I was litigating Clare's case at the same time as I was representing the brother of Charles Stuart, the man who had killed his pregnant wife in what nearly every article described as "a crime that shocked the nation."

On October 23, 1989, Carol DiMaiti Stuart, eight months pregnant, was fatally shot, and her husband, Charles ("Chuck") Stuart, was badly wounded. It was 8:43 p.m. They were returning from a birthing class at the Brigham and Women's Hospital, joyously anticipating the arrival of their first child. Or so it seemed.

Chuck called the police on his cell phone. The 911 tapes were later replayed over and over again:

"My wife's been shot. I've been shot."

"Where is this, sir?"

"I have no idea. I was just coming from Tremont, Brigham and Women's Hospital."

"Where are you now, sir, can you indicate to me?"

"No, I don't know. I don't know. We drove, he made us go to an abandoned area. . . ."

"Okay. Has your wife been shot as well?"

"Yes, in the head. . . . Yeah. I ducked down. . . ." Chuck said, taking pains to explain, even to the 911 dispatcher, why he was only wounded while she was killed.

Chuck faded in and out of consciousness, all the while leaving the phone on. The dispatcher heard sirens; the police must be close. By 9:00 p.m., a Boston cruiser spotted Stuart's car parked adjacent to the curb on St. Alphonsus Street near McGreevey Way.

"It was a black man," Chuck told the officer. The man had asked for directions when they were stopped at a traffic light. Then he had forced himself into the back seat. He had told Chuck not to turn around, not even to look in the rear-view mirror. And then, in the dark, Chuck drove to where the man directed. The man demanded their watches, Carol's wedding ring, Chuck's money. Then, shouting, "I know you are 5–0, fuck 5–0," the slang for police officers, he shot Carol in the head, Chuck in the stomach.

Carol was pronounced dead shortly afterwards. Baby Christopher died seventeen days later.

The *Boston Globe* and *Boston Herald* the next day, the next week, and, indeed, months afterwards, told and retold the story: A photograph taken through the Toyota's windshield showed Carol crumpled against the steering wheel, her hair matted with blood. Headlines screamed the far-too-familiar story of urban crime. A total of 800 people attended Carol's funeral Mass, held in the same church in which she had married Chuck a few years before. Politician after politician called for the law enforcement version of a full court press.

As Sean Flynn, a *Globe* reporter, wrote:

So the police pursued three basic investigatory trails. The first was to race after every report of a black man with a gun, as two dozen officers did on the afternoon of October 24 when someone saw two men in Roxbury with a pistol. Wrong caliber. Wrong guys. The second was begging for help, pleading with the public to come forward with any scrap of information. And the third was more primitive: harass the bejeezus out of every known hoodlum, and some not known, until one of them finally gives up the shooter.

Countless black men between the ages of fifteen and sixty-five were stopped, searched, and questioned—often at gunpoint. Many of them claimed that they had been intimidated by the mainly white police officers, coerced to inform on their neighbors, some jailed on technicalities and squeezed to give false information. Despite outcries from the black community, the police did not relent until a black suspect, Willie Bennett, was arrested.

Then, on January 3, 1990, three months after the shooting, Matthew Stuart, seemingly out of the blue, implicated his older brother, Chuck, in Carol's murder. Believing that he had been granted immunity from prosecution, Matthew told the police what he knew: although they had been estranged for some time, Chuck asked for Matthew's help, first to stage a fake break-in at the DiMaiti-Stuart's Reading home, but when that failed, a phony street robbery. Chuck, Matthew said, would make some sort of "claim" based on the property taken from his car; he would pay Matthew for his trouble out of the insurance.

On the night of the shooting, Matthew met Chuck in Mission Hill. He borrowed a friend's car. The plan was for him to retrieve Chuck's property in a bag, return home, and then dispose of it. It was dark. Matthew was not wearing his glasses. The encounter took no more than twenty or twenty-five seconds. He pulled alongside his brother's blue Toyota on Gurney Street, the passenger side of Matthew's car beside the driver's side of Chuck's car. While the scene was strange, Matthew did not think twice about it. It must be some kind of insurance scam, he thought, but because it was Chuck, he didn't ask any questions. Chuck was his older brother (Chuck was twenty-nine; Matthew, twenty-six) and ostensibly the family success story. He was married, had a promising job at Kakas Furs earning over $100,000 a year, and was expecting a child. Matthew was the youngest of six, still living at home, drifting, purposeless.

When he got home, Matthew was curious. He looked in the bag and was shocked to find a gun, along with Carol's wedding ring and other personal effects. He had not seen Carol in Chuck's car. Nor had Chuck mentioned a gun. Leaving the bag in his room, Matthew went to return his friend's car.

When Matthew came back, his family was in an uproar. Chuck and Carol had been shot. Matthew left for the home of his best friend, Jack McMahon, and after telling Jack everything he knew, the two returned to Matthew's house. They examined the bag and decided to throw it over the bridge into the Pines River in Revere. Except for Carol's wedding ring. If Carol died, they thought, Chuck might want it for sentimental purposes. They hid it in McMahon's attic.

It was not until the eleven o'clock news that night that Matthew put it all together. Not only had Chuck and Carol been shot, but Chuck was claiming that an unknown black man had robbed the Stuarts of the very items that Chuck had tossed to Matthew. Jack and Matthew were convinced that Chuck was the murderer.

By November 1989, the papers reported that Chuck had identified Willie Bennett as the perpetrator. Bennett was a black man, an ex-con, twice before sent to state prison. Matthew decided to go to the police. On January 3, 1990, he gave a statement implicating his brother. Divers found the bag with the gun in the river where Matthew told them it would be. McMahon retrieved Carol's wedding ring. One day later, Chuck Stuart jumped to his death off the Tobin Bridge that spans Boston Harbor.

The media were relentless, asking one question over and over again: "Will we ever know the real story?" Funny. When the assailant was supposed to be a black man, about whom the public knew next to nothing, when he was vaguely described by a white man who had caught only the barest glimpse of him in a dark car, the public thought they had all the answers. A black man? Of course. From Mission Hill—the racially mixed part of town? Naturally. No further explanation was needed.

But when the likely assailant was the husband in a not-so-unusual story of domestic violence, when they had Matthew's account, even physical evidence, and Chuck's suicide, the press asked, "Will we ever know the real story?"

It was all about race, with the public and the media filling in the gaps in the stories with stereotypes and a criminal justice system lurching first in one direction and then another.

After Carol Stuart's murder, residents of the Mission Hill area were enraged. My husband, John, whose work focused on civil rights litigation involving police, was meeting with community leaders to fashion a response. And their rage doubled when Matthew came forward. Two things were now clear: Chuck was the killer, and he had callously exploited the city's racism.

Two weeks after Chuck's death, Matthew Stuart had called, asking for me. Even though he had come forward to give an account of his brother's crime, he was now facing charges of insurance fraud. He had been referred by, among others, Alan Dershowitz, a friend of ours. In many ways, the case was irresistible—the city was up in arms about the Stuarts; there was every reason to believe that in the frenzy of the moment, truth, let alone justice, would be abandoned. Matthew was being pilloried in the press despite his voluntary cooperation. In some ways, in fact, it felt like the Saxe case: What would it take to make the system fair? How much work would it take to keep the wheels of justice from grinding him up and making him pay for his brother's sins?

The problem was John. So deeply had this case polarized the African American community that I feared that his relationship with his black clients would be undermined by my representation of Matthew. He talked to his clients and his colleagues, and true to form, encouraged me to take the case.

———•———

In a closing argument in a murder case I was handling shortly before the Stuart trial was to start, I compared the government's case to one of Stephen and Peter's dot games. I told the jury that each piece of evidence from the government was one dot. And I put each dot on a blackboard. And like the child's game, after you connected all the dots, a picture was supposed to emerge. The government said it was a picture of the defendant. But it was not. All sorts of dots—pieces of evidence—were left out. In fact, if there was any face that came close to tying all the dots together—and even that was vague—it was the face of another man; in this case, the slain woman's son.

But I feared that rational argument—what the evidence was, what the appropriate inferences were—wasn't enough. My client was Travis Burch, a young black man accused of murdering his white neighbor, Judy Bell. I feared that the jury would fill in the gaps in the evidence, not with data, but with their stereotypes. "Don't connect the dots with your biases," I said. "Don't say, 'Travis Burch *must have* done it, I can believe it of him—people *like* him'— even though the dots don't line up. If there are gaps here, holes in the picture, then the government has not proved its case." Racial generalizations, in short, are not evidence.

No one accused me of playing "the race card," as O. J. Simpson's lawyers had been accused of doing, although what I did was not demonstrably different. Like O. J.'s legal team, I tried to warn the jury that the prosecution would appeal to their deeply in-grained racial biases to make them find Travis guilty. Trial narratives frequently, if not indirectly, play the race card just as they play the gender card, the "fine upstanding citizen" card, the "woman victimized by husband" card, the "How could someone who looks like this do this crime?" card. Because trials cannot tell the entire story of a complex reality, lawyers use shorthand expressions, the popular, one-dimensional images. The best example was the trial of the white officers accused of beating Rodney King in Los Angeles. The videotaped beating of a black man at the hands of these officers could not be expunged; the jury would see that with their own eyes. But what the jury also heard and believed was what the officers said had happened before, out of the view of the cameras. They painted a picture of a hulking, "out-of-control" black man, a picture informed by their stereotypes. "Yes," the jury must have said. "We can believe that of Rodney King." If King were white, a woman, or an old man, they would probably not have believed that testimony so quickly—if at all.

While waiting for the Stuart case to be heard, I watched a young woman lawyer who was representing a young black man. The judge was a woman about my age. She had in front of her the probation record that represented the man's criminal history, but the paper was largely blank. It had only his name, race, and address. The judge looked up at the young black man and said, "I don't believe this. Mr. X, I don't believe you don't have a record." She knew nothing about this man except the color of his skin, where he lived, and what he was charged with. She turned to the lawyer and said, "I want you to put your client on the stand so he can swear that he doesn't have a record." And the lawyer did.

———

In the literature on racism and the police, the Carol Stuart investigation will be Exhibit A. Stereotypes, perhaps unconscious, affected how the police "connected the dots"—which leads they accepted and which they rejected, when they were satisfied they had "cracked" the case.

They started with Chuck's story, not just because it was the victim's account but also because it "fit"—black-on-white crime, even the gratuitous shooting of a pregnant woman. There were other credible theories, to be sure—a husband killing a wife was one, especially when she was pregnant. In fact, Chuck's story was the less probable one; most crime is not interracial; victims of African American crime are more likely to be African American. And some of the facts were strained: as Ralph Martin, soon-to-be DA of Suffolk County, said when he read a transcript of the 911 tapes: "[Stuart] ducked? How in the hell do you duck in a Toyota?"

When Willie Bennett's name was mentioned in two "hotline" calls to the Boston Police Department, it too seemed to "fit." One detective noted that he "had a criminal record consisting of shooting police and civilians, indicating that he was capable of the crime of shooting and robbing Carol Stuart." Fill in the dots: from what we know of him, his background, or worse, his "profile," we can believe that he committed this abomination.

The day after the murder, Willie Bennett's fifteen-year-old nephew, Joey "Toot" Bennett, bragged about his uncle's violent exploits to a group of his friends. When someone in the room added the Stuart murder to the list, Toot giggled and said "yes." Like the child's game of telephone, the ramblings of a fifteen-year-old somehow turned into "evidence" against Willie Bennett; the account of the conversation kept changing as it was retold. There were various versions—that Toot recounted details of the crime (the "don't look in the rear-view-mirror comment," the "5–0 remark"), that Toot showed the group the murder weapon, and even credit cards that belonged to the Stuarts, that Willie himself came in and reenacted the crime to the assembled group of teenagers.

A joint task force of the U.S. Attorney's Office and the FBI convened after Chuck's suicide and concluded in a fifty-four-page report that there had been coercion and intimidation of civilian witnesses, particularly two, Erick Whitney and Derek Jackson, who were allegedly present when Toot made the incriminating comment.

———

At the scene, going in and out of consciousness and in considerable pain, Chuck could muster only a few details: the assailant was a black male, in his thirties, wearing a black running suit with red stripes and a black baseball hat. That made sense. Chuck had only a brief glimpse of the assailant, at eight thirty at night, or maybe, when he cast a furtive glance in the rear-view mirror of the darkened car.

Three days later in the hospital, however, he did better, much better: "brown-skinned, about 5'10", 150/160 pounds, short Afro, twenty-eight to thirty-four years old, thin build, splotchy facial hair." Then he repeated the description of the assailant's clothes—"black baseball cap, black jogging jacket with two or three red stripes running down the sleeves," but added "black driving gloves with the knuckles exposed, dark colored shirt under the jacket, a raspy voice."

On November 16, 1989, over a month later, he improved still more. He picked out two photographs from a photo array, saying "That's the best one so far." The suspect, he said, was "a little thinner and was a little bit lighter in skin coloring" than that best picture. And, he added, "I didn't realize that his nose was so broad." The officer taking all of this down reported that when he saw the photo of Willie Bennett, Stuart "started to breathe heavy [*sic*] and trembled."

But the virtuoso performance was on December 28, 1989. Chuck was presented a lineup that included Willie Bennett, whose photo had been shown to him earlier. (The other man whose photo he had picked out was not included.) Chuck knew that there was a suspect in the mix.

After lengthy commentary, Chuck was "99 percent sure . . ." that Bennett was the man.

Word on the street had been that it was Bennett, and now Chuck confirmed it.

But there was also "word on the street" that the police had it all wrong—indeed, pretty reliable, detailed "word"—that Chuck had killed Carol. The problem was that this was from a different street, in a different neighborhood, and no one was paying attention.

During the fall of 1990, when the police were pounding the two or three people who claimed to have heard Bennett confess, perhaps twenty people had already heard Matthew's suspicions, friends and siblings alike. But the police did nothing.

There was Jack McMahon, whom Matthew had told the evening of the crime. The next day, Matthew told his girlfriend, Janet Monteforte. They visited Matthew Stuart's uncle, a lawyer named Ronald Corbett (although both Matthew and Jack were rather drunk and not particularly coherent). Then Matthew told his brother Michael, and McMahon told Donna Rosa, his girlfriend, his mother, his father, his father's girlfriend, his brother, and his brother's girlfriend. By mid-December, Janet's parents knew, and then Maria Stuart, Michael's wife, found out, and, by the first of the year, Mark Stuart and Shelley Yandolfi, two more Stuart siblings, and Shelley's husband learned about it, too. On the day before he came forward with his own lawyer, Matthew even told Chuck's lawyer, Jack Dawley.

And beyond the information that the police "should have known" had they probed and prodded the people in Revere in the same way they had the community in Mission Hill, there were facts that the police did know.

On Labor Day, in 1989, a month before the offense, David Frank McLean, a friend of Chuck's, and McLean's wife got together with Chuck and Carol. Chuck said that he wanted to talk to McLean about something, and wanted David to call him on the following Tuesday at work. Then "he started telling [McLean] about [*sic*] that he wanted to have someone killed." Chuck wanted to know if McLean had any connections, people who could do this. McLean said he did not. Chuck called McLean that Tuesday, following up the earlier conversation.

And, on the following Friday, Chuck disclosed why: his wife was pregnant, he said, but he did not want to have children. He was at a point in his life where he wanted to invest in something, but children put everything "on the back burner." And then, Chuck reported, he saw something in her an attitude that he had never seen, that she had the upper hand in the relationship. That's when he told McLean that he wanted to kill her. In fact, he kept on calling every couple of days, even asking if McLean could help him get a gun.

At Carol's funeral, McLean told his brother Dennis what Chuck had said before the shooting. Dennis told John Carlson, a friend of the family. Carlson suggested that they call a state trooper named Danny Grimbowski. Calling Grimbowski first, Carlson told him that Chuck killed his wife.

The McLean brothers and Carlson never heard anything more from the state police.

In November 1989, Carlson called his brother-in-law, Philip Scarpaci, a Metropolitan Police officer stationed in Clinton, Massachusetts. He told Scarpaci that "Willie Bennett did not do it, and that he had information that Charles Stuart had done it." He then went on to relate David McLean's account about being approached before the shooting.

Scarpaci said, "I contacted my detectives, explained what was going on, and then I contacted the Boston Police Department, Homicide, Detective Robert Ahearn. He returned the call, and I explained to him what was going on and what happened and what was told to me. And Detective Ahearn had taken it from there in going forward."

Ahearn, who had been present during the interrogation of Eric Whitney in November 1989, when Whitney tried to retract incriminating statements about Bennett, somehow had trouble setting up a meeting with David McLean. He claimed that McLean "just didn't seem to want to open up, and suggested that the possibility was that he was frightened or something along there."

No one tried to interview McLean over and over again, as they had done with Whitney and Jackson. No one harassed McLean's friends and associates. While a fifteen-year-old boy bragging about his supposedly violent uncle was followed up with a vengeance, a husband's comments about killing his wife the month before her death—to a friend, no less, who had no reason to lie—were ignored. While they would not take "no" for an answer with Whitney or Jackson, with McLean the matter was just dropped.

A grand juror summed it up: "When this was all in the paper and we were looking at Willie Bennett, didn't anybody think that someone should do something? I mean, the people that really thought they knew something, that something should have been done at that point, or get in touch with this office, or letting all these people think this up until the last minute? . . . I mean, we were ready to indict a man." He added, "I mean, but nobody was even looking at Charles."

It may well be that no one was out to "get" Willie Bennett or any other particular suspect. It may well be that there was no official policy to degrade and demean an entire neighborhood, as the Mission Hill community believed. It may well be that the officers assumed that the witnesses were equivocating or changing their stories because Bennett had threatened them or because of their relationship to Bennett. Maybe they simply couldn't believe that the early reports—that the black man with the bad reputation did the deed, which of course made sense—were in fact wrong.

———

I want to say that once Chuck died, the pendulum swung in the other direction, now subjecting the Stuart family and their community to merciless scrutiny. That is not entirely true, although Matthew did bear the brunt of the redirected wrath of the people and the press. Bennett was exonerated of the murder but punished for everything else he had ever done. In October 1990, ten months after Charles Stuart's suicide, he was sentenced to a twelve-to-twenty-five-year term for robbery, an offense wholly unrelated to the Stuart murder.

Although Matthew was a first offender, and had ultimately

solved the crime for the police to boot, he was vilified. Much of the moral outrage initially directed at his brother when the truth came out was transferred to him. For sure, he had not covered himself with glory. But it had been difficult for him to turn on his brother, to be responsible for his prosecution. In fact, Massachusetts law did not require relatives to turn in their kin. A man could not be charged with being an accessory after the fact of murder for acts covering up his brother's crime.

So the government investigated him for months, seeking a murder indictment. Every family member, every friend, everyone overlooked before January 3, 1990, was brought before the grand jury. This was the investigation that they had neglected before.

Still, the police believed they were not getting the "whole story." They subpoenaed Jack Dawley, who had represented Chuck. Dawley testified that after he met with Matthew in January 1990 and learned the outlines of Matthew's story, he wanted to stop his representation of Chuck. He met Chuck the next day; he may well be one of the last to talk to him before he committed suicide. But Dawley would not disclose his privileged communications with Chuck Stuart, even though Chuck was dead.

Dorothy, Chuck's mother, was the executor of Chuck's estate. She had authority to waive Chuck's attorney-client privilege, to allow Dawley to testify to the content of that last conversation with her oldest son; but she refused to do so. The prosecutors were furious at her. Rights and privileges are so damned inefficient. It would be so much easier just to ask the lawyer of a dead person what the client had said, just as it is easier to break down doors, threaten witnesses, or plant evidence.

The grand jury transcript of Ms. Stuart's testimony was extraordinary, hardly the usual dispassionate proceedings. The assistant DA, Francis O'Meara, repeated over and over again that Ms. Stuart had the right to disregard the advice of her own counsel, which had been to assert Charles Stuart's attorney-client privilege. Then, denigrating that advice, he suggested that there was "something improper, if not decidedly immoral, about invoking the privilege in this case." The grand jurors followed his lead, deriding Ms. Stuart. She was wrong to try to protect her son Matthew. And they badgered her, asking the same questions over and over again. The prosecutor did not stop them.

The prosecutor went to the courts. There was, he claimed, a public interest exception to the attorney-client privilege. I opposed. Candidly, this was in Matthew's interest. I knew nothing about the Dawley–Chuck Stuart conversation. All I knew is that nothing Chuck Stuart had said about this crime had been true from the first; why assume his words to Dawley were any different?

Larger issues were at stake. The attorney-client privilege encourages people to confide in their counsel. Advocacy depends upon it. And, in any event, there was a right to keep secrets from the government, even to death.

The Supreme Judicial Court ruled against the government. The attorney-client privilege was sacrosanct.

I saw the Stuart family regularly—in their home, in my office, at court proceedings. To avoid the press crush for every hearing, we would meet in my office and I would drive them to the court, getting in through the underground garage. My car—no longer the dying "Iffy" but a new Saab—was regularly covered with kid stuff, cracker and cookie crumbs, apple juice containers, and games. Matthew, used to hanging out with his sibling's children, felt right at home. He had my home number. Dianne Gamere, my dear friend and now a paralegal for our firm, would harangue him regularly about his hair ("too long") or his life ("get a job"). My secretary, Gail MacDonald, who knew something about the neighborhood that Stuart came from, chimed in as well.

While the DA's office had spent months presenting scores of witnesses to the grand jury to develop evidence of Matthew's knowing participation in his brother's plan to murder Carol, no such evidence materialized. The failure was telling. A grand jury, as Harvey was wont to say, would indict a "ham sandwich," if the government wanted it. And yet they had refused to bring an indictment for murder.

Instead, after all that, Matthew was charged only with offenses that derived from the statements that he had made in January—statements about his possession and disposal of items that he received from Chuck the night of the murder. He was charged with conspiracy to commit insurance fraud by agreeing to participate in Chuck's plan to make some sort of "claim" for the property that he took away. He was charged with carrying an unregistered firearm (from his admission that he had carried the bag that he had received from Charles; an unregistered handgun was one of the items), compounding a felony (from his statement that he had given Christmas gifts to his siblings in December 1989, as he always did, at about the same time that he had told them about his suspicions), receipt of stolen property (from Matthew's statement that the bag also contained Carol's jewelry, allegedly "stolen" from her by Charles), and conspiracy to obstruct justice (based on Matthew's statement that he had thrown the bag and its contents into the Pines River and had failed to come forward sooner to the police). McMahon was charged with accessory after the fact of murder, among other offenses.

———

By the time the case was ready for trial in 1990, I had just joined Dwyer, Collora, & Gertner. They knew that when they got me, they got Stuart. And Tom's help—he knew everyone—was invaluable.

The only question was whether Matthew's statements to the DA in January 1990 would be admissible. If it was, there was no defense. The argument was straightforward: Matthew had a right to remain silent, as do all citizens. Giving a statement to the police meant that he waived that right. Massachusetts law required that the government prove the waiver of the right to remain silent was knowing and voluntary. Voluntariness meant more than the absence of the thumbscrew and rack. It involved a particular state of mind. If you believe that the statement you are giving to the police cannot be used against you in a court of law, and you are wrong, then you have not understood the consequences of waiving your rights. And if you didn't understand that fundamental point, your statement was not voluntary. It didn't matter if you believed that you had immunity because of your own mistake, your lawyer's negligence, or police misconduct. Massachusetts applied the strictest standard to measure whether a statement was voluntary, "beyond a reasonable doubt."

I thought the question was not even close. Matthew would not have made the statement on January 3, 1990, if he had known that his words would be used against him. Typically, the lawyer outlines to the prosecutor what the client will say and what the client will get in return for the information. The government says this: If that information pans out, we will immunize your client for it, and the privilege against self-incrimination is waived. If the information does not, then your client will be charged, but the statement that he gave cannot be used against him. Only after the deal is struck does the lawyer allow the government to have access to the client.

Matthew told his lawyer, John Perenyi, that he wanted immunity in exchange for helping the police. They met for hours to talk about how this might occur. Matthew instructed Perenyi to get in touch with the DA to make the arrangements. Perenyi told Matthew that if he couldn't get him immunity, Perenyi would turn around and walk out.

Late in the afternoon of January 3, 1990, Perenyi called the DA's office, reporting that he could produce a witness who could "solve the Carol Stuart murder case." He arranged a meeting at Suffolk County Courthouse that evening. At the DA's office, Perenyi instructed Matthew to wait in the hallway while he spoke with O'Meara and another ADA. He took the first step: he summarized the information that Matthew would later tell the police, information bearing on Charles Stuart's role in the murder of his wife, and physical evidence (namely, Carol Stuart's wedding ring) that proved that the Stuarts had not been robbed at all. O'Meara said that the conversation would be "informal," that Matthew would not be given Miranda warnings. Perenyi went no further—no writing, no clarification of what "informal" meant. So certain was he that the Commonwealth would reward Matthew for his information that he did not bother to seek anything more explicit. If Chuck Stuart had not committed suicide, the odds are that this give-and-take—the "old boy" network—would have been enough.

Perenyi told Matthew that he had "nothing to worry about," that "it was all right for them [Matthew and his friend Jack] to go in and cooperate." Then Matthew took the police to the Pines River Bridge and pointed out where he and McMahon had thrown the items. Divers recovered the bag immediately; the gun was found at that location a few days later. It was registered to Kakas Furs, where Chuck Stuart worked. Matthew arranged to have Carol Stuart's ring delivered to the DA's office.

The government agreed with Perenyi's view of their conversation, although they claimed that they would not have given Matthew immunity "at that time" had his lawyer expressly asked. And they agreed that Perenyi had not asked for it, and they were not about to clarify the situation. They played "gotcha" with Matthew's liberty. The only source of information about what was happening, its legal significance, was Perenyi, and he led Matthew to believe that there was a deal.

Matthew's statement had to be suppressed. Either the government lied—in fact they had meant to immunize him, as Perenyi believed, and were now reneging—or they had deceived him, winking about informality but not meaning immunity. Or else Perenyi was negligent, telling Matthew that he had immunity when the situation was not at all clear. Or neither—Matthew might just be mistaken about a critical issue. Whatever the reason, Matthew had every reason to believe, by word and deed, not to mention by common sense, that his words would be used in an effort to prosecute the man who had murdered his pregnant wife and duped an entire city, not against himself.

———•———

The trial judge found otherwise. The statement, he concluded, was volunteered by Matthew, who had made a "strategic" decision to rush to the courthouse because he feared others might come forward to frame him in the murder. He hired counsel, the judge found, only to make the appointment with the prosecutor and not for what lawyers typically do—negotiate a deal. He "was not influenced to give his statement by anything Perenyi said or did." He would have gone to the police no matter what.

The findings were belied by every shred of testimony, every morsel of evidence. No one testified that Matthew was concerned about being framed for the murder. (Indeed, while the government tried to paint Matthew in the worst possible light, coming forward to save his skin, witness after witness agreed that Matthew had come forward in part because of his concerns that the wrong man was about to be indicted for Charles Stuart's crime.) There was absolutely no reason to believe that the police, who seemed to be completely intent on pursuing Willie Bennett, would do an about-face and go after the Stuarts instead. O'Meara said as much: up until January 3, 1990, the police had "no evidence" linking Charles Stuart or Matthew Stuart to the murder of Carol DiMaiti Stuart.

Nor was Matthew self-destructive. He was not about to fall on his sword. Every single witness—government and defense—confirmed that McMahon and Matthew had sought immunity for their statements. Indeed, to their friends and family, they justified their delay in coming forward because they were seeking counsel and trying to get immunity. There was no evidence supporting the judge's conclusions, much less evidence "beyond a reasonable doubt," as state law required.

Four months later, the same judge had no problem suppressing an incriminating statement made by a defendant who was also a police officer. While the facts were different, the parallels were striking. The standard for determining that someone had waived his rights was high. The government has the burden; they must prove that the defendant knew full well what he was doing. Counsel is terribly important, and effective counsel at that. The lawyer in the police case was negligent and had a conflict of interest (he was both a police officer and a lawyer). Because the defendant relied on his lawyer's advice—which was flawed, not unlike Perenyi's—it was not considered a voluntary statement; hence, the judge suppressed it.

I appealed the Stuart decision to the Supreme Judicial Court. Surely, someone would see this for what it was. Instead, we lost.

I hit a wall. Some lawyers talked about "the big case" exception to the Constitution. In high-profile cases, courts seem unwilling to enforce constitutional guarantees that might hobble the prosecution. In twenty years of high-profile cases, however, I had not encountered that one before.

———

We convinced the court to try the case in Northampton because of the publicity, which was overwhelming—including several books (such as *Murder in Boston,* by Ken Englade), a television movie (*Good Night, Sweet Wife: A Murder in Boston*), even a rap song ("Wildside," by Marky Mark and the Funky Bunch)—suggested that Matthew was guilty of murder. While much of this publicity was national, there had been fevered local interest, too. The government was responsible for much of it—the articles and books quoted police sources, district attorneys, even grand jury witnesses. Northampton, located two hours north of Boston, was a marginally better locale.

The media expected to cover jury selection in Northampton on Monday, November 2, 1992. But secretly, on the previous Friday, we were negotiating with the DA for a plea. There was a new DA, Ralph Martin, the first black DA in the Commonwealth of Massachusetts, who had participated in the investigation of the Boston police for their pursuit of Bennett. All we wanted was proportionality, treating Matthew like any other nonviolent first offender who had cooperated with the police. The government wanted five sentences of three to five years, each running concurrently, with Matthew eligible for parole in one year. We agreed, and in exchange, Matthew would say precisely what had been in his January 3 statement. We agreed that Matthew's statement was all that was needed to convict him of the offense.

We called the judge to alert him to the decision to plead guilty. The judge asked, "What will Matthew say about his role?"

I said, "He will adopt everything in his statement to the police."

The judge retorted: "That's not good enough!"

"What?" I countered. "What more do you want?"

"You know what I want, with all the press surrounding this case," he said. And I did.

I was furious. He plainly wanted Matthew to take responsibility for Carol Stuart's murder. And he had no right to do so. He was acting not as a judge, but as a protector of the prosecutor, and the former prosecutor at that.

But I was powerless. I could not disclose the conversation, not if I wanted to practice in the Suffolk County court again, not if I wanted to make certain that any ire directed at me would not be vented against my client.

The plea went forward. No matter what the judge had said, Matthew stuck to his story, as he had from the beginning. He had done wrong, no question about it, in participating in the insurance scam. But he had no idea what his brother was up to. He was as snookered by his brother as were the Boston police, the media, the Suffolk County DA's office, the entire city. The only question, I said, was whether he was going to pay for his crime or for the sins of Charles Stuart, the sins of the city, the sins of the police.

The judge ended up accepting the plea and the sentence. It was a good outcome, as these things go. I had to be "realistic." I did the best I could. The next day was the 1992 presidential election, with Bill Clinton running against George Bush. I flew to Little Rock, Arkansas, to celebrate Clinton's victory with my old friends from law school.

———

Several months before, in the Travis Burch trial, in sketching the "dot game," I told the jury that the dots did not add up, even though one dot—and an important one at that—pointed to Travis: his bloody palm print at the threshold of the house. Her blood, her hair, his palm print. But there was no motive. There was no evidence that anything of value had been taken.

There were many, many dots—fingerprints, boot prints, telephone numbers, hair fibers—that pointed to others. Apart from the palm print at the threshold of the house, there was no other evidence of Travis's presence—as if he had come upon the scene and then left. There was a clear footprint—not Travis's—a blond hair, fingerprints of the victim's twenty-one-year-old son, a noose over the mother's body, and a piece of paper with the telephone number of a local drug dealer that the son had double-crossed. There was evidence that the killer, apparently comfortable in the house, had taken time to clean the scene, washing off blood here and there, opening the refrigerator. There was a curious symbolism; the body had been specifically dragged into the son's room. In fact, the victim's son was the police's first suspect. She had gotten a restraining order against him. Then the police turned to a second suspect, a young man passing through town who had given Travis a ride home that evening. But although there was evidence of bloody towels in his hotel room, it was too late to test them when the police found out about them.

The picture was not Travis Burch, I argued. It was someone else—or at least there was reasonable doubt.

He was acquitted. It was an extraordinary victory.

———•———

So you win some and lose some, I should have said to myself after Matthew was sentenced. But that's not what I felt. Madeline Kunin had it right, describing her fascination with politics in *Living a Political Life*:

> This cycle of risk taking, followed by fear followed by euphoria, followed by new risk taking, must be akin to what a gambler experiences each time he rolls the dice. There was part of me that thrilled to the game, but another part felt trapped by the addiction.

Trials had become a sort of addiction, getting harder and harder to satisfy. The Burch euphoria lasted a few minutes. Matthew was a downer.

CHAPTER FIFTEEN

From Red Dress to Black Robe

Almost everyone I cared about was crowded into the room—friends, clients, all the people in this book. Members of the Susan Saxe defense committee, Clare Dalton, my relatives, my partners. Families with children crying, some dressed in jeans, in leather, or in business suits. Susan wanted to come. She would have moved heaven and earth to do so, she told me, but she feared that her presence and the attention it would attract would take away from "my day."

Chief Judge Stephen Breyer (then on the First Circuit Court of Appeals, not yet an Associate Justice of the Supreme Court) introduced me. Chief Judge Joseph Tauro administered the oath of office as a judge of the U.S. District Court for the District of Massachusetts.

Then I walked up to the podium.

"I have waited a long time to tell this story. It puts today's events in context for me, and I would like to share it with you.

"It was June 1971. I was graduating from Yale Law School, well on my way to a prestigious position with the Chief Judge of the Seventh Circuit Court of Appeals in Chicago.

"My mother and I were having a huge fight—the kind of fights only mothers and daughters can have. Shrieking at each other in the small kitchen of our apartment in Flushing, Queens; you could have heard us up and down the stairs of the building.

"My mother wanted me to take the Triborough Bridge toll taker's test—just in case!"

The audience exploded in laughter.

And then I added, eyes to heaven, "Excuse me for a moment. Ma! At last, a government job!"

Sitting proudly in the audience were my sister and her family, my father's brothers and their families (Seymour and Teddy, Ceil and Florence, Yussie and Selma). Stephen and Peter, John, Sarah, and Rachel. Mom and Dad could not have imagined this moment, not in their wildest dreams.

Mom had died long before. But Dad was only recently gone. Three days before President Clinton nominated me as a federal judge, he died. He was found in his easy chair, in the living room where we had argued about the *Eleventh Hour News* for hours, until my mother would scream and he finally gave up. "Go be a lawyer," he said, with his eyes twinkling.

Dad knew that I had applied. Months before, in my law office, he went over the letters of support that Tom Dwyer, my partner, had organized. Every single prosecutor I had opposed, from the beginning of my career to the end, including U.S. Attorney William Weld, Attorney General Scott Harshbarger, the DAs of every county, and nearly every opponent in civil cases had written in support.

Still, he didn't get it. "You will go before the state legislature, right?" he said.

"No, Dad, this is federal. I am going to seek confirmation in the U.S. Senate."

"Not the Anita Hill committee?"

"Yes, Dad. In Washington, the Anita Hill committee."

Long pause. He looks up, tears in his eyes. "Have I mentioned, Nance, how proud I am of you? My daughter, the judge."

I would not forget where I came from. But I wasn't certain I wanted the job. I had never planned for it, never courted people for it. Then Bill Clinton was elected president.

Other friends were seizing the chance to be in public service, and I was tempted. I had done everything there was to do in law—taught and practiced, handled civil and criminal cases, trials and appeals, local and national. I had written and given speeches, participated in bar association activities and lectures. My qualifications were undeniable. Still, the confirmation process had become so political. I had been an advocate for controversial clients, and an outspoken one at that. I would try, because the time seemed right, but would not be disappointed with the rejection I would inevitably get.

——

Senator Ted Kennedy interviewed me. I had never met him before, never worked for him, but my partner Tom was quite close with members of his staff, which was surely helpful.

I was relaxed, loose, the way you are when you believe you haven't a prayer of succeeding. We talked about my background. He knew it well. He wanted to know what I really thought about the 1991 Civil Rights Act, which he had sponsored. I told him, honestly—its good points and its limitations. We chatted for over an hour. Aides indicated that it was time to end the interview.

That's when I let him know that I had "a bone to pick with him." I thought I could hear a staff member's sharp intake of breath, as in "Oh my God, where is she going now?"

"A judgeship is supposed to reward a distinguished career," I said. And I went on to make the point that if he valued civil liberties and civil rights work, then once, just once—it didn't have to be me—he needed to recommend such a person for a judgeship.

He recommended me to President Clinton. He was in the middle of a hotly contested reelection campaign. There were safer choices.

I was in the middle of another murder trial, directly following the settlement of Clare Dalton's case and the sentencing of Matthew Stuart. Tom Shay and Alfred Trenkler were accused of putting a bomb under Shay's father's car. When the Boston police came to defuse the bomb, it exploded. One police officer was killed; a second was seriously injured. The presiding judge was the only woman on the court, Rya Zobel, a distinguished judge and mentor to me.

The papers were filled with word of Kennedy's recommendation. The prosecutor asked the judge to instruct the jury to ignore the publicity. She did: "Ladies and gentlemen," she said, "you probably know that the defense lawyer in this case has been nominated to be a federal judge. It should not affect you one way or the other." Then she looked at me and added, with a smile, "But I can't wait."

———

I had no idea how long the confirmation process would last. Clinton's nominees were taking a beating. I had my doubts as to whether the president would support me if my nomination became a lightning rod for opposition, our friendship notwithstanding. But I knew I could count on Kennedy.

The nomination papers were extensive. I went over every case I had ever done. I would withhold nothing. "What are the cases you are proudest of?" the application asked. My reply was *Moe v. Hanley*, the Massachusetts case establishing the right to choose abortion under the Massachusetts constitution.

"Any [other] unfavorable information that may affect your nomination?" Yes. For ten years, as a matter of law, I would not disclose the names of clients from whom I had received cash. The law required that I, like Anzalone, had to report cash transactions to the government, and I did. But when the form asked whose cash it was, I wrote a brief in reply, citing the attorney-client privilege— what I had fought for in Matthew Stuart's case, the principle that I had upheld when I refused to appear before a grand jury. I would not disclose this information unless a court ordered me to.

———

During the summer, Seymour Hersh, the Pulitzer Prize-winning columnist, called me. Clinton had ordered the bombing of Baghdad because he suspected the Iraqis of planting a bomb near President George Bush when he had visited Egypt some time before. The government's suspicions were based on the Exis Computer, the same computer that the government had used in the Shay case to link Shay and his co-defendant, Trenkler, to the type of bomb that killed the Boston police officer. I had spent months challenging this computer, its data, its conclusions. Junk information—hearsay of every manner—was fed into the computer, and—not surprisingly—junk (in my view, at least) was what it spit out. Please, Hersh begged. Give me a quote about the computer for the *New Yorker* article I'm working on. I said, I have applied to be a judge. How would it look to be criticizing the president under these circumstances? Oh, he said. I understand. Minutes later, I called him back. I had never pulled my punches, and I would not do so now. So I told him: the computer information was garbage, and a troubling basis for making foreign-policy decisions.

I tried gamely to keep up my practice, but the nomination distorted everything. For some, I had suddenly achieved a new status—a gravitas, if you will. For others, it was a way to threaten me. "You know, we think what you did was unethical. If you continue, we will tell the Board of Bar Overseers about this. How would that look for you?"

"Do whatever you like," I would say. "As long as I am still a lawyer, I will practice law as I have always done, ethically, in my judgment, and regardless of the consequences to me."

In November 1993, less than a month after Dad died, my confirmation hearing was scheduled. While the press response to my nomination had been favorable, a week before, a local columnist for the *Boston Herald*, Don Feder, attacked me in print. He compared me to Lorena Bobbitt, the woman who had just been arrested for cutting off a piece of her abusive husband's penis. "Judge Gertner," he said, "would do to justice with her gavel what Lorena did to her husband with a kitchen knife."

Perfect. I had never been caricatured before. Scratch the surface of any woman's image and come up with a stereotype—here, the castrating bitch—whether it remotely fit, whether it remotely made sense.

I flew to Washington before the hearing. My partner Tom

came with me to prepare. He was my stalwart. He read everything and orchestrated the letter-writing campaign on my behalf.

While Supreme Court Justice Ruth Bader Ginsburg had to prepare only three days for her confirmation, I needed four. Questions were fired at me by representatives from the Department of Justice; Jeff Blattner, of Kennedy's staff; and Ron Klain, of the White House staff. They had prepared three loose-leaf binders. One had my cases in it—briefs, decisions, etc. A second had articles I had written for law reviews, bar journals, and the occasional op-ed piece. The third loose-leaf was the problem; it contained speeches that I had given on Boston Common.

These guys were good. The goal was to prepare me for the worst. It worked. I felt like everything I had ever done in my life was subject to attack.

At the hearing, I was the first of the four judges from Massachusetts slated to be confirmed that day. Stephen, Peter, Sarah, and John were sitting there proudly. Even Rachel, John's eighty-four-year-old mother, had come, although she was terribly frail. My friends, Dianne Gamere, Judy Mizner, and Clare Dalton, all came to cheer me on.

I was nervous. I thought Kennedy had made a woeful error scheduling my hearing first. I feared that my nomination would then consume much of the day. But Kennedy knew better. My hearing was scheduled between the NAFTA vote and the Thanksgiving recess. The senators asked only four questions. And when it was over, Senator Kennedy recommended that we leave quickly. We did.

All four of us were approved by the Judiciary Committee. Confirmation by the full Senate seemed a foregone conclusion. When we returned to Boston, we huddled in front of the television, watching C-SPAN, expecting to hear my name mentioned on the floor of the Senate.

Then Kennedy called to tell me that I would not be confirmed that week or any time soon. Senator Jesse Helms had objected, based on the Don Feder piece. All my work reduced to this caricature. It seemed absurd.

Four months later, John and I were eating breakfast when I

read in the paper that Kennedy had voted for a Helms-sponsored school prayer amendment. I called Kennedy and told him that I was not worth it. By that afternoon, I was confirmed. The amendment never made it out of the legislative conference committee.

———

It should have been over—I should have been exulting—but it was not. The day after the hearing before the Senate Judiciary Committee, I received a call from a young lawyer in the tax division of the Department of Justice. "Ms. Gertner," this lawyer said, "we believe that you have violated the law by not providing the government with information about an individual who had provided you with cash. We intend to start a civil enforcement proceeding against you to secure the identity of your client." Of all the lawyers in the Commonwealth of Massachusetts who had taken the same stand, I alone would be prosecuted for it. I knew the implications. This would kill my nomination. I did not mention the pending judicial application. I told the young man that I thought he should look at the issue more closely, that the case law in Massachusetts—which I had help create—strongly supported my position. I heard nothing. I was holding my breath, waiting for the other shoe to drop.

The day after the Senate voted to confirm me, an FBI agent walked into the office of Dwyer, Collora, & Gertner, asked to see me, and served me with a summons in the case of *United States v. Gertner.* It was a civil enforcement proceeding to get me to disclose my client's identity.

Close friends urged me to call the client and ask his permission to disclose his name. I started to; I stopped mid-dial. What was I asking? That he put himself in harm's way for the sake of my career advancement? It was an unimaginable question. It violated everything that I cared about. I had refused to disclose his identity as a matter of principle. I would stand by that until a court ordered me to do otherwise, no matter what.

Because of the complexity of winding down my practice, I set up my swearing-in ceremony two months after the Senate confirmed my nomination. I was in the office, frantically finishing cases, referring some clients to other lawyers. My secretary, Gail MacDonald, buzzed. "Lloyd Cutler, the president's counsel, is on the phone."

"Who?" I said, incredulous.

She said it again: "It is Lloyd Cutler, the president's counsel."

Heart in mouth, I took the phone. "Yes, Mr. Cutler," I said. "What can I do for you?"

"Let me get right to the point," he said. "The president wants you to put off your swearing-in until this nasty business, this civil enforcement action, is taken care of."

I gulped. "Well, thank the president for his interest, but no, I won't put it off."

Abruptly, Cutler terminated the conversation.

A week later, he called again. "If this action becomes public, it will be embarrassing for the president. And if it does, the president would like you to announce that you would recuse yourself in all cases involving the government."

"What?" I said. "All cases involving the government!"

"Yes," he said, "until the case is over."

"I will confer with the federal judiciary's Ethics Committee to see what my obligations are. I will call you back."

I spoke to Judge Tauro, who was on the committee, and then I called Cutler back. "No," I said. "I have been advised that it is not unusual for a judge to be sued, and that all I am obliged to do is disqualify myself from cases involving the IRS, the agency arguably seeking the information. I will not follow your recommendation."

Furious, he threatened an investigation of me and hung up. I was in over my head. If the president became embarrassed by this litigation against me, he wanted to be able to say that he had no idea about it when I was recommended, that I had kept it under wraps. The stakes were high. Because I had been confirmed by the Senate, the only way to stop my swearing-in would be to impeach me—impeach me before I was—"peached."

An investigation did indeed follow, run by the Department of Justice. I was told that this information—about my stand on currency transaction forms—was not in the version of the nomination that had been sent to the Judiciary Committee. I felt in grave danger.

We dug. As it turned out, one arm of the Department of Justice, with people trying to shepherd through my nomination, had edited the information out of the petition that had gone to the committee. They thought so little of it—it was in the miscellaneous section anyhow—that they excised it. At the same time, another arm of the Department of Justice was preparing to prosecute me for it.

I could prove that I disclosed everything. The version of my nomination that had been sent to the president and the DOJ included everything. The swearing-in would go on as scheduled.

We heard later that some officials in the Department of Justice knew what was going on—that the tax division of the Justice Department was investigating me while others in the department were trying to get me confirmed as a judge. If they took my nomination off the floor of the Senate, it would be over, and I might never get another chance. So a plot was hatched, one that would have the president simply delay the signing of my judicial commission until the disclosure business was taken care of. Either Clinton ignored the advice or was too distracted to pay attention. He signed the commission. By April 1994, I was sworn in.

Several years later, the IRS's enforcement action—to get me to disclose my client's identity—failed. The case was moved to Maine, and I won.

When Clarence Thomas was confirmed to the Supreme Court, his metaphor for the kind of judge that he would be was "stripped down like a runner," "without entangling opinions or prejudgments." Unlikely.

We pick judges in their forties and fifties for what they know and what they have lived through. We understand that they have opinions, feelings, positions. We expect it.

Every person who decides he or she is going to be a judge has to move to neutral. And that move should be no more difficult for a civil rights advocate than for a prosecutor or corporate lawyer. I have always been suspect of the juror who said: I know nothing, read nothing, and have no opinions. I have always felt more comfortable with the juror who acknowledges his or her opinions, who would struggle with them.

I knew who I was, what I had been, what I believed in. A passion for justice. A determination to work until I found an answer. Looking at the people before me as people I might have represented, I might have opposed, I might have lived next to. Talking to Moishe through them. Feeling empathy, and yet learning detachment.

———•———

I have been a judge for all of one week when I get a call in the middle of a proceeding. I am told that Peter is on the phone.

"No," I say to my clerk, Maryellen Molloy. "That can't possibly be. Peter can't dial. He is only six."

"But judge," she says insistently, "it *is* Peter on the phone."

I say to the lawyers in front of me, very solemnly, "Excuse me. I have to take a moment for a very important call."

I go into the judge's lobby and pick up the phone.

"Peter," I say, "what's the matter?"

"Mama, there's no chocolate pudding in my snack!"

Melting at the sound of his small voice, I say: "Sweetie, it is in the paper bag in your pack."

"Oh," he says. "Bye."

I ascend the bench.

The world has come back in perspective.

ACKNOWLEDGMENTS

It is difficult to imagine where to begin in thanking the people who have contributed to this memoir. There are the people I write about—the clients who gave me the opportunity to know them and be their public face in their most difficult and challenging times, the lawyers and staff with whom I worked who made me look good and cheered me on. And, of course, there is my family, who patiently watched this process—the process of living these stories, then writing about them—unfold over many, many years.

I give special thanks to my best friend, co-counsel, partner, husband, sweetheart, teammate, sous-chef or executive chef (depending on the day), John Reinstein. It is hard to disentangle where one role ends and the others begin. This book reflects the work and the family we share and nurture, the *Enterprise,* as we liked to call it (with a nod to *Star Trek*). Writing a memoir involves a certain level of narcissism, which made John, who doesn't have a narcissistic bone in his body, decidedly uncomfortable. Still, he was my rock, keeping the house together when I was squirreled away writing, comforting me when the process seemed endless and endlessly disappointing, all the while doing his extraordinary legal work at the American Civil Liberties Union of Massachusetts. Then, when he realized the book would actually be published, he focused on it with the rigor that he would apply to the briefs on which we collaborated. That meant long discussions and debates, en route to New Hampshire, on plane trips to Europe or wherever, on walks around the lake, often late into the night. That particular part of the *Enterprise* makes me wish I'd never finished.

And I thank my dear, dear children, Sarah, Stephen, and Peter, who have patiently heard many of the stories in this book, rolled their eyes as I repeated them over and over again until they finished my sentences. Now that it is done, I put them on notice: I will just say, page 30, or, chapter 6, and they should understand. Their unending love, their bright futures, our quirky family makes this work (again, the *Enterprise*) worthwhile.

I thank my sister, Roz, who also has heard most of the stories here far too many times. When she was not accusing me of appropriating *her* stories ("I was the one who did that, not you"), she was recounting family accounts that totally contradicted mine ("Nance, that just did not happen!"). She keeps me connected to our parents and relatives, and to the narrative of our little family on the Lower East Side of Manhattan and Flushing, Queens. And she is my cheerleader, particularly now that our parents, Sadie and Moishe, are gone.

Thanks too to Gail MacDonald Marchione, secretary, executive assistant, paralegal, chief cook and bottle washer, who has worked with me over nearly two decades and whose humanity and sense of humor encourages me to show mine.

And in many ways I owe a special debt to Harvey Silverglate, who, over the twenty years of our partnership, taught me that one could and should align your work and your heart, that money didn't matter but principle did. Over the course of any single day, I remember as many "Harvey-isms" as "Moishe-isms." And I thank Judy Mizner, lawyer extraordinaire, unparalleled workaholic, with whom I worked on case after case, and who could stay up even later than I.

And thanks to Tom Dwyer, who was my partner for only four years but who worked ceaselessly to transform this improbable lawyer's career into a federal district court nomination, as well as to Dianne Gamere, paralegal and then firm office manager but, more importantly, dear, dear friend, whose contribution to many of the cases described here was invaluable.

I also thank my editors at Beacon Press, Helene Atwan and Allison Trzop, who cared not just for the words on the page but for the principles they reflected. I thank my agent Helen Rees, another indomitable support; Betsy Groban, who encouraged me to do this book; as well as Anita Diamant, Doe Coover, Bill Patrick, Linda Kerber, Joyce Antler, Alan Dershowitz, and Phyllis Segal.

And I thank the many women who led the way for me and others of my generation, most especially, U.S. District Court judge Rya Zobel.

Finally, I give special thanks to Moishe and Sadie Gertner, my father and mother, whose absence I feel every single day of my life.